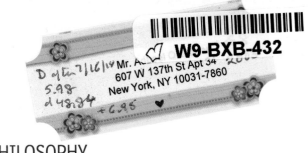

SEX AND PHILOSOPHY

Also available from Continuum:

The Sartre Dictionary, Gary Cox
Sartre: A Guide for the Perplexed, Gary Cox
The New Sartre, Nik Farrell Fox
Sartre's 'Being and Nothingness': A Reader's Guide, Sebastian Gardner

SEX AND PHILOSOPHY

Rethinking de Beauvoir and Sartre

Edward Fullbrook and Kate Fullbrook

continuum

Continuum

Continuum International Publishing Group
The Tower Building   80 Maiden Lane
11 York Road   Suite 704
London SE1 7NX   New York NY 10038

www.continuumbooks.com

British Library Cataloguing-in-Publication Data
A catalogue record for this book is available from the British Library.

ISBN-10: HB: 1-8470-6065-X
          PB: 1-8470-6066-8
ISBN-13: HB: 978-1-8470-6065-5
          PB: 978-1-8470-6066-2

Library of Congress Cataloging-in-Publication Data

Fullbrook, Edward.
   Sex and philosophy : Jean-Paul Sartre and Simone de Beauvoir / Edward Fullbrook and
Kate Fullbrook.
     p. cm.
   ISBN 978-1-84706-065-5 -- ISBN 978-1-84706-066-2 1.   Sartre, Jean-Paul, 1905–1980.
2. Beauvoir, Simone de, 1908–1986. 3   Philosophers--France--Biography. 4. Sartre,
Jean-Pual, 1905–1980--Sexual behavior. 5.   Beauvoir, Simone de, 1908–1986--Sexual
behavior. I. Fullbrook, Kate. II. Title.

   B2430.S34F85 2008
   194--dc22
   [B]

                                    2007034574

Typeset by Fakenham Photosetting Ltd, Fakenham, Norfolk
Printed and bound in Great Britain by MPG Books Ltd, Bodmin, Cornwall

To

Margaret Simons,

whose example gave us the courage to ask the questions

Contents

Acknowledgements

This book brings together 15 years of research on the works and lives of Simone de Beauvoir and Jean-Paul Sartre by myself and my late wife, Kate Fullbrook. In that time we have been assisted in various ways by many people and most especially by fellow Beauvoir and Sartre scholars. We particularly want to thank Margaret A. Simons, for her personal encouragement, for the exemplary standards set by her own foundational work on Beauvoir's philosophy, and for all her work in publishing Beauvoir's posthumous papers. Special thanks are also due to Christine Delphy, Sylvie Chaperon, Sylvie Le Bon de Beauvoir and Alice Schwarzer. We also want to thank Eleanore Holveck, Debra Bergoffen and William McBride for kindly allowing us access to their own research on Beauvoir and Sartre. Yolanda Patterson's dedication to Beauvoir scholarship deserves special thanks from all who value the philosopher's legacy. We are grateful to the British Academy's Humanities Research Board and the University of the West of England's Faculty of Humanities Research Committee for providing funding for aspects of the work which went into this book. We also want to thank Geoff Channon, Bill Greenslade, Jean Grimshaw, Sue Habeshaw, Robin Jarvis, Renee Slater and Helen Taylor for the kind of support which would have been difficult to do without. Like all scholars, we owe an immeasurable debt to the librarians who helped to secure the documents which made our work possible; in this case, the more than patient librarians at the University of the West of England. Thanks are also due to our editor, Sarah Campbell, who has expedited this book in time for Beauvoir's centennial. Finally, deep thanks must go to Zita Adamson for her moral support and editorial advice in putting this volume together.

I wish to thank Polity Press for permission to reproduce two chapters from our book *Simone de Beauvoir: A Critical Introduction*, and the University of Illinois Press for permission to reproduce our essay 'Introduction to Two Unpublished Chapters' that appeared in *Simone de Beauvoir: Philosophical Writings*, edited by Margaret A. Simons.

Introduction

Jean-Paul Sartre and Simone de Beauvoir were two of the most brilliant, influential, unorthodox and scandalous intellectuals of the twentieth century. The impact of their interconnected writings on the modern world cannot be overestimated. But Beauvoir and Sartre are remembered almost as much for the lives they led as for their influence on the way we think. From 1929 until Sartre's death in 1980 they remained 'essential' to each other but never monogamous. Their committed but notoriously open union created huge controversy in their lifetime. And even before their deaths they had become one of history's legendary couples, renowned for the passion, daring, humour and intellectual intensity of their relationship.

Sartre

In his 30s Sartre published three books on pyschology that went largely unnoticed. But the publication in 1938 of his first novel *Nausea* and of a collection of stories *Intimacy* brought him immediate recognition and success. These works express his early existentialist themes of alienation and commitment. In 1943 he published *Being and Nothingness*, a 600-page philosophical treatise on which his reputation as one of the most important and original philosophers of the twentieth century primarily rests. This book is recognized as the work out of which much of modern existentialism derives. Sartre popularized its ideas through his best-selling essay *Existentialism is a Humanism* (1946), a series of novels (*The Reprieve*, *The Age of Reason* and *Iron in the Soul*) in *The Roads to Freedom* (1945–9) and as the author of numerous successful plays, including *The Flies* (1943), *No Exit* (1947) and *The Devil and the Good Lord* (1951). In the 1960s he published two more major philosophical essays, *Critique of Dialectical Reason* (1960), and *Search for a Method* (1967). Sartre also wrote much literary criticism including *What Is Literature?* (1948) and books on Baudelaire (1947) and Jean Genet (1952). In 1964 his autobiography of his childhood, *The Words*, became an international bestseller. Also in 1964, keeping to his lifelong commitment of refusing prizes, he turned down the Nobel Prize for Literature. When he died in 1980 over 50,000 people joined his funeral cortege as it crawled through the streets of Paris.

Beauvoir

Simone de Beauvoir was the most famous and emblematic intellectual woman of the twentieth century. She was a philosopher, novelist, essayist, biographer, autobiographer, playwright, journalist, editor and pre-eminent feminist theorist. Like Sartre, she worked as a schoolteacher for over a decade before becoming a professional writer. She was 35 when in 1943 she first broke into print with her novel *She Came To Stay*. It won her instant acclaim and an international readership. The following year her essay *Pyrrhus and Cinéas* served as one of the primary vehicles by which existentalism was introduced to the French public. Increasingly, Beauvoir became a public figure, first in France and soon worldwide. Her book *The Second Sex*, published in 1949, is widely acknowledged as the founding text of modern feminism. It has been translated into many languages and, despite the intellectual intensity of its 700 pages, has sold over 3 million copies. In 1954 her novel *The Mandarins* won her France's highest literary prize, the Prix Concourt. Her four volumes of autobiography, still widely read, became a primary source of the Sartre–Beauvoir legend. When she died in 1986, 5,000 people joined her funeral cortege on its way to Montparnasse cemetery where she was buried next to Sartre.

The Two False Presumptions of the Sartre–Beauvoir Legend

As the Sartre–Beauvoir story developed and became part of contemporary mythology, it was increasingly filtered through two presumptions regarding the nature of the partnership. *One concerned sex, the other philosophy*. The classic view of Beauvoir, encouraged by her own writing and by Sartre's acquiescence, has been one of Sartre as womanizer and Beauvoir as the patient, loyal female victim. The legend also consistently portrayed Beauvoir as the midwife of Sartre's philosophy rather than a thinker in her own right, encouraging the view that her philosophical writings were mere echoes of the thoughts of her man. But over the past 25 years big chunks of documentary evidence have become public which show that both of these traditional interpretations of the Sartre–Beauvoir story are profoundly false. It is now clear, as this book explains, that it was Beauvoir's demand for sexual freedom that dictated the open terms of their relationship and that it fell to Sartre at least as often as to Beauvoir to perform the role of midwife for the other's philosophy.

It was the English translator of Sartre's *Being and Nothingness*, Hazel Barnes, who first unwittingly undermined Sartre's claim to the philosophical system contained in that work. Barnes's *The Literature of Possibility* (1959), a comparative study of the works of Beauvoir, Sartre and Albert Camus, treated Beauvoir's novel *She Came To Stay* as a philosophical text. By doing so, Barnes was merely applying to the woman writer a practice that was already a standard method of analysis for Sartre's fiction. The Cambridge philosopher Mary Warnock has explained the logic behind this method.

This insistence on the particularity and concreteness of descriptions, from which ontological and metaphysical and general statements may be drawn, is what most clearly characterizes existentialist writing – and what, incidentally, makes it perfectly plausible for Sartre to use novels and plays as well as straight philosophical expositions to convey philosophical doctrines.[1]

Beauvoir's *She Came To Stay* was published in 1943, the same year as Sartre's *Being and Nothingness*. Barnes's reading of Beauvoir's novel demonstrated that it contained a full statement of the theories of bad faith and of inter-subjectivity (being-for-others) found in Sartre's treatise. The latter point is, with hindsight, particularly significant. Over a third of Sartre's book (pp. 219–430) is taken up by his statement of the theory of intersub-jectivity, which, writes Warnock, 'is by far the richest and the most extraordinary part of the whole book'.[2]

At the end of the 1950s, when Barnes was writing, it was culturally unthinkable (nor was it then known which of the two books had been written first) that the philosophy shared by these two works and their authors could have originated with the woman. Nonetheless, Barnes dared to append the following footnote:

I do not at all preclude the possibility that de Beauvoir has contributed to the formation of Sartre's philosophy. I suspect that his debt to her is considerable. All I mean in the present instance is that the novel serves as documentation for the theory, regardless of who had which idea first.[3]

No one disputed Barnes's observations regarding the close correspondence between the two texts. But neither did scholars investigate the scandalous 'possibility' it suggested. The prejudices of the day opposed it too violently. So the presumption of Beauvoir's intellectual subservience to Sartre continued unchanged as an essential theme of the increasingly iconic Sartre–Beauvoir story.

A decade later the legend's other primary theme, the presumption of Beauvoir's sexual subservience to Sartre, was also jeopardized. This time, the person who undermined it was Sartre himself. In his old age he became careless about the legend he and Beauvoir had constructed around themselves. In an interview in March 1971 he mentioned that he had not been Beauvoir's first lover, and named as her first sexual partner a man still living who, when contacted, confirmed the revelation.[4] It was not the fact itself that was startling, but rather the implications it might hold for the credibility of Sartre and Beauvoir's many-volumed and often-told version of their connected lives. Her sexual innocence was integral to the most hallowed of all Sartre-and-Beauvoir stories, that of the initial meeting and romance, which culminated in their oath-taking in the shadow of the Louvre. If *this* story was based on a fabrication, then so might any of their others be. And what did this suggest about the *real* nature of the relationship that existed between them? What was it that was being hidden? Surely it was not simply the fact that Beauvoir was no longer a virgin when she first had sex with Sartre. Sartre's perhaps unintentional revelation pointed to something dubious about the legend he and Beauvoir had invented about themselves, something that had to do with the terms on which they had founded that relationship.

Western culture, however, was still not ready to call into question the legend that it had come to love, and so, like Barnes's comparative readings, Sartre's revelation passed virtually unnoticed. Not until near the end of the century did the traditional accounts of Sartre and Beauvoir's romantic and intellectual relationships began to publicly unravel, and then only gradually as scholars digested the significance of a series of events:

1 Some interviews given by Beauvoir not long before she died
2 The publication of the original opening chapters of Beauvoir's first novel
3 The posthumous publication of Sartre's letters to Beauvoir
4 The discovery and posthumous publication of Beauvoir's letters to Sartre
5 The posthumous publication of Sartre's war diaries
6 The posthumous publication of Beauvoir's war diaries
7 The growing acceptance of people in the West that women as well as men can be the primary source of important ideas
8 The discovery of Beauvoir's student diaries.

Out of this mountain of documents the true story of Sartre and Beauvoir has gradually emerged. It is even more fascinating than the false one that has been told and retold so many times. In the light of these new bodies of evidence and in the open-mindedness of the changed moral climate regarding gender relations, this book brings together 15 years of research on the shared lives of Beauvoir and Sartre.

Our Research

When my late wife Kate and I began our research into Sartre and Beauvoir, three problems of belief regarding the stories of their lives confronted us. One, the story surrounding the couple presumed a radical and almost overnight reversal of the nature of the relationship between them and also of Beauvoir's character. These changes did not appear to us as plausible. Second, the various accounts of their relationship that Beauvoir gave were seriously inconsistent. Some supported the traditional legend and some contradicted it. Among scholars, with the notable exceptions of Margaret Simons and Linda Singer, it had become standard practice to accept the former and ignore the latter. But we found that when we stepped out from under the legend's spell we could not honestly say that we knew in which of her accounts Beauvoir had been telling the truth and in which she had been lying. And in any case, why had Beauvoir at times felt it necessary to lie about the nature of her relationship with Sartre? Our third problem of belief concerned only Sartre, or rather in our continuing state of ignorance, appeared to concern only him. The number of sizeable feats that biographers attributed to Sartre between

17 February 1940 and October 1942 (when he submitted his manuscript of *Being and Nothingness* for publication) was preposterous. The feats claimed for Sartre in this period of two years and eight months include the following:

1 He read and closely analysed the philosophical works of Hegel and Heidegger.
2 He invented from scratch his own highly original and monumental philosophical system.
3 He single-handedly wrote a 700-page account of his philosophy.
4 He wrote, produced and acted in a play.
5 He wrote and published another one.
6 He wrote one and a half long novels.
7 For half this period he wrote long letters every day and kept a diary.
8 He wrote numerous articles.
9 He spent four months as a soldier in an army at war.
10 He spent nine months as a prisoner of war.
11 He escaped from a German prison camp.
12 He worked for a year as a full-time lycée teacher.
13 He seduced many young women.
14 He organized a resistance movement.
15 He travelled for a whole summer by bicycle through France.

On paper Sartre looked like an intellectual Arnold Schwarzenegger character, a stereotypical male fantasy.

Most of these undertakings attributed to Sartre were well documented, but numbers 1, 2 and 3 were not. Even so, months passed before a trivial chance observation had the effect of crystallizing our suspicions enough so that henceforth we gave up trying to banish them and decided instead to investigate them. For some time we had possessed a book titled *Sartre* by the philosopher Peter Caws, part of a venerable series and self-described as a 'systematic reading of the entire corpus of Jean-Paul Sartre's philosophical writings'. Its cover featured a photo of a page of handwritten manuscript, which of course we had presumed was Sartre's. But one day a note on the back cover caught our attention. It read: 'The cover shows a page of unpublished text by Sartre. The handwriting is that of Simone de Beauvoir.' This proved absolutely nothing. But as a cultural artefact the cover now suggested to us that in the philosophy community an ethic of gender roles sometimes existed which if applied to the shared lives of

Sartre and Beauvoir could conceivably have generated a radically false account. With this as a cautionary principle, our research into Sartre and Beauvoir began in earnest.

This Book

Because the romantic and intellectual relationships between Sartre and Beauvoir were so inextricably intertwined, the one cannot be understood without understanding the other. This makes the biographer's task extremely demanding. He/she must not only be familiar with the worldly details of Sartre and Beauvoir's personal and professional existences, but also have a strong grasp of the ideas which, both for the individuals and for the couple, were the gravitational centre of their lives.

There have been many fine books written about Beauvoir and Sartre. But this book is arguably the first one that fully combines explorations of the two primary dimensions of their relationship. Part I explores biographically their first 12 years together. It closely traces the formation of their relationship, their subsequent numerous sexual liaisons and the parts each played in the development of their most important ideas. Part II, through a combining of textural analysis and biographical detail, apportions credit for their shared ideas. In the light of this apportionment, Part III looks at Beauvoir's ethics, her concept of gender and her writing of *The Second Sex*.

PART I
SARTRE AND BEAUVOIR

Chapter 1
Final Exams

'You girls will never marry ... you have no dowries; you'll have to work for a living.'[1] This often repeated lament by Simone de Beauvoir's father for his two daughters, was for her a signal for hope rather than despair. When her 11 years of primary school education at *Le Cours Désir* ended in 1924 when she was 16, her family debated her next step. Her father thought Simone should study law and qualify for a civil service post which would give her security and a pension; her mother thought librarianship would be more genteel.[2] Beauvoir had other ideas. Philosophy attracted her. It had the benefits of being considered with suspicion by her family and with interest by the young man whom she fancied at the time. Further, Beauvoir had come across an article on a woman who had a doctorate in philosophy, a pioneer, who seemed to have 'succeeded in reconciling her intellectual life with the demands of feminine sensibility'. Beauvoir was impressed: she, too, wanted to be such a pioneer. Philosophy also suited Beauvoir's own intellectual proclivities:

> The thing that attracted me about philosophy was that it went straight to essentials. I perceived the general significance of things rather than their singularities, and I preferred understanding to seeing; I had always wanted to know *everything*; philosophy would allow me to appease this desire, for it aimed at total reality; philosophy went right to the heart of truth and revealed to me, instead of an illusory whirlwind of facts or empirical laws, an order, a reason, a necessity in everything.[3]

Her ambition was irresistible and in 1925 she began work for the series of examinations for certificates and diplomas which would lead her to her first adult career as a teacher of philosophy in the lycées.

During the four years of her higher education, during which Beauvoir progressively moved out of the all-female and Catholic educational milieu of her childhood into the coeducational and humanist atmosphere of the Sorbonne, her family's influence on her steadily waned. At first carefully placing her in institutions where she could not become 'infected' with the secularism of the age – the Institut Catholique and the Institut Sainte-Marie de Neuilly – Beauvoir's parents' ability to control her life disappeared almost completely as she gravitated to the Sorbonne and to the Ecole Normale Supérieure toward the end of her studies, where she made important friendships with the outstanding students of her educational generation. Beauvoir's independence as well as her new friends led her to experiment with visits to some of the more dangerous and colourful low-life areas of Paris. Yet for all this, Beauvoir's parents' approval of their daughter also grew as her studies progressed. As a woman who merely had to earn her living, Simone was, for her father, 'a living confirmation of his own failure'. If, however, she became 'a sort of intellectual prodigy' she would be, not a source of shame, but a 'phenomenon who could not be judged by normal standards', someone who 'could be explained away as the result of a strange and unaccountable gift'.[4] Beauvoir, the dutiful daughter after all, became that prodigy, an adept at passing examinations, one of the youngest students in her cohort.

In 1925, however, this success was still in the future, and the all female Institut Sainte-Marie was, in fact, a very good place for Beauvoir to begin her studies. Two of the women there were particularly important. The Institut was run by Madame Charles Daniélou, a passionate proponent of education for women, who held more degrees than any other woman at the time in France.[5] Beauvoir's philosophy tutor, Mademoiselle Mercier was an *agrégée* in philosophy, one of the handful of women in the country who had passed the highly competitive examination for this qualification.[6] These were precisely the right intellectual models at the right time for Beauvoir. They set high standards, they demanded respect, their praise had to be earned. The other teacher of importance to Beauvoir at this time was Robert Garric, a young, left-wing, charismatic and intensely religious lecturer at the coeducational Institut Catholique. Garric taught literature and numbered Jacques among his devotees. Garric, a kind of secular saint, lived in the working-class district of Belleville, to which

Beauvoir once made a disappointed sentimental pilgrimage to gaze at his house. Garric represented Beauvoir's first serious brush with the political left. Her father's views, as might be expected from a man who valued Gobineau and Maurras, were that of a far right-wing, paternalist nationalist. Beauvoir's political views seem to have been largely unformed. She was never a particularly engaged political animal, in any conventional sense, but her adulation of Garric directed her toward the anarchist-leftist political stance that she was to retain as her most characteristic political position. Garric ran a series of youth groups, *Les Equipes Sociales*, dedicated to bringing high culture to the working class. When she was 18, Beauvoir joined one of these groups and spent time in Belleville teaching classes in literature to young, working-class women. It was her first (and largely unsuccessful) attempt at teaching, as well as her first extended view of life outside her own caste. The experience was useful, and the girls of Belleville seem to have taught Beauvoir more than she taught them. Beauvoir identified with her students' need to escape their homes, and used her teaching as an excuse to escape her own. Beauvoir worked hard for both Garric and Mademoiselle Mercier. They encouraged and praised her. The time-honoured process of the gifted student working first to gratify admired teachers before launching into their own work operated well for Beauvoir, whose persona of the dutiful daughter transferred easily to her new role of star (female) student.[7]

The grounding Beauvoir received in continental philosophy at this time laid the foundations for her thought throughout her lifetime. Kant developed in her a passion for 'critical idealism'; Bergson was valued for his theories about 'the social ego and the personal ego'; later, Beauvoir read Descartes and Spinoza with attention and admiration, and still later her enthusiasms covered Plato, Schopenhauer, Leibnitz, Hamelin, and, especially, Nietzsche.[8] Her final year thesis, on Leibnitz, was written under the direction of the influential neo-Kantian, Léon Brunschvig, and, indeed Kant remained the most important of Beauvoir's philosophical predecessors.

At the same time as her philosophical studies proceeded with great success and ever more complex development, Beauvoir not only maintained her interest in literature, but felt that her chief ambition – unlike Sartre, who thought of himself as the future author of a grand philosophical system – was not to join the ranks of those skilled in philosophical abstractions, but to write 'the novel of the inner life'. At the age of 18 she made her first adult attempts at writing fiction: the results were not successful and Beauvoir knew it, but she was nonetheless pleased with the process of writing itself and felt that fiction provided a mode of discourse in which she could put her 'own experience into words.'[9]

That experience, the experience of a woman moving out of known territory into a singular life for which she had not been prepared, and which she had to shape in her own individual way became more absorbing for Beauvoir as she moved out of her adolescent phase of imaginary friends and into closer contact with other individuals of her own age who liked and valued her as the possessor of a body as well as of a mind and who had no connection with the opinions, favourable or otherwise, of Beauvoir's parents. Beauvoir's education, during the period of 1925 to 1929 consisted of more than the formal arrangements bounded by courses, examinations and solitary literary experiments. In her late teens, and despite her academic success, Beauvoir felt she was profoundly alone and directionless: 'I ... was breaking away from the class to which I belonged: where was I to go? Whereas Sartre's life, at this time, was proceeding agreeably and smoothly along familiar gender-based paths for a young man of his class and aspirations, Beauvoir felt, at 18, 'condemned to exile', unable to imagine her future, while determinedly abandoning her past.[10] Her lack of perceived direction often meant she drifted close to despair. However, while scarcely realizing it, and like many intelligent rebels, whether male or female, Beauvoir was in the process of finding her tribe. The search was especially precarious for a woman and Beauvoir scarcely understood the urges behind some of her own actions. Looking for alternatives to the life she knew, Beauvoir, whose reckless streak sometimes outbalanced her caution, sought out adventures. In a spirit of somewhat foolhardy desperation she and her sister, who in some ways was an earlier and even more formidable rebel than Simone, played sexual games in cafés and bars, picking up men and then escaping when matters looked like turning serious. Beauvoir developed a taste for alcohol, and went drinking when she claimed to be teaching in Belleville. The element of risk in these escapades helped her in the process of changing her rather timid ideas about the nature of the relationships between men and women.

In this process of revising her notion of women's possibilities, Beauvoir had a stroke of great good fortune when she was 20 and on a visit to Zaza's family's country estate in the Landes region. There, Beauvoir made an important friendship, one that was to serve as a healthy counterbalance to her febrile tie to Elisabeth herself. Beauvoir's new friend was a Polish-Ukranian emigrée, Stépha Awdykovicz, who was working for the Le Coin family as a governess that summer. Stépha was outlandish, exotic, lively, and daring; further, she had a keen sense of her own sexuality, and dared to talk to Beauvoir about sexual matters which Beauvoir's own prudish upbringing had excluded almost from thought, much less mention. Stépha, who had been sent by her parents from Lvov to study in Paris, seems to have simply laughed Beauvoir out of some of her reserve and over-propriety. Certainly, when the young women returned to Paris and kept up the connection that had begun on holiday (indeed Stépha was to be Beauvoir's lifelong friend, and this affection was to extend to Stépha's son, John Gerassi, who became one of Sartre's most perceptive biographers), Beauvoir was both delighted and appalled at the new bohemian set to which Stépha introduced her. Stépha was living with a Spanish painter, Fernando Gerassi, and Beauvoir was shocked and impressed when she discovered that Stépha posed for him in the nude. Indeed, one of Stépha's most important functions for Beauvoir was that she allowed her to take possession of her own body. In contrast to the stiff and untouchable manners that Beauvoir had previously encountered in her ultra-proper milieu, Stépha insisted on touch as a way to signal their friendship. She took Beauvoir's arm in the street, she held her hand in the cinema, she kissed her. Stépha simply accepted the facts of bodily life and refused to be shocked when the two young women caught sight of a pimp being arrested by police in the street. 'But Simone, that's life!,' said Stépha when Beauvoir thought she was going to faint at the sight of the pimp and his whores.[11] Stépha explained men's sexuality to Beauvoir; she talked to her about clothes; she introduced Beauvoir to her bohemian political and artistic friends. She brought, in short, not only daring but pleasure into Beauvoir's life.

Hélène, too, made a contribution to Beauvoir's development. Perhaps even more determined than Beauvoir to make her own way, and, by training as an artist, choosing an even more dangerous path for a woman of her class, Hélène and her friend Gégé Pardo enhanced Beauvoir's network of female friends who were braving the disapproval and difficulties of their novel position to carve out lives for themselves in unorthodox ways. Through these other women, Beauvoir took possession of the world that was, in fact, her adult milieu. The 'pacifists, internationalists, and revolutionaries', the artists and experimenters with whom this prim daughter of the bourgeoisie now associated opened her eyes to new political and aesthetic possibilities.[12] And, as has been noted, the sexual freedom of her new circle was a revelation.

Flirting with an alternative way of living, bowled over by surrealism and Ballet Russe,[13] tempted by bohemianism and revolt, Beauvoir also found her colleagues at the Sorbonne, at which she began her studies in 1928, a source of discovery. In 1928 the pass list in the moral science and psychology examinations was particularly impressive. Simone Weil, who was, with Beauvoir, to be one of the most distinguished philosophers of her generation, headed the list, followed by Beauvoir. After them came the future existentialist philosopher who was to be a close friend of both Sartre and Beauvoir, Merleau-Ponty. Weil was an opportunity missed for Beauvoir. Her revolutionary sympathies were already developed and she clearly thought Beauvoir a bourgeois fool (a judgement with which Beauvoir, many years later, was happy to concur). Their only encounter recorded by Beauvoir concerned a conversation about the relative merits of ontology and revolution. Weil terminated the discussion with the declaration that 'It's easy to see you've never gone hungry'. Beauvoir was annoyed.[14]

Merleau-Ponty was a different matter. A student at the Ecole Normale Supérieure, from a background sympathetic to Beauvoir's own, and still wrestling with the vestiges of his own lost faith, he sought out Beauvoir after the publication of the general philosophy results list. The two students became close friends and philosophical associates. Beauvoir liked him so much that she introduced him to Zaza. Merleau-Ponty, in turn, introduced Beauvoir to Maurice de Gandillac, who took an interest in the state of her faith and who was effusive in his admiration of her brilliance.[15] It was all very flattering for Beauvoir, and her success with these two *normaliens* led her to pursue the acquaintance of another of their number in whom she was especially interested.

René Maheu seemed the most accessible of a threesome that included the future novelist, Paul Nizan, and Jean-Paul Sartre. Their clique, which was composed, in the main, of former students of Alain, the only radical philosopher teaching at the Lycée Henri IV, had a reputation for daring and 'brutality', and was the last group of fellow students to remain closed to Beauvoir.[16] Maheu, like Nizan, was married, but Beauvoir was taken with him from her first close contact with him in a talk that he gave in one of Brunschvig's lectures early in 1929. The attraction was physical and fit in well with her newly discovered talent for pleasure. Beauvoir liked Maheu's face, his eyes, his hair, she found his voice charming. She decided to make his acquaintance and approached him during lunch in the Bibliothèque Nationale. The two hit it off immediately and soon Maheu was writing poems for Beauvoir and bringing her drawings and magazines.[17] Beauvoir found him thrilling, not least for the vigour of his sensuality. Writing her memoirs in 1958, Beauvoir remembered with affection 'how proud' Maheu 'was of the young red blood pulsing in his veins!' She is careful to note the symmetry of Maheu's liberating influence with that of her new female friend, Stépha. In 1929, Beauvoir said, 'I was tired of saintliness and I was overjoyed that [Maheu] should treat me – as only Stépha had done – as a creature of the earth.' For Beauvoir, Maheu was 'a real man' and 'he opened up paths that [she] longed to explore without as yet having the courage to do so.' Somewhat to her own surprise, she found herself arguing with him against the case for premarital female virginity.[18] Exactly when the two became lovers is not clear, but what is certain is that Beauvoir remembered Maheu and the first year of her affair with him with pleasure and affection. He helped her complete her own liberation.

Maheu also rechristened her. As Beauvoir, who was known as 'le Castor' to her adult intimates, tells the story, it was Maheu who provided her with her new identity. 'One day he wrote on my exercise-book, in large capital letters: BEAUVOIR = BEAVER. "You are a beaver," he said. "Beavers like company and they have a constructive bent."'[19] It was all more apt than either could have known.

For Beauvoir, 1929 was a turning point. In January, she did her teaching practice. She was the first woman to teach philosophy in France in a boys' lycée, at the Lycée Janson-de-Sailly with Merleau-Ponty and Claude Lévi-Strauss.[20] Beauvoir recalled her feelings of exclusion and inadequacy when she used to pass the Collége Stanislas. Now she was in charge of a classroom of just the sort of boys she used to envy. She was an integral member of the next generation of the French intellectual aristocracy in the making. She had discovered pleasure. In one year, racing ahead of her colleagues, she was studying both for her final diploma and for the *agrégation*. Her world had opened up and she felt that she was on the 'road to final liberation'. She was sure 'that there was nothing in the world I couldn't attain now'.[21] Her childish sense of superiority had been vindicated as she triumphantly passed her written exams and was taken by her now proud father for a celebratory dinner at the Café Lipp. Beauvoir, indeed a pioneer, was preparing to face the adult world not only with confidence but with an appetite for experience that would never falter.

If Beauvoir's romance with Sartre's married friend, Maheu, ripened with the spring of 1929, so too did Sartre's interest in Beauvoir. Maheu was so aware of his friend as a potential rival for Beauvoir's affections that, whenever he was with Sartre, he snubbed her so as not to have to introduce them.[22] Then, at the beginning of May, just after her grandfather died, Sartre saw Beauvoir in a corridor in the Sorbonne dressed all in black, like Simone Jollivet on the day he met her. The sight seems to have moved him, and he made his first gesture in her direction by making a sketch for her of a man surrounded by mermaids, which he signed and labelled 'Leibniz bathing with the Monads': the philosopher was Beauvoir's thesis subject, the monads were the seventeenth-century philosopher's elementary units of being. The next day Maheu forgot his caution and presented the drawing to Beauvoir. She may have been charmed by the gesture which flattered both her intellect and her sense of the fantastic, but another month passed and Sartre still had not met her. Yet he was, in his words, 'dead set on making her acquaintance'.[23] He knew from Maheu what lectures she attended and so could easily have approached her, as was his habit with other women students he wanted to know. With Beauvoir, he was inhibited in a way that had not affected him during his earlier deep infatuation with Simone Jollivet. To understand Sartre's uncharacteristic behaviour, it may help to imagine what Beauvoir may have represented for him.

As a fellow candidate for the philosophy *agrégation*, Beauvoir offered herself for judgement against the same standards as Sartre. And, assuming that she would pass the examination on her first attempt, whereas he had failed, Sartre knew he would never be placed as highly in the competitive academic hierarchy of their generation as Beauvoir. Even if he had genuinely persuaded himself that his examination failure was due to excessive genius, there remained the fact that Beauvoir, age 21, was reaching the academic finishing line nearly three years faster then he. But these were not the only facts regarding Beauvoir that held dangers both for Sartre's traditional male ego and for his perception of himself as, with the exception of Raymond Aron, intellectually superior to his peers. Whereas Beauvoir had struggled with poor schools and often contrary parents, Sartre, as he well understood, had enjoyed, from cradle to *agrégation* nearly every possible educational advantage and encouragement that family, money, connections and masculinity could secure. For months, Maheu brought back reports to Sartre about the amazing Beaver, and so Sartre was well aware of the radical differences in their educational backgrounds and may have wondered what heights Beauvoir might have scaled had she received her fair share of the educational privileges that had been lavished on him and his friends.

In mid-June, after the candidates for the philosophy *agrégation* had sat several days of written exams, Maheu told Beauvoir he was leaving Paris with his wife and would return in ten days to prepare, with Sartre and Nizan, for his oral examination. He said that the men wanted her to join their study group, and that Sartre wanted to take her out. She was delighted with the first invitation and probably would have agreed to the second, having heard Maheu praise Sartre's charm and intellect. But Maheu, fearing the effect Sartre would have on her in his absence and not wanting his own affair with her to end, persuaded Beauvoir to send her sister in her place. On the evening Hélène went out with Sartre, Beauvoir, musing on her future, wrote in her journal:

> Curious certainty that this reserve of riches that I feel within me will make its mark, that I shall utter words that will be listened to, that this life of mine will be a well-spring from which others will drink.

Hélène reported back to Simone that 'she had done well to stay at home' and that everything Maheu said about Sartre's virtues was 'pure invention'.[24]

When June ended, Sartre, the womanizer, had still not met the friendly fellow student he was so 'dead set' on knowing. There remained a three-week study period before their oral examinations, after which their student days would be over. The legendary meeting between Beauvoir and Sartre finally occurred on the morning of the first Monday in July, when Beauvoir, full of apprehension, reported for the first group study session. This event, surely one of the most important meetings in twentieth-century intellectual history, is invariably related from Beauvoir's point of view, as she was the only one of the couple who wrote about it. But the encounter is perhaps more interesting considered from Sartre's perspective, given that he almost certainly had a much larger psychological investment in the meeting than Beauvoir. When she received the invitation to study with the three *normaliens*, she was pleased because it meant she 'would soon be seeing [Maheu] again' and because she 'was accepted by his group'.[25] Sartre, as an individual, appears not to have figured significantly in her anticipation of that momentous Monday. For Sartre, Beauvoir's arrival in his cluttered dormitory room was the realization of a desire that had lasted throughout the spring and into summer. Presumably, his unreturned interest in Beauvoir had been fuelled, not only by Maheu's

11

reports of the Beaver's critical intelligence and good humour, but also by her attractiveness, which, though not overly apparent in photographs, was much remembered by those who knew her in her youth. Recalling her in 1973, Maheu said, 'what a heart! She was so authentic, so courageously rebellious, so genuine, and as generous as Sartre. And she was so distinctly attractive, her own genre and her own style, no woman has ever been like her.' Nizan's widow, Henriette, who resented Beauvoir, and who still thought, 50 years later, that Beauvoir 'should have helped me butter the toast while the two pals [Sartre and Nizan] were together,' remembered Beauvoir as:

> a very pretty girl [with] ravishing eyes, a pretty little nose. She was extremely pretty, and even that voice, the same voice she has now, rather curious and a little broken, somewhat harsh – that voice added to her attractiveness. I don't think I ever saw her then dressed in anything but black ... As I said, she was a very serious girl, very intellectual, and these qualities and the black dress actually enhanced her glamour, her unselfconscious beauty.[26]

Beauvoir's confirmed intellectuality and independence of mind, and her rebellious insistence on never covering up these traits or even playing them down when in the presence of men must have provided a new experience for the young Maheu, whose notion of proper gender roles, Beauvoir said, corresponded to the prejudices of his day.[27] Yet as a well-married man enjoying an affair, Beauvoir posed no fundamental or permanent challenge to Maheu's perceived male role. With Sartre, however, a relationship with Beauvoir which took place on the margins of his existence was, as he surely realized, unlikely. He was romantically adrift, his happy cloistered college days were ending, and his 10-year-old couple relationship with Nizan was disintegrating as his friend settled ever more deeply into marriage and into the Communist Party. Worse still, in November, Sartre faced a year and a half of compulsory military service. More and more his immediate future must have appeared to him as a replay of the most traumatic event of his life: his fall from paradise at 1 rue le Goff into his La Rochelle hell of Others.[28] If he was going to save himself from a second fall, he quickly needed to form a new partnership. His only ready prospect was a woman unlike any he or his time had imagined, and the more Sartre learned of Beauvoir the more he must have realized that this way out of his predicament would lead him into a relationship as new, original and daring as the woman herself.

Sartre could hardly have been proud of the way he finally engineered his meeting with Beauvoir. That winter, when the sight of Maheu in the National Library had made Beauvoir desire his acquaintance, she had simply followed him into the restaurant, sat down at his table and engaged him in conversation about Hume and Kant. After three months of wanting to meet Beauvoir and having unlimited opportunities to do so, Sartre finally, backed up by Maheu and Nizan, gained his wish as she entered his room, feeling, she says, 'a bit scared'.[29] Decades later in an interview, she explained why.

> Maheu, Nizan, and Sartre were always inseparable. They came to very few courses because they despised the students at the Sorbonne and the classes there, while the Sorbonne students used to talk about them and say how terrible they were, that they were men without heart, without soul. And of the three, they would say the worst is Sartre, because they considered him a womanizer, a drunk, and a just plain bad person.... People looked at him with a kind of terror. No one dared say a word to any of them, and they on the other hand refused to lower themselves to talk with anyone else.[30]

Instead of giving Beauvoir a chance to find her feet, the three *normaliens* made her begin by leading them in a discussion of Leibniz, which she did 'all day long, petrified with fear'. But each day she went back and soon 'began to thaw out'. Eventually, dropping Leibniz for Rousseau, Sartre took charge of their revision.[31] Beauvoir recalled that she soon began to see in Sartre:

> someone who was generous with everyone, I mean really generous, who spent endless hours elaborating on difficult points of philosophy to help make them clear to others, without ever receiving anything in return. He was also very entertaining, very funny, and forever singing Offenbach and all sorts of other tunes. In other words, he was a totally different person from the one the Sorbonne students saw.[32]

The quartet met every day for two weeks, although they were soon taking afternoons and evenings off. Nizan's wife often joined them and they attended the fun fair at the Porte d'Orléans and drove around Paris in the Nizans' car. One day Beauvoir slipped off with Maheu and 'rented a room in a small hotel in the rue Vanneau' where she was, she says, 'ostensibly helping him to translate' Aristotle's *Nicomachean Ethics*.[33] Maheu was worried he had failed the written exams. A few days later the results were posted at the Sorbonne, and at the door Beauvoir met Sartre who told her that he, she and Nizan had passed, but Maheu had indeed failed. She knew it meant the departure of Maheu from Paris and possibly the end of their affair.

It was at this time that Sartre famously said to Beauvoir, 'From now on, I'm going to take you under my wing,' a remark that frequently has been quoted out of context, giving the impression that this paternalistic offer of protection permanently set the terms of their relationship.[34] In fact, however, this appears to be the first time Sartre had spoken to Beauvoir on his own, and the question of forming an intimate relationship with her was not in question. Sartre's remark, reported by Beauvoir in *Memoirs of a Dutiful Daughter*, is placed after accounts of her own bold and manifold confidence. It is presented as a contrast to Sartre's protracted hesitation at making her acquaintance, and has a comic ring, which was undoubtedly intended, as Beauvoir uses Sartre's remark as the introduction to a mocking, sarcastic portrait of his pretensions as a ladies' man:

> 'From now on, I'm going to take you under my wing,' Sartre told me when he had brought me the news that I had passed. He had a liking for feminine friendships. The first time I had ever seen him, at the Sorbonne, he was wearing a hat and talking animatedly to a great gawk of a woman student who I thought was excessively ugly; he had soon tired of her, and he had taken up with another, rather prettier, but who turned out to be rather a menace, and with whom he had very soon quarrelled.[35]

What Beauvoir later said first attracted her to Sartre was not his preemptory claiming of her as a lively disciple, but, far more believably, his qualities of vitality, generosity, warmth and uniqueness.[36] As she turned from Maheu to Sartre, she turned not to a protector but to an equal.

Sartre understood the choice that Beauvoir now had to make. As he explained to Gerassi, Sartre knew perfectly well that Maheu and Beauvoir's relationship was an intimate one: 'Maheu was in love with her … And she was in love with Maheu; in fact he was her first lover.'[37] But Sartre also felt that Maheu's examination failure had altered the circumstances significantly, and in a way that worked in his favour. With his romantic rival absent, and two weeks of oral examinations about to begin, Sartre pressed his opportunity. With the good impression he had made on Beauvoir over the previous fortnight, he had something upon which to build. He also must have been more determined than ever as he now knew that Maheu's reports regarding Beauvoir's personality and intellectual talent had not been exaggerated. Sartre's plans worked well; he and Beauvoir became recognized companions. Raymond Aron has spoken of the impact Sartre and Beauvoir's partnership had on his own life from the first:

I think that our relationship changed the day Sartre met Simone de Beauvoir. There was a time when he was pleased to use me as a sounding board for his ideas; then there was that meeting, which resulted in that, suddenly, I no longer interested him as an interlocutor.[38]

In cafés and on the paths of the Luxembourg, where they met every morning, Sartre and Beauvoir began the conversation that would last 51 years. They immediately found 'a great resemblance' in their attitudes.[39] But more important by far was their discovery that they were committed to similar dreams, whose extravagance required that they think inordinately well of themselves. Their deep-seated ambitions to become writers – in Sartre's case a great writer – had sprung directly from their childhood fantasies rather than from adult or even late teenage assessments of their aptitudes and possibilities. Of course, dreams of literary fame were common in their student milieu, but it was also customary to abandon them when graduation forced their holders out into 'the adult world'. With Sartre and Beauvoir, however, and especially with Sartre, there is a suspicion that they were psychologically incapable of forgoing belief in their literary futures without suffering mental collapse. If Beauvoir did not aspire to be a philosopher, or believe she was predestined for literary immortality, her aspirations, nevertheless, were more complex than Sartre's and, in total, more immodest. She gradually had become totally committed to leading the life of what today is called a 'liberated woman', *and by doing so she intended above all else to win happiness*.[40] Since his days on his grandfather's knee, Sartre could name scores of men who had succeeded in his dream, but Beauvoir could name no woman who had succeeded in hers. The price that women traditionally had to pay for rejecting conventional values was high, and Beauvoir did not intend to

15

pay it. She wanted both liberty *and* happiness, and her relationship with Sartre was to be structured in the light of both of her goals.

For Sartre, taking Beauvoir 'under his wing' meant re-enacting his most cherished moments with his mother. In Beauvoir's autobiography, she tells how, in their first days together, Sartre led her on searches of the riverside bookstalls for his favourite childhood comics, took her to cowboy films, invited her to share his belief in his destiny as a great writer, and enumerated the adventures he would have when, as he once travelled from A to Z through the *Larousse*, he began his intended world travels – fraternizing with the dockworkers, pimps and whiteslavers of Constantinople, the pariahs of India, the monks of Mount Athos and the fishermen of Newfoundland – all the while collecting material for his future masterpieces. To encourage Beauvoir's credulity about his ambitions, Sartre offered her his own credulity regarding her dreams. She had not encountered this before. He also encouraged her to talk about herself and, says Beauvoir, 'always tried to see me as part of my own scheme of things, to understand me in the light of my own set of values and attitudes' and explained to her how 'I would have to try to preserve what was best in me: my love of personal freedom, my passion for life, my curiosity, my determination to be a writer.'[41] But he also warned her, as was his standard tactic with young women he desired, to take care not to infringe his freedom, as, above all else, it was necessary that he remain free to fulfil his destiny as a great writer and great man.[42]

That year's three-man *agrégation* jury agonized over whether to give first place to Beauvoir or Sartre, although all agreed that of the two she was the 'true philosopher'. One judge held out for Beauvoir, but the others, after initially favouring the woman, decided that since Sartre was a *normalien*, that is, a man, he should receive first place.[43]

Chapter 2
Courtship and Union

Meanwhile, Sartre's friendship with the *sorbonnarde* was less than two weeks old and he was already hinting at marriage. Beauvoir, who never forgot his speech to her about preserving his freedom, was too embarrassed to reply, although Sartre was beginning to make her think that perhaps she could both remain true to herself and not have to face the future all on her own.[1] But if they were to have a more permanent relationship it would have to be on some basis other than the conventional one Sartre was suggesting, and, besides, she had yet to be won away from Maheu. She and Sartre were not yet lovers, and at the beginning of August, Beauvoir left him to spend the rest of the summer with her family in the country.[2] There, shortly after arriving, she borrowed money from her cousin, Madeleine, and travelled to nearby Uzerche were she rendezvoused with Maheu and spent three days with him before returning to Limousin.[3] Meanwhile, Sartre was about to redeem himself for the procrastination he had shown when seeking Beauvoir's acquaintance.

Beauvoir was at the kitchen table drinking her breakfast coffee when Madeleine rushed in to whisper that a very short man was waiting for her in the meadows beyond the tower. At once Beauvoir ran out to meet him. Sartre, who was not expected, had arrived the night before and taken a room at the local hotel. They picked up their discussion at the point where they had left off in Paris. Soon they realized that even if they carried on talking 'till Judgement Day', they would 'still find the time all too short'. Early every morning they met in the meadows. When the luncheon bell rang, Simone would go home to eat with her family, while Jean-Paul stayed and ate the cheese or gingerbread deposited by Simone's cousin Madeleine in an abandoned dovecote down the road. Immediately after lunch Beauvoir returned. 'Hardly had the afternoon begun before it was over, and darkness falling.'[4] Sartre would return to his hotel and eat alone. Beauvoir told her parents that they were writing a book together, a critical study of Marxism. She hoped that her parents' hatred of Communism would win their approval of her daily all-day rendezvous with an unknown man. But on the fourth day she saw them appear at the edge of the meadow where she and Sartre were sitting.

Sartre, wearing a bright red shirt, 'sprang to his feet'. Simone's father began a prepared speech in which he asked Sartre to leave the district because his day-long meetings with his daughter were causing a scandal that was damaging the entire family's reputation. When Simone protested, her mother screamed. Sartre spoke, forcefully but calmly, saying that they were in a hurry to complete their philosophical inquiry and so could not postpone their daily consultations, and Monsieur Beauvoir would have to explain that necessity to those whom he thought it concerned.[5] Sartre was victorious: the parents left without replying. Beauvoir realized that, 'My father and mother no longer controlled my life. I was truly responsible for myself now. I could do as I pleased, there was nothing they could say or do to stop me.' And Sartre? It was a performance of which any young man would be proud. He and Beauvoir were now lovers and he proposed marriage. 'I told him,' said Beauvoir in 1984, 'not to be silly and of course I rejected marriage.' Sartre, feeling it was the institution rather than himself that she was rejecting, argued for several days on behalf of marriage, not just in general but as a framework for their immediate lives.[6] Eventually, Beauvoir was forced to remind Sartre of his commitment to maintaining his complete freedom and of his extensive plans for bachelor travels. 'I was,' recalled Sartre ten years later, 'hoist with my own petard. The Beaver accepted that freedom and kept it. It was 1929. I was foolish enough to be upset by it: instead of understanding the extraordinary luck I'd had, I fell into a certain melancholy.'[7] When Sartre still remained in Limousin a week after Beauvoir's parents had told him to leave, Beauvoir told him that he had made his point. He should return to Paris and she would join him there. The infatuated Sartre left, clearly uncertain as to whether he had secured Beauvoir's affections on an other than temporary basis.

Sartre's worries may have been justified. The new lovers were now to be separated for a month and a half. During this time, the pair exchanged letters daily. When Beauvoir returned to Paris in the middle of September, Sartre was absent, and, in the month before his return, there were three major developments in Beauvoir's life. First, she set about clarifying her relationship with her cousin Jacques. That her intentions toward Sartre, and perhaps Maheu too, were still ambiguous is shown by the fact that it was not until after she called on her first love that she wrote of Jacques in her journal: 'I shall never marry him. I don't love him any more.' A few days later she learned that Jacques was engaged to marry a young woman, not for love but for her connections and large dowry; Beauvoir was shocked by how far she had misjudged him and 'heart-broken at the thought of seeing the hero of [her] youth transformed into a calculating bourgeois'. But a much greater jolt, as well as a more pointed warning of the dangers that lurked in the conventions of marriage, was the death of Zaza. Earlier that summer, as Beauvoir watched her friends Zaza and Merleau-Ponty fall in love and become engaged, she had thought: 'One of my dearest dreams was about to be realized: Zaza's life would be a happy one!' While stiff opposition to the marriage was expected from Zaza's parents, who by custom expected to choose their daughter's husband, Beauvoir thought that, at last, Zaza believed that she, though a woman, had a right to claim her own happiness. But by the end of summer Zaza's letters to Beauvoir had become despairing: she was caving in to her family's will and she had been forbidden by her mother to see or even write to Merleau-Ponty. When Beauvoir saw Zaza again in late September she 'was in a very low state; she had grown thin and pale; she had frequent headaches'. Beauvoir 'urged her to make a fight for her happiness', and urged Merleau-Ponty, who was worried about his own mother's reactions, to do the same.[8]

Two weeks later Beauvoir received a note from Zaza's mother informing her that her friend was gravely ill, with a high temperature and 'frightful pains in the head'. From Merleau-Ponty, Beauvoir learned that the day after she urged Zaza to fight for her happiness, she had gone to Merleau-Ponty's flat and in a 'confused state' questioned his mother on her opposition to their marriage. Later, Merleau-Ponty arrived, noted Zaza had a high fever and took her home in a taxi. Beauvoir tells how when she next saw Zaza she was in a chapel 'laid on a bier surrounded by candles and flowers. She was wearing a long nightdress of rough cloth. Her hair had grown, and now hung stiffly round a yellow face that was so thin I hardly recognized her.' The doctors were uncertain of the cause of her death. 'Had it been a contagious disease, or an accident?' asks Beauvoir. 'Or had Zaza succumbed to exhaustion and anxiety?' Although decades later she learned more about the events leading up to her friend's death, the tragedy's significance to Beauvoir remains the same: 'We had fought together against the revolting fate that had lain ahead of us, and for a long time I believed that I had paid for my own freedom with her death.[9] With those words Beauvoir concluded *Memoirs of a Dutiful Daughter* in which, she later said, 'my main desire really was to discharge a debt.'[10]

Beauvoir's entire adolescence had been given to her fight 'against the revolting fate', and the most important event in her life that autumn was that, when she returned from the country, she began her long dreamed of existence as an independent woman. Teaching jobs were assigned nationally and in the first instance were invariably in the provinces, so Beauvoir had decided, *before her first meeting with Sartre*, that she would take her rebellion still further and refuse a post so that she could remain in Paris and have time to write. Ironically, it was Maheu who had pushed her in this radical direction. She says that as she got to know him:

> I had the feeling of finding myself: he was the shadow thrown by my future. He was neither a pillar of the Church, nor a book-worm, nor did he spend his time propping up bars; he proved by personal example that one can build for oneself, *outside the accepted categories*, a self-respecting, happy, and responsible existence: exactly the sort of life I wanted for myself.[11]

Moving out of her parents' flat, Beauvoir rented a room in her grandmother's sixth-floor walk-up apartment. Her grandmother treated her 'with the same unobtrusive respect she showed her other lodgers'. There Beauvoir was free to come, go and entertain as she pleased and, for the first time in her life, she had a room of her own.[12] Some private tutoring and part-time teaching of Latin and Greek at a lycée earned her enough money to live.

When Sartre returned to Paris in mid-October, Beauvoir says she had decided that he 'corresponded exactly to the dream-companion I had longed for since I was fifteen ...'. Beauvoir's ideal needs closer examination as its complexity makes it easily misunderstood, and yet it is a factor of crucial importance in determining the nature of the Beauvoir–Sartre relationship. For her dream-companion, who at 15 she still imagined as her husband, Beauvoir says she 'had no particular type in mind' but 'a very precise idea of what our relationship would be'. Rather than be 'a man's companion', she would write and have a life of her own. She and her ideal would 'be two comrades' who would 'be able to discuss everything'. This required, she said, that they:

have everything in common; each was to fulfil for the other the role of exact observer which I had formerly attributed to God. That ruled out the possibility of loving anyone *different*; I should not marry unless I met someone more accomplished than myself, yet my equal, my double.

Someone more accomplished than herself, yet her equal, her double: this, of course, is a paradox and Beauvoir tries to resolve it. It emerges that she has two types of equality in mind: equality in terms of achievements and equality in terms of innate potential for achievement, or, as she calls these concepts, equality 'from without' and equality 'from within'. Her ideal companion is her equal from within and must also be nearly her equal from without or else they will not be able to discuss everything. But he cannot, at least in the beginning, be completely her equal from without; it is necessary to her concept of equality from within, which as an idealist she holds as the more important of the two, that he be superior to her from without. At the age of 15, Beauvoir had already understood the basic sociological facts of her female existence. Under the existing state of society and culture, males, vis-à-vis females, were favoured with better education and, perhaps more importantly, were encouraged at all points to have higher opinions of themselves and to cultivate loftier ambitions. Thus, any man of similar age, class and interests as her own would, as the recipient of decades of this positive discrimination, have had 'a flying start' over her. If he failed to show superiority of accomplishments, it would only testify to his inferiority within.[13]

On coming of age, Beauvoir defined herself on the basis of four values which, when situated in the existing sociology of the sexes, came perilously close to being self-contradictory. She was, as explained, committed to the pursuit of happiness, achievement and independence and, finally, placed great store on having a permanent partnership with her male double. But, without limiting her ambitions, it was extremely improbable that she could find her alter ego, and, if she did, then it was also unlikely he would join with her unless she bowed to social conventions regarding gender roles and unions between the sexes. Alternatively, without an approximation of her ideal relationship, her long-term happiness looked unlikely, and without happiness, her authorial aspirations would also be thrown into doubt. Some may wish to argue that Beauvoir (as she herself once thought) could have steeled herself and got on successfully without her ideal union, but the psychological intensity with which she engaged with Sartre for half a century shows beyond any reasonable doubt that her need for such a relationship was no less integral to her character than her unilateral commitments.

The question remains of how Beauvoir set up Sartre in her mind as her superior from without so that she would not see him as her inferior from within. Even for someone as intelligent as Beauvoir, this could not have been an easy task. If, with his flying start, Sartre had got through the *agrégation* two and half years quicker than Beauvoir, all would have been well, but, of course, the opposite was the case. Sartre had, in fact, at first failed where she had succeeded. Lesser writers would have let this problem with their narrative slip by when composing their memoirs, but not Beauvoir: she attempts to tackle it head on:

> Two years older than myself ... and having got off to a better start much earlier than I had, he had a deeper and wider knowledge of everything. But what he himself recognized as a true superiority over me, and one which was immediately obvious to myself, was the calm and yet almost frenzied passion with which he was preparing for the books he was going to write ... I couldn't imagine living and not writing: but he only lived in order to write.[14]

This, as she realizes, scarcely gets Sartre off the ground, but a few pages later Beauvoir succeeds in lifting him onto a very shaky pedestal. She focuses on his ambition to be a 'philosopher' – an ambition she did not share – and claims that he had already brought into existence 'a whole philosophy'. For evidence she recalls that the 'originality and coherence' of his philosophical talk 'astounded his friends' and quotes from Sartre's 'detailed outline' of his 'system of ideas' which had appeared as a letter in a student journal:

> It is a paradox of the human mind that Man, whose business it is to create the necessary conditions, cannot raise himself above a certain level of existence, like those fortune-tellers who can tell other people's future, but not their own. This is why, as the root of humanity, as at the root of nature, I can see only sadness and boredom.[15]

The 24-year-old's letter continues in this pompous, inflated, unsystematic and undergraduate vein, which, ten years later, a more mature Sartre himself characterized harshly if humorously as his attempt 'to translate craggy, unpolished thoughts into the style of Anatole France'. Beauvoir, however, decided that the young man's verbiage 'was positive proof that he would one day write a philosophical work of the first importance'.[16] Beauvoir's excess of confidence in Sartre needs to be seen as more than a stereotypical exaggeration of the talents of the beloved. This kind of extraordinary (indeed unreasonable) leap of faith is usually a precondition for the creation of such comprehensive works as those that Sartre intended to produce, and, by believing in Sartre, not only had Beauvoir found her ideal companion, but Sartre had found someone whose belief and commitment to his future greatness was as profound as he had once imagined his mother's to be. But Sartre was getting a great deal more than a new, improved version of his mother, because Beauvoir would never believe in Sartre uncritically. Like his grandmother, Beauvoir was inherently sceptical and questioning. She no sooner proclaimed the inevitability of his great writer's future than she began noting his considerable shortcomings, which, if his greatness was really to emerge, he would first have to overcome. She observed that he did not write very well, a serious handicap for one who wants to be a writer, an even more profound one for the individual who wants to be a great writer. He 'refused', she says, 'to separate philosophy from literature' and she was 'disconcerted by the clumsiness' of his essays. And when she read to him the novel she was writing, he responded in kind: 'I was alarmed,' says Beauvoir, 'to discover that the novel sets countless problems whose existence I had not even suspected.'[17]

No part of the Sartre–Beauvoir legend is more central or retold so often as the oath-taking that followed Sartre's October return to Paris in 1929. The story is usually told in something like the following way:

When Sartre returned to Paris, he and Beauvoir resumed their conversations, read each other's manuscripts, played games of man and wife, and began to think seriously about their future together. Beauvoir, being a woman and having waited for Sartre's return like a bride-to-be, surely hoped for marriage. But Sartre, the independent male, demurred and so 'it was essentially Sartre who explained to de Beauvoir what the nature of their relationship would be.'[18] He informed her that, as he was not monogamous by nature, he could not offer her sexual fidelity or even the opportunity to live with him under the same roof. But, 'to temper this revelation' he explained that theirs was an 'essential love', whereas any others they had would be only 'contingent'. The difference was, Sartre said, that they were two of a kind and their relationship would endure for as long as they did. Even so, they signed 'a two-year lease', meaning that in that time they would not have contingent love affairs – a promise which, of course, Sartre did not keep. They also agreed that the ideal to which they would peg their essential love was never to lie to or conceal anything from the other, that is, 'to tell one another everything'.[19] This meant that they would describe in intimate detail to each other their contingent loves, a practice that soon caused the naturally monogamous Beauvoir a great deal of distress.

This story, with its obvious sexual stereotypes, is plausible only if one is both committed to a literal and flat-footed reading of Beauvoir's very literary autobiographies and prepared to forget Sartre's marriage proposals, Beauvoir's affair with his friend, and a wide range of facts regarding the couple's individual pasts and characters.

A review of the timescale and chronology of events will highlight the improbability of the traditional account. Maheu did not leave Paris until some days after the Bastille Day celebrations of 14 July 1929. Beauvoir left Paris at the beginning of August. That gives Sartre and Beauvoir two weeks or less together, in which he, to her astonishment, hints at marriage. In late summer, Sartre appears at Limousin, while Beauvoir has had three days with Maheu in Uzerche. Beauvoir now becomes Sartre's lover and he immediately proposes marriage. She warns him not to be silly, but for several days he presses for marriage. In the end, she is forced to point out that his behaviour contradicts the claim he made for himself in Paris, and a few days later, at her request, he leaves. They next see each other in Paris in mid-October, and Sartre leaves for military service at the beginning of November. They were left with only two further weeks together.

The traditional account is rationalized by appeals to sexual stereotypes and to Beauvoir's memoirs. But her autobiographies are open to other readings, and, even if they were not, it is difficult to accept the old story as the true one: too much has become known. More plausible is the explanation that Sartre, in his self-reported melancholy, came to accept the fact that Beauvoir was not going to marry him and that the famous terms they laid down for their relationship were merely the best *he* could get. Of course, Sartre was not monogamous by nature, but neither was Beauvoir's father, or Beauvoir herself, for that matter, and one feels she would have done almost anything not to undergo a marriage like her mother's. Besides, Beauvoir, as she says when describing how she and Sartre came to their understanding, 'had broken free of [her] past, and was now self-sufficient and self-determining'; and had established her 'autonomy once and forever, and nothing could now deprive [her] of it', whereas Sartre had only 'more or less shed the irresponsibility of adolescence'.[20] Also, Sartre had two 'partnerships' – with his mother and with Nizan – and with each he had lived in the same room, but there was no such precedent in Beauvoir's life: she had never lived with Zaza or with Jacques. Her domestic dream of dreams was to have a room of her own, and now she had it.

The manner (highly reminiscent of her treatment of Sartre's 'take you under my wing' remark) in which Beauvoir embeds Sartre's request for 'a two-year lease' in a metaphorical incident in *The Prime of Life* should leave the reader in no doubt as to where Beauvoir thought the balance of power lay on the occasion of their oath.

We walked down as far as the Carrousel Gardens, and sat down on a stone bench beneath one wing of the Louvre. There was a kind of balustrade which served as a back-rest, a little way out from the wall; and in the cagelike space behind it a cat miaowing. The poor thing was too big to get out; how had it ever got in? Evening was drawing on; a woman came up to the bench, a paper in one hand, and produced some scraps of meat. These she fed to the cat, stroking it tenderly the while. It was at this moment that Sartre said: 'Let's sign a two-year lease.'[21]

Chapter 3
Carousing

Sartre and Beauvoir's relationship, like the balustrade in Carrousel Gardens, was to have openings in it. Like the miaowing cat caught in the cage, the petitioning Sartre had become variously swollen through the intermittent attentions of Beauvoir who was now obliging him with the two-year lease, as his army induction, like the evening, was drawing near.

What the usual accounts of Sartre and Beauvoir's initial pledge to each other also tend to devalue is the fact that there were other clauses in their agreement, compared to which their sexual arrangements are of subsidiary importance: for example, they promised they would 'tell each other everything' and would never allow anything to 'prevail against this alliance'. But the putative two-year sexual lease is of interest for what it has for so long covered up. The two years were to be special because in them, says Beauvoir, 'There was no question of our actually taking advantage ... of those "freedoms" which in theory we had the right to enjoy.'[1] This implies she had agreed to end her affair with Maheu. Indeed, at this point Maheu drops out of her memoirs and their veracity on this matter has always been accepted. But as Beauvoir and Sartre sat on the stone bench in the Carrousel Gardens with the evening drawing on, Maheu was due back in Paris to begin another year studying for the *agrégation*.

A letter, first published in 1990, from Beauvoir to Sartre, and which includes a letter from Maheu to her, sheds further light on the events in the Carrousel Gardens in 1929. Dated Tuesday 6 January 1930, Beauvoir's letter was written only two months after the oath taken in the shadows of the Louvre. The relevant section reads as follows:

I was very annoyed yesterday by a *pneu* I got from the Llama [Maheu's nickname] ... I'm copying out his note ...

Can you be at home on *Wednesday afternoon?* ... I have some quite important things to tell you, since it is possible I shall never see you again. For you must understand that I have had my fill of the pretty situation that now exists, as a result of that September of yours and the two months of lying which followed it, and that I deserve something better than the crumbs – the relations continued out of charity 'because I am unhappy' – that you both offer me with such elegance.

> I shall tell him, all the same, how astonishing I find this note of his ... he always said that he accepted this situation, and that what he feared was seeing it change. He, who finds it so easy to reconcile his affections for his wife, for me and for the Humous Lady, is really the last person who can reproach me for loving somebody besides him.... I was very upset that day at the Napoli and the Café des Sports, when I saw the Llama being so nice after the letter was discovered. I was still a bit upset at the Closeries des Lilas the other day. But this note hasn't upset me at all, because I see it as mere jealousy of a thoroughly disagreeable kind.
>
> How are you, little man? I'm really longing for a letter from you tomorrow. We'll be seeing each other soon, won't we, my love? You promised, so I'm taking good care of myself. I love you. I am, most tenderly, your own Beaver.[2]

From Beauvoir's letter it can be concluded that she did not end her liaison with Maheu, and the famous two-year lease on sexual fidelity was merely a fiction constructed, not for Beauvoir and Sartre, but for the readers of Beauvoir's memoirs. In fact, the distinction between essential and contingent loves was operational from the first day of the Sartre–Beauvoir pact, and Beauvoir's letter illustrates how the difference, when combined with the full-disclosure principle, actually worked to create their 'morganatic marriage'. By practising 'translucence' with Sartre and not with Maheu, Beauvoir causes the latter to feel that he is receiving only the 'crumbs' left by his rival, despite Sartre's absence from Paris. It is also important to note how far Beauvoir takes her translucence by admitting to Sartre that she was 'very upset' when Maheu, after discovering the truth about Beauvoir and Sartre in the letter, did not initially react. Beauvoir's letter also reveals something about her autobiographical technique. *The Prime of Life* begins with Sartre's arrival at Limousin at the end of August 1929, but Maheu is not given a direct appearance in the book until she relates the events of early February 1931, a year and a month after the above letter. Yet, surely, it is this same letter to which Beauvoir now misleadingly refers.

> For some time our relationship had rested on an equivocal basis. He [Maheu] had no intention of admitting what Sartre meant to me, and I had no intention of enlightening him on the subject. Two months previously he had found a letter in my room which made the situation quite clear: he had laughed at the time, but had shown some annoyance too – although he had never concealed the fact that he was highly interested in a girl from Coutances.[3]

If Beauvoir's readers are surprised by her authorial rearranging of the facts, they have only themselves to blame: in the preface to her second volume of autobiography, she clearly states her ground rules.

> At the same time I must warn them [her readers] that I have no intention of telling them everything.... . I have no intention of filling these pages with spiteful gossip about myself and my friends; I lack the instincts of the scandalmonger. There are many things which I firmly intend to leave in obscurity.[4]

Foremost, it seems, among those 'many things' to be kept out of the public domain were the precise details of her sexual relations. Contrary to popular trends, sex remained for Beauvoir largely a private and personal matter, and it has become customary to attribute this preference to an innate prudishness fostered by her generation and class. But perhaps rationality was also at work. Perhaps, as someone whose life's work centred on exposing the tyrannies of the Other, she was, in the face of celebrity, committed to preserving her own subjectivity, no less than her privacy. And as someone renowned for her gift for genuine and lasting friendships, perhaps she also was motivated, and not irrationally, to practise discretion out of loyalty to her friends. Beauvoir wrote *The Prime of Life* in the late 1950s, and it would have been unhelpful then to Sartre's public image, and to her own, if she had made it known widely that it was her promiscuity, even more than Sartre's, that had determined the terms of their relationship. Furthermore, as shall be seen, the fiction of the two-year lease served to hide more of Beauvoir's sexual activity in the early 1930s than solely her continuing affair with Maheu.

In November 1929, a month after the New York Stock Market crashed, Sartre's status as a *normalien* cushioned his army induction. He and his classmate, Pierre Guille, were assigned to a meteorology training centre on the outskirts of Paris, where they launched paper aeroplanes at their colleague and instructor, Raymond Aron. But, in January 1930, this arrangement, which so neatly parodied his student life, ended, and Sartre was sent to a post near Tours without his fellow *normaliens*. He was now three hours by train from Paris and he tasted ordinary adult existence devoid of educational privilege for the first time. 'Just think,' he wrote to Beauvoir:

> the details of my life here are so well regulated, minute by minute, that I know for certain that in eight times twenty-four hours, at 18:15 I will take the same readings, which will begin with the same numbers, after performing the same actions. This will always be mechanical, but I know that the same thoughts will recur, the same hope and despair and all the schizophrenic fabrications which I notice I'm trusting more and more.[5]

If Sartre was tormented by the mechanistic regularity of army life, in Paris, Beauvoir's life radically shifted towards the other extreme of disorder and unpredictability as she settled into a bohemian existence which was as alien to her as Sartre's enforced monotony was to him. For as long as she could remember, Beauvoir's personal reality had been dominated by her preparation for examinations and by the accelerated pace at which she had taken them. She had judged every hour, even those given to recreation, in terms of the series of hurdles society placed between her and the *agrégation*. Now, except for a few hours of simple teaching, her time was free from the demands of any externally defined system of goals. No longer a student, not yet a committed teacher or writer, and actively refusing to honour the rules attendant on her female status, she found herself without a social role to play and cut off from any structured future. In short, Beauvoir had placed herself in a position where she could no longer define herself, even vaguely, by compliance with a pre-established order.

According to the philosophy Sartre later outlined in *Being and Nothingness*, Beauvoir's situation was both psychologically dangerous and epistemologically privileged. Sartrean existentialism begins with the idea that a person is nothing but a series of undertakings which they *choose* in given sets of circumstances; and Sartre's lengthy treatise seeks to explain the consequences of this inalienable freedom. He begins by arguing, in his first chapter, that individuals apprehend their existential freedom with anguish, but, with rare exceptions, evade this apprehension by immersion in routines and values imagined as beyond freedom of choice. However, when an individual is exiled from the everyday world, as Beauvoir was for the two years following her student days, the consequence may be not only anguish, but also fundamental insight into the human condition. It was Beauvoir's experience that Sartre was almost certainly drawing upon when he wrote the following in *Being and Nothingness*:

> There exists concretely alarm clocks, signboards, tax forms, policemen, so many guard rails against anguish. But as soon as the enterprise is held at a distance from me, as soon as I am referred to myself because I must await myself in the future, then I discover myself suddenly as the one who gives its meaning to the alarm clock, the one who by a signboard forbids himself to walk on a flower bed or on the lawn, the one from whom the boss's order borrows its urgency, the one who decides the interest of the book which he is writing, the one finally who makes the values exist in order to determine his action by their demands. I emerge alone and in anguish confronting the unique and original project which constitutes my being; all the barriers, all the guard rails collapse, nihilated by the consciousness of my freedom. I do not have nor can I have recourse to any value against the fact that it is I who sustain values in being. Nothing can ensure me against myself, cut off from the world and from my essence by this nothingness which I *am*. I have to realize the meaning of the world and of my essence; I make my decision concerning them – without justification and without excuse.[6]

Instead of having an imposed schedule of lectures to attend and examinations to take, Beauvoir now faced only the amorphous goal of becoming a published writer. There was no daily network of support, no prescribed way for her to proceed and little likelihood that, whatever way she chose to pursue her ambition, she would be successful. Meanwhile, the pleasures of being young, daring, high-spirited and at liberty in Paris cried out to her, and, within a few months, Beauvoir's literary ambitions were submerged beneath a vivacious hedonism. Moreover, writing for one's self, she found, was not as easy as she had imagined. Ensconced in her own room and faced with blank sheets of paper, Beauvoir discovered that she 'had no idea what to write *about'*. She says she 'found the world's crude immediacy stupefying' and 'had no viewpoint of it to present' and, in default, fell into a crude pastiche of her favourite novels: Alain-Fournier's *Le Grand Meaulnes* and Rosamond Lehmann's *Dusty Answer*.[7] From these she patched together a story that was to be her first novel. She abandoned it at the third chapter.

Beauvoir, however, was scarcely short of things to do: that was half the problem. Besides devouring many novels, often in English, while hunched beside the fire in Sylvia Beach's bookshop and lending library, Shakespeare and Company, Beauvoir found herself in demand by an eclectic and shifting assortment of people. With her sister and Gégé she frequented the Jockey Club and La Jungle where, she says, she 'made dates and went out with anyone – or almost anyone'. Fernando Gerassi, before he and Stépha moved to Madrid to join the struggle to establish the Republic, introduced her into the group of mostly foreign artists, musicians and poets, which included the Delauneys and Tristan Tzara, who drank late into the night at the Café des Arts. Beauvoir attended their gatherings 'regularly', and, on at least one occasion, accompanied the group afterwards to the Sphinx, a famous brothel of the day, whose pimps included Henry Miller, and which had the distinction of being the first air-conditioned building in Paris.[8] On other nights Beauvoir entertained various artists and writers from Madrid and Budapest, sent to her by Fernando and by a Hungarian friend. 'Night after night,' she wrote:

> I showed them around Paris, while they talked to me of other great unknown cities. I also went out occasionally with a young Chez Burma salesgirl, ... whom I found a very likable character ... We went to dance halls on the rue de Lappe, our faces smothered in powder and lipstick, and we were a great success. My favourite partner was a young butcher's assistant.

'It was seldom,' she adds, 'that I got to bed before two in the morning.'[9]
During Beauvoir's two years 'alone' in Paris, Sartre's friends also played

a part in her frenetic social life. There was Maheu, of course, who divided his time between the provinces and Paris, but, increasingly, his position as Beauvoir's second lover was threatened by Guille, who, when Sartre was shipped off to Tours, had the good fortune to be assigned to the capital. Since his university days, Guille had enjoyed the favours of a Madame Morel, a wealthy, highly educated, fashionable lady in her 40s, who had been raised in the Argentine and who, with the encouragement of her invalid husband, had taken Guille both as her lover and as the tutor of her two teenage children. Along with a country house and a villa on the Riviera, the Morels maintained a large flat on the Boulevard Raspail, where Guille had his own room. Sartre, though less frequently, had also enjoyed the multifaceted hospitality of Madame Morel. During his absence in the army, Beauvoir became an habituée of the Morel household. Several times a week she dined there, or with the household's various members in restaurants, and she often joined Guille and Madame Morel for long drives in the country. In Sartre's absence, Beauvoir quickly found favour with Guille. Madame Morel, far from standing in the way, encouraged the new liaison by loaning the couple her car for trips to Chartres, to the Château de Chaumont and, three or four times, to Tours, presumably to visit Sartre.[10]

On Sundays either Sartre came to Paris, or Beauvoir, with an armful of borrowed books, made the long rail journey to Tours, returning by the 5 am train, which arrived at the Gare d'Austerlitz just in time to allow her a few hours of teaching. In the late summer of 1930, Beauvoir took up residence for a month in a small hotel on the banks of the Loire, ten minutes from where Sartre carried out his weather observations using 'a sort of miniature Eiffel Tower'. He recently had inherited the equivalent of a few thousand dollars from his grandmother which, with Beauvoir, he ran through by patronizing expensive restaurants – a lifelong enthusiasm – and by chartering taxis to tour the valley's châteaux. Like Beauvoir, Sartre had plenty of free time, but, in her absence, was not tempted by the local diversions. Instead he applied himself to fulfilling his imagined destiny of becoming a great writer. Yet his vision of the form his greatness would take seems to have remained embarrassingly vague. He initially wrote poetry, which, when read by Beauvoir and Guille, evoked unintended hilarity. He switched to a novel based on the story Beauvoir had given him of Zaza's death. When this was also rejected by his two critics, he moved on to 'The Legend of Truth', a 'philosophical work' related as a story in the manner of Nietzsche. Beauvoir deplored its 'antiquated method' and 'the stiffness of his style', but, this time, Sartre persisted with the exercise.[11]

In her autobiography, Beauvoir relates how during the two years following university, she was more interested in sex than in literary pursuits. In 1929, she says she learned 'to take unconstrained pleasure' in her body, and in 1930–1, 'separated from Sartre for days or even weeks at a time', she frequently 'fell a victim' to sexual desire. Even in the hours immediately after being with Sartre, her appetite for sex could put her at risk. 'In the night train from Tours to Paris the touch of an anonymous hand along my leg could arouse feelings – against my conscious will – of quite shattering intensity.' The anonymous hand may not have been beyond her powers of resistance, but on other nights of the week she was with men she more or less knew and also liked, and with them, resistance was not so easy, or even attempted. Beauvoir's account of her struggle with her sexuality during this period is full of images which imply that, except on the night train, she was incapable of resisting her 'burning pangs of desire' and frequently enjoyed sex with partners other than her mainstays, Sartre, Maheu and Guille. She speaks of 'my tyrannical desires', of 'the discrepancy between my physical emotions and my conscious will', of how 'my body compromised me completely', and of 'lurid desires that ... struck me with the force of a thunderbolt'. She says, 'I ... felt my freedom being engulfed by the flesh' and also felt 'condemned to a subordinate rather than a commanding role where the private movements of my body were concerned.'

Despite her unease, this all accorded well with her romantic belief that 'The pleasures of love-making should be as unforseen and as irresistible as the surge of the sea or a peach tree breaking into blossom.' 'My body had its own whims,' she writes, 'and I was powerless to control them; their violence overrode all my defenses', and although in the morning she would find her desire sated, 'by nightfall my obsession would rouse itself once more'. She said she 'dared not confess such things' to Sartre, thereby breaking their 'policy of absolute frankness'. 'By driving me to such secrecy,' she continues, 'my body became a stumbling block rather than a bond of union between us, and I felt a burning resentment against it.'[12]

In February 1931, several weeks before Sartre, Guille was discharged from the army. He borrowed Madame Morel's car, and invited Beauvoir to join him on a tour of France. She says she 'went straight into a kind of daze, exhilarated ... at the thought of ten days' tête-à-tête with' Guille. But, two days before their departure, Maheu turned up in Paris without his wife, expecting to spend the next two weeks with Beauvoir. He issued an ultimatum: if she went off with Guille, he would break off their long-standing affair. Beauvoir says she chose Guille, because she 'now valued his intimacy more than' Maheu's. [13]

If his partner's sexual promiscuity disturbed Sartre – and, even given the sexual adventurism of their set of friends, it is difficult to think that it would not – neither his nor Beauvoir's writing gives any indication of it. But the fact that they both saw Beauvoir as 'well on the road to self-betrayal and self-destruction' was another matter and one about which Sartre's concern appears to have outstripped Beauvoir's. In fact, the manner in which Sartre responded actively to Beauvoir's existential breakdown was thoroughly admirable. Both he and Beauvoir realized that she was in great danger. It was not only that she was losing sight of her goal of becoming a writer, she was also becoming intellectually passive. In the face of Sartre's mental energies, she, by default, was accepting a secondary status, 'that of a merely ancillary being'. It was Beauvoir's good fortune – and without it, it seems unlikely that she would be of interest today – that in Sartre she had found perhaps the only male intellectual of his generation in all of France who was not pleased to see his lover lapse into her traditional gender role. Increasingly, Sartre threw his energies into reviving Beauvoir's ambition, her appetite for ideas, and her habit of saying what *she thought* about things. He told her that he especially missed the flood of ideas that used to originate with her which had formed so much of the basis of their discussions. And he warned her not to turn herself into a 'female introvert' or a 'man's helpmeet'. Beauvoir accepted his criticism: 'I was furious with myself,' she says, 'for disappointing him in this way.'[14]

Both Beauvoir and Sartre had talked about going abroad separately to work for a few years, but in the spring of 1931 Sartre went straight from the army into a teaching post at a boys' lycée in Le Havre, while Beauvoir accepted a post at a girls lycée in Marseille which would begin in October. Le Havre was two and a half hours from Paris, but Marseille was 500 miles from the capital and even further from Le Havre. The prospect of this radical separation from both Sartre and Paris fuelled Beauvoir's despair and disillusionment. Sartre offered marriage, as, under the rules of the central French educational bureaucracy, this would have entitled them to teaching assignments in the same town. Beauvoir declined. Instead they revised their original pact, agreeing to postpone their separation at least until they reached their 30s. In June their lives brightened when the

Gerassis returned to Paris long enough for Stépha to give birth to her son before leaving for Spain. To their satisfaction, the Republic had been established, and Beauvoir and Sartre were urged to come to Madrid to join the celebrations. In August 1931, the French couple, with almost no money but with their generous friends awaiting them, crossed into Spain. It was their first trip outside of France. It set the pattern for their travels together over the next half century, with Beauvoir making all the arrangements and Sartre obligingly trailing after her as she, ravenous for experience, sought to visit every known sight. At the end of September, after six happy weeks, they crossed back into France to take up their new and separate lives as provincial schoolteachers. At Bayonne, Beauvoir, awash with tears, left the Paris train to pick up the Marseille express.

Chapter 4
Would-be Authors

A week later, from Le Havre, Sartre wrote Beauvoir a long letter describing his new life.[1] He lived in a seedy hotel situated between the train station, the docks and the red light district, patronized the local cafés, taught five hours a day, went to Paris on his Wednesdays off, and walked aimlessly around Le Havre thinking about his new project, an essay on contingency. This was a topic then very much in vogue, rather like 'structure' in the 1970s, and on which he and Beauvoir were required to write in their examinations for the *agrégation*.[2] The idea of contingency is a key concept in the phenomenological philosophical tradition to which Sartre and Beauvoir belong. It refers to the proposition that existence of all forms, including physical matter, cannot be identified with necessity. In Sartre's letter to Beauvoir of 9 October 1931, he describes his discovery of a chestnut tree in a local park, which subsequently he would use to famous effect as a symbol for contingency. But the work in which Sartre would utilize this observation from his early days in Le Havre would only appear in the future after a long and sometimes desperate struggle. Meanwhile, he missed his alter ego, and told her so:

My dearest, you cannot know how I think of you every minute of the day, in this world of mine which is so filled with you. Sometimes I miss you and I suffer a little (a very tiny little bit), at other times I'm happy to think that the Beaver exists, buys herself some chestnuts, takes a stroll; the thought of you never leaves me and I carry on little conversations with you in my head.[3]

If Sartre saw himself in Le Havre as an exile, Beauvoir's autobiography explains that she treated her arrival in Marseille as a second chance, having, over the previous two years, failed so miserably to establish the self-discipline needed to succeed as a writer. In this Mediterranean city where she knew no one, she hoped to find within her enforced solitude the 'greater familiarity with [her]self' that would give her the power to control her daily existence in a manner consistent with her goals. Removed from temptations offered by friends, she set out to free herself, too, from those of her body, subjecting herself to large and regular doses of strenuous physical exercise: tennis in the mornings before teaching, and walking and climbing alone in the rugged hills and mountains above Marseille on her days off. 'I never once,' she writes, 'found myself wondering how to spend my Thursdays and Sundays. I made it a rule to be out of the house by dawn, winter and summer alike, and never to return before nightfall.' She continues:

> At first I limited myself to some five or six hours' walking; then I chose routes that would take nine to ten hours; in time I was doing over twenty-five miles in a day. I worked my way systematically through the entire area: I climbed every peak ... and clambered down every gully; I explored every valley, gorge, and defile.

Beauvoir's solitary rambles developed in her a lifelong taste for 'pleasure in driving [her] body to the very limits of endurance,' and for the exhilaration of coping with physical dangers, in this case, from the very different threats of rape and of falls.

On one of her rambles she struggled up a series of steep gorges that she thought would lead her out onto a plateau. The further she climbed the more difficult it became and the more impossible it became for her to get back down by the route she had clambered up. So she kept on. Eventually 'a sheer wall of rock blocked any further advance'. So she had no choice but to retrace her steps from one gorge to the next. Eventually she came to fault in the rock across which she was afraid to jump. She could hear nothing except the rustling of snakes slithering on the stones. 'No living soul would ever pass through this defile: suppose I broke a leg or twisted an ankle; what would become of me?' For a quarter of an hour she shouted for help, but of course got no reply. In the end she leaped and landed unscathed. [4]

The tough physical regime that Beauvoir initiated to pull herself out of her intellectual torpor worked. Before long, she says, 'I had subdued my rebellious body, and ... I no longer despised myself.'[5] Her reading again became purposeful, and, as usual, related to her situation. She was fascinated by the stories, journals and letters of Katherine Mansfield, and by their exploration of the concept of the 'solitary woman'. Beauvoir also began a new novel, and, unlike the previous one, stuck with it until it was finished. For the first time, Beauvoir felt she did have something to say. There was the previous year's breakdown of her will and self-respect, and her attempt to use Sartre to 'release her from the burden of supporting the weight of her own life' upon which to reflect in her writing.[6] And, recalling how she had once tried to use Zaza in the same way, she progressed to the formulation of a general concept which she called 'the mirage of the Other'. This was the decisive beginning of a lifetime of intellectual originality. The Other became a theme in Beauvoir's new novel and in most of those that followed but more importantly, in the idea of the Other, she – at the age of 23 – had found a rich and almost untouched topic for philosophical research. Gradually, over the next two decades, Beauvoir would develop her theory of the Other which would have a profound influence on her career, and an even greater one on Sartre's. The concept, with its supporting theoretical apparatus, would be Beauvoir's gift to the social and intellectual history of the century.

In the autumn of 1932, after her year in Marseille and a summer travelling with Sartre in Spain and Morocco, Beauvoir was posted to a lycée in Rouen, a mere hour from Le Havre and an hour and a half from Paris. It meant the couple could have Thursdays – their day off – together, as well as the weekends, which they frequently spent in the capital. Beauvoir took a room in a hotel near Rouen's train station and began work on another novel. She was now fully committed to serving a hard literary apprenticeship and was heartened by having Sartre's support near at hand. Beauvoir regarded her new novel, on which she would work for two years and take through several drafts, as purely a learning exercise, intended not for publication but to sharpen and deepen her skills as a novelist.

Sartre also was coming to terms with the fact that, unlike Nizan, he was not going to be an overnight success as a writer. Sartre's friend's account of his year abroad, *Aden-Arabie*, had won critical acclaim. Nizan tried, unsuccessfully, to put his nascent influence to work on Sartre's behalf. He attempted, but failed, to find a publisher for Sartre's student novel, *A*

Defeat, and for his philosophical fable, 'The Legend of Truth'. Sartre kept writing. Gradually, with Beauvoir's help, Sartre's essay on contingency was turning into a novel. Whenever the couple met, Beauvoir read what Sartre had written or rewritten in her absence. He had learned, as she explains, to accept her criticism:

I knew exactly what he was after, and I could more nearly put myself in a reader's place than he could when it came to judging whether he had hit the mark or not. The result was that he invariably took my advice. I criticized him with minute and meticulous severity, taking him to task for, among other things, overdoing his adjectives and similes.[7]

Their association, however, was not confined to ideas and writing. They shared an avid taste both for gossip and for psychological analysis. Whenever they were together, Beauvoir and Sartre's main topic of conversation was the various people they knew, he especially being fascinated with 'reading their characters'. Beauvoir found Sartre's 'psychological penetration' deeper than hers, but, as she explains in *The Prime of Life*, ultimately her interest in the existence of other people at this time was largely attuned to metaphysical and philosophical speculation, rather than Sartre's more purely psychological interest. In her apprentice novels Beauvoir had undertaken the analysis of 'the mirage of the Other', but she says, on a more general level:

The existence of Otherness remained a danger for me, and one which I could not bring myself to face openly. At the age of eighteen I had fought hard against sorcery that aimed to turn me into a monster, and I was still on the defensive.

Her first method of defence was to pretend that other people 'had not eyes with which to observe' her, but, in a few years, Beauvoir would find the confidence to drop her shield so as to explore and analyse the existence of Otherness.[8] The philosophical prize she would gain by so doing would be enormous.

Meanwhile, she and Sartre were also working out their notion of bad faith, which was intended to embrace 'all those phenomena which other people attributed to the unconscious mind'. Such a concept, which went beyond psychological determinism, was essential to the success of what had become their joint project of developing a philosophy that was both logically coherent – an absolute requirement for the more rigorous Beauvoir – and consistent with their mutual devotion to the idea of human freedom. By observing themselves and the people around them, they set out together to describe self-deceit in all its forms. 'We rejoiced,' says Beauvoir, 'every time we unearthed ... another type of deception.'[9] These discoveries, together with the system of analysis they were slowly constructing, would figure prominently in their future writings.

Sometime during the 1932–3 academic year, Beauvoir and Sartre had an important conversation with Raymond Aron. Aron was in Paris on holiday from Berlin, where, with a year's fellowship at the French Institute, he was finishing a thesis and studying the philosophy of Edmund Husserl. Sartre and Beauvoir were already familiar with the German phenomenologist, thanks to the many-talented Fernando Gerassi, who had studied under Husserl in Berlin, where one of his classmates had been Martin Heidegger.[10] But it was Aron who sparked the couple's interest in Husserl's approach to philosophy and, more importantly at the time, offered Sartre a year's respite from his dull life as a provincial schoolteacher. It could be arranged, explained Aron to his fellow *normalien*, for them to exchange positions for a year. Sartre was delighted with the prospect. He immediately bought his first book on phenomenology.[11]

With Beauvoir, Sartre visited England at Easter 1933 and toured Mussolini's Italy in the summer, before going on to begin his year in Berlin. Hitler had been Chancellor since January, but there is no evidence that Sartre took special notice of the uniformed thugs who were to be seen in the streets terrorizing Jews. Sartre, without Beauvoir's hunger for exploration, rarely, it seems, ventured far from the French Institute, where he spent his mornings studying Husserl and his evenings working on a new draft of his novel. He had arrived with high hopes of sexual conquests with the local women, but these quickly evaporated in the face of his inadequate German. He settled instead for an affair with the emotionally disturbed wife of one of the other French fellows. When Beauvoir visited him in February 1934, Sartre introduced her to his lover, thereby forcing Beauvoir to walk the same kind of psychological minefield she had for so long forced him to tread vis-à-vis herself, Maheu and Guille. She seems not to have been put off her stride. In Sartre's absence she had rekindled her longstanding affair with Guille. In her autobiography she says that during this period she told Guille everything that happened to her and that 'he occupied a most important place' in her life.[12]

When, in October 1934, Sartre returned to his teaching post in Le Havre, he turned over to Beauvoir his German text of Husserl's *Leçons sur la conscience interne du temps*.[13] Having finished her second apprentice novel and with no new writing projects in mind, Beauvoir threw herself into the study of phenomenology. She was an exceptionally fast reader, in contrast to Sartre, who, in an interview in 1972, admitted that he had always been a very slow one. In the same interview he went on to say:

> it takes me far too long to understand things ... It takes me a lot longer, for instance, than it does the Beaver here. The Beaver is much faster than I am. I'm more like a snail.[14]

After his return from Berlin, Sartre soon acknowledged that, as with other philosophical doctrines, Beauvoir's grasp of Husserl's 'was quicker and more precise than his own'. Every time she and Sartre met, they discussed Husserl's work, and Beauvoir recalls that 'the novelty and richness of phenomenology filled me with enthusiasm; I felt I had never come so close to the real truth.'[15] Despite its intimidating name, phenomenology's project is the mundane one of the description of experience. Although such an undertaking might seem an obvious starting point to the non-philosopher, it was, in fact, an approach radically neglected by philosophy, not just by French rationalism and German idealism, but also by British empiricism.

Husserl's phenomenological method (called 'epoché', which is the Greek word for 'bracketing') is to focus on some part of one's experience and then to describe it by 'removing' oneself from its immediacy. This psychical distancing is achieved by analysing away the preconceptions one brings to the objects of one's perceptions. The method's rewards were thought to be two-fold: it would reveal the structures of experience, thereby leading to metaphysical insights, and it would bring philosophy back into contact with the real world. But despite these worthy intentions, Husserl's philosophical programme very soon reached an impasse. From the Austrian philosopher Franz Brentano, Husserl adopted the principle of intentionality, which holds that consciousness is always conscious of something, that is, that consciousness intends an object. To this, Husserl added his notion of a 'pure' ego or inner self, separated from one's spatio-temporal self, not derived from experience, and residing pristine and soul-like at the 'core' of consciousness. The impasse arose when it turned out that it was this 'transcendental ego', and not the outside world, to which Husserl's bracketing led. The objects of consciousness would be revealed only through the mediation of the transcendental ego and in the form of 'essences'. Not for the first time, a sincere effort by philosophy to engage with the empirical world had the opposite effect of submerging it in idealism.

It is not clear at what point Beauvoir realized that, ultimately, Husserl's method led her and Sartre away from rather than toward their goal of direct philosophical engagement with the world around them. For Sartre, as will be shown in the next chapter, the decisive break with Husserl's method did not come until 1940. Nevertheless, it was in Berlin in 1934 that he began a short essay, 'The Transcendence of the Ego', which, when published in a philosophical journal in 1937, contained a radical revision of the Husserlian position. Sartre had always been opposed strenuously to any notion of a pre-existential inner life and so, regardless of what consequences it might hold for phenomenology, was forced to reject Husserl's transcendental ego. 'We would like to show here,' he writes in his essay, 'that the ego is neither formally nor materially *in* consciousness: it is outside, *in the world*.'[16] Sartre builds his case for the empirical ego by observing that, when one is fully engaged with the world of objects, such as when reading the words on this page, there is no *I* in one's consciousness. It is only when one stops to reflect on what one was doing that the *I* appears in one's consciousness, and then not as its subject but as its object. Sartre's essay argues that it is by a consciousness reflecting like this on its own activities that one's ego comes into being. These ideas about the structure of consciousness were to prove a critical breakthrough for Sartre and Beauvoir, not so much for the ideas themselves, but because they pointed the young couple in an uncharted direction that would, in time, force them into further original thought.

In literature, Sartre and Beauvoir looked for new techniques that corresponded to the ones they sought in philosophy. Here, in the first instance, they were much more successful. The motto of Husserlian phenomenology was 'to the things themselves', and, for their fiction, the couple, especially Beauvoir, had a similar aspiration. In *The Prime of Life*, she recounts how, from the first days of her literary apprenticeship, she was anxious to find techniques that would reduce 'the gulf that yawned between literature and life' and 'between things and words', that could capture the 'here-and-now presence' of reality.[17] Beauvoir explained how, at the beginning of the 1930s, she and Sartre seemed to find in the fiction of Hemingway a method for reducing that gulf. His technique, says Beauvoir, 'accommodated to our philosophical requirements'. Traditional realism rested on the false assumption that things could be described 'just as they were', and Proust and Joyce had opted for forms of subjectivism. Hemingway had found a middle ground. The world was externalized but always seen through the eyes of a particular character. He 'only gave us what could be grasped by the mind of the character he was interpreting'. By never separating the physical objects from the mind of his protagonist he gave them an 'extraordinary reality', one that emphasized 'the enduring quality of things' and thereby evoked the passage of time. 'A great number of the rules which we observed in our own novels,' says Beauvoir, 'were inspired by Hemingway.'

Yet Sartre's indebtedness to Hemingway may be rather greater than Beauvoir's remarks reveal. Sartre's *Nausea*, which in 1931 began as an essay and was six years in the making, could not be more different in narrative tone from Hemingway's *A Farewell to Arms* (1929), but beneath the two novels' distinctive surfaces there are some remarkable similarities. There is no hard evidence that either Beauvoir or Sartre ever read *A Farewell to Arms*. But given the avowed importance which the couple attributed to the American's method, and Beauvoir's longstanding frequenting of Shakespeare and Company, the then Paris headquarters of contemporary American writing, it seems unlikely that Beauvoir, at least, had not by 1932 read Hemingway's most celebrated work. That was the year, says Beauvoir in *The Prime of Life*, she persuaded Sartre that he could change his 'lengthy, abstract dissertation on contingency' into a novel. She even suggests that she showed him how to plot it, and it is in plot and theme that *A Farewell to Arms* and *Nausea* are so remarkably similar.[18]

Hemingway's tragic novel has as its theme and villain the contingency of existence, which, as in a detective story is slowly revealed to the outsider hero (a young American caught up in the Italian army) through eternal processes – rain, war, pestilence and childbirth. Lieutenant Henry comes to Italy expecting adventure and believing in the honour and glory of war. Instead he passes time in bordellos before a random shell blows open his knee. Later, as the rain brings his army's advance to a halt in the mud, contingency begins to shed its verbal disguise.

> I had seen nothing sacred, and the things that were glorious had no glory and the sacrifices were like the stockyards at Chicago if nothing was done with the meat except to bury it. There were many words that you could not stand to hear and finally only the names of places had dignity.[19]

In retreat, Lieutenant Henry finds himself about to face a firing squad as he stands beside a river in flood, the novel's ultimate symbol of contingency. He escapes by diving into the water, nearly drowns, but eventually pulls himself onto a bank, where, after his physical struggle with contingency, he experiences nausea.[20] He attempts to forge a separate peace by escaping with his pregnant girlfriend to Switzerland, where, for a while, the rain turns to snow. But when his lover dies in childbirth along with their child, the hero realizes that the villain is not simply war but a more general and inescapable condition.

With a few simple inversions and a failure of nerve at the end, Hemingway's plot is repeated in *Nausea*. Again, contingency doubles as theme and villain, and the narrative proceeds – even more obviously than in *Farewell to Arms* – like a detective story. Roquentin, the outsider hero, is a man past his first youth, who, after lengthy travels, comes to a drab provincial town to do research for a thesis on an eighteenth-century adventurer. Sartre's protagonist gradually sinks, like the Italian army in the mud, into an insular present. As his life sheds its meaning, he loses his belief that he has had great adventures; and, when he decides that there are no adventures, only stories, he deserts his project. Language and routine continue to lose their grip on reality until the full absurdity of the provincial bourgeoisie is revealed to Roquentin, like that of war to Lieutenant Henry. Finally, sitting on a park bench, Roquentin sees a chestnut root, and, by extension, his own body, as manifesting a bare existence beyond all explanation, and, like Lieutenant Henry, he is overcome with a feeling of nausea arising from his desire to escape contingency. His hope for escaping rests with a former girlfriend who is due to visit him, but, when she arrives, her faded self fails to heal Roquentin's psyche. It is then that Sartre evades the force of his own ideas, ending his novel with optimism surging in his hero as he contemplates writing an adventure story that would be 'beautiful and hard as steel and make people ashamed of their existence'.[21]

Ultimately, however, *Nausea* is driven, not by a Sartrean variation on Hemingway's plot, but by what Beauvoir called its 'central purpose – that is, the expression in literary form of metaphysical truths and feelings'.[22] Paramount among these was Sartre's phenomenologist's nostalgia to return to things themselves, and, for that reason, it is things, rather than processes, that are the focal points of Roquentin's apprehensions of contingency. *Nausea*'s language and imagery are often overtly philosophical, as befits a novel whose principal aim is to show that a material world exists independently of whatever consciousness makes of it, and to offer, in evidence, Roquentin's nausea as a visceral intuition of that reality.

The text of *Nausea* was already close to its final form when, in 1934, Sartre returned to his schoolteacher's life, and, under Beauvoir's supervision, began 'a scrupulous revision of every single page'. Yet now, quite suddenly, the couple's belief in their authorial futures waned nearly to extinction. Beauvoir recalls a day in November when together in Le Havre they complained 'at length about the monotony of [their] future existence'.

> Our two lives were bound up together; our friendships were fixed and determined to all eternity; our careers were traced out, and our world moving forward on its predestined track. We were both still the right side of thirty, and yet nothing new would ever happen to us![23]

Individually, Sartre and Beauvoir reacted differently to their falling expectations. Sartre fell into depression and then slid toward madness as his boyhood dreams of the great man's life faded. Beauvoir adjusted, since, as she explained, being a woman then meant that the teaching 'career in which Sartre saw his freedom foundering still meant liberation to me'.[24] It was her turn to nurse him through a mental breakdown.

Sartre's unstable mental condition did not stop him from writing. In 1935 one of Sartre's professors at the *Ecole Normale* commissioned him to write a book for a series. Sartre's contribution, *L'Imagination* (1936), was a survey of psychological theories of the imagination, made up largely of an elaboration of a thesis he wrote as a student. After quickly completing this book at the end of 1935, Sartre set about trying to create his own theory of the imagination. This led him to an interest in dreams and anomalies of perception, which, in turn, had led him to ask to be injected with mescaline at a hospital in February 1935. While under the drug's influence, he reported to Beauvoir by telephone that he was having 'a battle with several devil fish'. Following his unhappy experiment with the drug, Sartre's depression deepened and he began to suffer from hallucinations, usually of a lobster that trotted along behind him. After an Easter holiday with Beauvoir in the Italian Lakes, not only did Sartre's depression become even worse, but he also often felt himself followed, no longer by a lone lobster, but by a whole army of giant crustaceans. Despite Sartre's clear mental distress, a doctor he consulted refused to provide him with a certificate of leave from his teaching post and, instead, prescribed belladonna which added to Sartre's difficulties. Beauvoir's strategy for dealing with Sartre's breakdown was similar to the one he, a few years previously, had employed against hers. Rather than indulge him with psychological analysis, she 'attacked him for the resigned way in which he accepted ... as a fact' what for him was the intolerable fate of being only a schoolteacher who at best could only write books that restated other people's theories.[25]

That summer, while Beauvoir climbed mountains alone in France for three weeks, and often slept rough, Sartre went on a Norwegian cruise with his parents. Afterwards, he joined Beauvoir, with whom he walked in the mountains in France for several weeks, all the while followed by his lobsters. But, in the end he declared that he had 'sent them packing', and he and Beauvoir returned to their jobs, very much hoping for a better year.[26]

During the previous academic year, Beauvoir had put aside her writing to concentrate on studying philosophy. Now, in autumn 1935, she began a connected series of short stories, while Sartre continued with his psychological studies and his revision of *Nausea*. His turning away from philosophy at this point may have been Beauvoir's doing. In separate interviews given in old age, both Beauvoir and Sartre indicated that she, with familiarity, became so radically disenchanted with Sartre's philosophical talents that she repeatedly advised him to abandon any thought of writing as a philosopher. 'I said to him,' recalled Beauvoir, 'I think you ought to devote yourself to literature rather than philosophy.'[27] Sartre remembered her stating the matter rather more bluntly: 'Actually, there was a long period during which Simone de Beauvoir advised me against spending too much time on philosophy, saying, "If you haven't a talent for it, don't waste time on it!"'[28] Presumably, it was not only his time, but her own, that she had in mind. It was clear to her by now that any philosophical projects undertaken by Sartre would call for a great deal of advice and effort from her if they were to reach an acceptable standard of sophistication. She was more certain of Sartre's literary talents and she did what she could to push him in the writerly direction she thought would make his name.

Chapter 5
More Carousing

It was also at the end of 1935 that the couple became increasingly entangled with two 19-year-olds, who had entered Sartre and Beauvoir's joint lives in the previous spring as a direct consequence of Sartre's illness. Not wanting him to be left alone with his giant shellfish, Beauvoir recruited two former students – one Sartre's and the other her own – to act as 'nurse-companions' for the ailing teacher. Jacques-Laurent Bost, whose older brother was already an established novelist, was befriended by Sartre while still his student at the lycée in Le Havre. Beauvoir describes Bost as 'both quick-witted and droll', 'with a dazzling smile and a most princely ease of bearing'.[1] Bost also was handsome, and, in a few years, would pose a direct and prolonged threat to Beauvoir and Sartre's relationship. Meanwhile, it was the unpredictable daughter of a French mother and an exiled Russian nobleman who, at this point, threw Sartre and Beauvoir's relationship into disarray.

Olga Kosakievicz, even more than Bost, 'personified youth' for the now 30ish Sartre and Beauvoir. Blonde, impetuous, and categorically opposed to conventional values, Olga had dreamt of becoming a ballet dancer, but, after passing the *baccalauréat* in 1934 under Beauvoir's tutelage, her parents insisted that she begin medical studies in Rouen, a project at which Olga was determined to fail spectacularly. Beauvoir explains that, initially, Sartre valued Olga's company only as a means of deflecting his terrifying lobster hallucinations, but when, in the autumn of 1935, 'the crustaceans withdrew they left a kind of vast empty beach behind them, all ready to be filled with new obsessional fancies'. Sartre now began to pay 'fanatical attention to Olga's every twitch or blink'.

He was increasingly determined to seduce her, but something rather the inverse of this occurred. In addition to Olga's continuing resistance to Sartre's sexual advances, she gradually seduced him into adopting her system of values, one which Beauvoir says contradicted her own and which she previously had shared with Sartre. Beauvoir, in turn, and anxious to agree with Sartre, found herself compromising formerly mutual beliefs. Despite the fact that some of the deepest principles that had held them together were now becoming ever less firm under the influence of Olga, Beauvoir agreed with Sartre that they should annex the young woman to their relationship, and that from now on they would be a trio rather than a couple.[2]

It is usually assumed that Sartre and Olga became lovers, thereby causing Beauvoir much distress, but, as so often seems to be the case when dealing with Sartre and Beauvoir, the legend appears to be the opposite of the truth. In an interview with Sartre near the end of his life, Beauvoir asked:

> Have you sometimes been rebuffed by women? Were there women you would have liked to have certain relations with – women you have not had?
> Sartre: Yes, like everything else.
> De Beauvoir: There was Olga.
> Sartre: Ah, yes.
> De Beauvoir: But that was such a very confused situation![3]

From her letters, published in 1990, it is clear that it was Beauvoir, rather than Sartre, who became Olga's lover, and it is against this background that Beauvoir's account in *The Prime of Life* of Sartre's jealousy with respect to herself and Olga should be read.[4] Although, under Olga's influence, Sartre slid back toward adolescence, the trio's primary effect on Beauvoir seems to have been intellectual advancement. In discussions, she now not only sometimes found herself opposing Sartre, but, for a period in mid-1936 his jealousy was such that he no longer thought of her as an 'ally' and there was a 'rift' between them that poisoned the air. Beauvoir says:

> I was led to revise certain postulates which hitherto I had thought we were agreed upon, and told myself it was wrong to bracket myself and another person in that equivocal and all-too-handy word 'we'.[5]

No less important for Beauvoir was the fact that, at times, Olga treated her in a manner that Sartre had never done. 'When she stood apart from me,' says Beauvoir, 'she looked at me with alien eyes, and I was transformed into an *object*'. Beauvoir and Sartre's relations had always been founded on a reciprocity between themselves as subjects. In contrast, the combination of Beauvoir's current partial alienation from Sartre, and Olga's tendency to 'look' at her as if she was a thing, prompted her to think deeply and philosophically, about the metaphysical basis of human relations.[6]

In another late conversation reproduced in *Adieux*, Sartre and Beauvoir reveal that, in 1936, despite their differences, they read and discussed the philosophy of Martin Heidegger, but that Sartre's German, even after his year in Germany, was not up to the task, leaving him dependent on Beauvoir's translations.[7] That summer the couple abandoned Olga for travels in Italy, where Sartre's lobster hallucinations recurred briefly in Venice. This seems to have been the final hallucinatory episode of Sartre's breakdown; when the summer was over, he had regained most of his equilibrium.

In the autumn, Beauvoir was assigned to a lycée in Paris, and, to her great pleasure, returned to live in Montparnasse, where she made the Dôme her headquarters. Olga moved into Beauvoir's hotel, and Sartre came to Paris from Laon twice a week. In the capital, the trio resumed its troubled existence, with Sartre still obsessed with seducing Olga. Bost became a philosophy student at the Sorbonne, and Fernando Gerassi, who with Stépha, two years previously, had returned to the Paris art scene and to Sartre and Beauvoir's lives, left to fight the fascists in the Spanish Civil War. Later, Sartre would immortalize Stépha and Fernando in his trilogy, *Roads to Freedom*, but, in December 1936, his plans to become a published novelist were thwarted when *Nausea* was turned down for publication.[8] Beauvoir says that Sartre was 'dreadfully taken aback' by its rejection and that, at the end of the year, when they went to Chamonix for skiing, he was still shedding tears over this setback.[9]

Sartre finally admitted defeat with Olga when she and Bost became lovers. Sartre compensated for this further disappointment by trying to seduce every young woman with whom he came in contact. He began a long campaign of seduction on Olga's younger sister, Wanda, who, though not as intelligent as Olga, was perhaps prettier.[10] But, in February 1937, Sartre's attention shifted back to Beauvoir, when, after months of overworking to finish her series of short stories, she fell dangerously ill with a lung infection. In the weeks that followed, her mother and sister,

Sartre, Bost, Olga and Madame Morel took turns sitting at her hospital bedside. In the spring, she was well enough to be moved into a hotel, but still too weak to walk across her room. Beauvoir recalled Sartre's care for her at this time with wry tenderness: 'The Easter holidays had come; at lunch time Sartre would go and get me a helping of the *plat du jour* from the Coupole, and bring it back to my room, taking short steps so as not to spill anything.'[11] She struggled to learn to stand up straight again, and it was a triumph for her when, with Bost and their gay friend, Marco, supporting her by the arms, she managed to walk as far as the Luxembourg Gardens. By April, she was strong enough to travel on doctors' orders to the Midi for convalescence, and while there, at the beginning of May, heard from a jubilant Sartre that Gallimard, after the intervention of Dullin, had accepted *Nausea* for publication.[12] Shortly afterwards, Beauvoir returned to Paris to help Sartre with the novel's final revisions. By mid-July she had her strength back completely, and, after the Bastille Day celebrations, she set off alone for several weeks of mountain-walking in the high Alps around the Col d'Allos. There she had another close encounter with death, when she lost her foothold and fell to the bottom of a ravine. To her astonishment, she had no broken bones, and she picked up her rucksack and continued on her way. Later, in Marseille, she joined up with Sartre and Bost, and the three of them sailed, deck passage, to Greece, where they toured for a month, before making their way back to Paris and to more changes than they could have envisioned.[13]

The year 1938 was momentous for Sartre and Beauvoir. As Europe turned irrevocably toward war, Gallimard's successful publication of *Nausea* in March brought the first secure public recognition that either of them had achieved. It was the first solid evidence that their lives, founded on anticipation of greatness, were not simply enactments of delusions by a pair of eccentric, and ultimately negligible, schoolteachers. The decade that followed was to 'belong', intellectually, to Sartre and Beauvoir to a rare degree. Between 1938 and 1949 they laid down an agenda of philosophical, moral, social and literary concerns central to the culture of the West in the mid-to-late twentieth century. The decade, as they lived it, looked quite different. It was a time, for them, not only of long-awaited success, but also of the shattering of their confident preconceptions, of being forced to realize that their freedom and their subjectivity were decisively bounded by the imperatives of history.

By 1938, Sartre and Beauvoir's lives were settling into the mature patterns which were to provide them with the necessary conditions for their most productive years. Sartre had now returned to Paris to work. Beauvoir was serving her second year at the Lycée Moliere in Passy, while Sartre obtained a post at the Lycée Pasteur in Neuilly. The pair had come to terms with their various sexual entanglements (Sartre had still not succeeded with Wanda), and their comradely intellectual liaison, so crucial for their careers as writers and thinkers, as well as mutual daily support was tested and intact. Sartre's mental illness was under control, while Beauvoir's physical collapse of 1937 was seemingly behind her. The gravity of the European political situation was pushing both of them towards new views regarding the importance of the social responsibilities of the intellectual. The hotel and café life that so suited the pair took on rhythms that were to become, after the cataclysmic interruption of Sartre's wartime internment, characteristic for them. The nucleus of their 'family', connected by ties of tutelage, friendship and sexual experience, was expanding. After nearly a decade of ambitious, anxious and, at times, despairing obscurity, Sartre and Beauvoir began to move into their influential place in French culture.

The publication of *Nausea* was a watershed for the fulfilment of Sartre's ambition to become a great writer. His previous failure to come anywhere near success had driven him, literally, mildly insane. In its final form, Sartre's first novel, in the running for the Prix Goncourt and the Prix Interallié,[14] and affectionately dedicated to Castor, attracted instant acclaim. It was followed, less than a year later, in February 1939, by the equally successful publication of *Intimacy* (*Le Mur*), the collection of Sartre's short stories which, together with *Nausea*, established his literary reputation in a remarkably brief period of time.

In contrast, Beauvoir was still floundering in 1938. Her collection of short stories dealing with the lives of a series of French women, *When Things of the Spirit Come First*, had been completed during her convalescence in 1937. Over the previous two years Beauvoir had continued to write, she says, only out of loyalty to her past and because Sartre 'pushed' her into it.[15] He thought highly of the result and persuaded her, in the wake of his own success, to allow him to submit her manuscript to Bruce Parain, his editor at Gallimard. Beauvoir was so certain of acceptance that she told her parents and friends of her stories' impending publication. Word of her success travelled quickly, especially through the exertions of Beauvoir's proud mother. The humiliation of the stories' subsequent rejection, not only by Gallimard, but also by Grasset, to whom Sartre next took the manuscript, was profound for Beauvoir. She would not allow the collection to appear until 1979. In 1982, Beauvoir described her feelings at the time:

> Two rejections were enough insult, enough humiliation. I was so naive then! If I had only known how many great writers are hurt by repeated rejection of their work, then I might have had the courage to try again with another publisher, but at the time I only believed that my work was inferior, undeserving of public attention. I saw myself as a failure and for a long time viewed myself as unworthy.[16]

Further, Sartre, careful of his own new-found success, warned her against complaining about her treatment by Gallimard. He told her 'not to say anything negative about Gallimard, because they were so powerful and he needed them'. Beauvoir said that she 'kept her mouth shut and swallowed the hurt and told everyone the book was poorly written and because it dealt with silly girls it would probably not have sold anyway'.[17] But the rejection was a bitter disappointment to her. While writing the stories, she had decided that they would be the means of her breakthrough into print after years of unpublished apprenticeship writing. She had, in fact, been 'sustained by the hope that a publisher would accept them', and buoyed up, too, by Sartre's approval of them. In the midst of Sartre's growing success, the double rejection was a severe blow for her. Worries about the obvious darkening of the international political scene, which she still wished to ignore, but no longer could, combined with her personal frustration, pushed Beauvoir into what she considered 'one of the most depressing periods' in her life. She was 30 and she felt her lack of public recognition keenly. Sartre seemed to be drawing uncatchably ahead of her. Word passed among her family and childhood acquaintances that she was a *fruit sec*; her father 'remarked irritably that if I had something inside me, why couldn't I hurry up and get it out?'[18]

Beauvoir claimed that it was during a delighted discussion of the success of *Nausea* with Sartre that the idea of both of them becoming 'really well-known writers', with 'public success, with all its attendant temptations' first entered her mind in a manner that made it seem realizable. In the light of this possibility, she felt their previous lives looked 'rather threadbare'. Beauvoir mustered all her forces of stubbornness and refused to admit defeat. Her ambition was clearly fired, rather than extinguished, by her initially depressing rejections. After another climbing holiday in the Alps, while Sartre spent time with his mother; a trip to Morocco with Sartre; and a self-centred reaction to the Munich Pact in September 1938, which consisted purely of delight at the avoidance of war, without 'the faintest pang of conscience', Beauvoir turned, with renewed commitment, to the composition of her new novel, *She Came To Stay*. Working with utter determination that this new book *would* be publishable, and taking advice while writing it from both Sartre and Parain, Beauvoir saw her fictionalization of the trio with Sartre and Olga as an act that would at last establish her as a writer.[19]

In 1938 and 1939 Sartre and Beauvoir placed their partnership on a new footing which was to remain the basis of their association for nearly the rest of their lives. In the summer of 1939, while they were on holiday in the south of France, Sartre proposed a new understanding to Beauvoir to replace their initial, renewable 'contract'. As Beauvoir recalled it, this new pact gave her a great deal of pleasure:

> Every October, Sartre and I used to drink a glass of wine to our first pact. But that summer at Madame Morel's villa, we were sitting in the dark one evening, just the two of us alone, and he turned to me and said, 'you know, Castor, we don't need any more temporary agreements. I believe we will be – we must always be – together, because no one could understand us as we do each other.' I don't remember what I said except that I was stunned to hear him say this, so out of the blue. Yes, of course, he often wrote such things in letters, but he wrote so many letters each day to so many people that I sometimes thought he made these statements more by rote than by real emotion. I think I just sat there. Then after a while I said, 'Yes.' I was so happy.[20]

That such a statement of permanent connection was valuable to both Sartre and Beauvoir at this point owed a great deal to the increasing emotional complexity of their association. Their union had never encompassed notions of sexual fidelity; it had, in fact, specifically precluded them. But it is difficult to imagine that Sartre and Beauvoir, pledging their youthful selves to one another, had ever imagined the convolutions of involvement with others that characterized their lives at the end of the 1930s. Yet accounts of the couple's relationship which cast Sartre as a typically sexually unreliable male while Beauvoir patiently tolerated his many affairs are simply misguidedly mapping out conventional notions of male–female relations onto a partnership which was anything but conventional. Since the publication of their letters to each other during this period, it is obvious that Beauvoir not only acquiesced to Sartre's promiscuousness (becoming worried only when Sartre made one of his periodic offers of marriage to another woman, or when another woman threatened to usurp her place as intellectual companion for Sartre), but joined him in vying for the honours in their mutually enjoyable and voyeuristic accounts of sexual athleticism. Beauvoir's bisexuality, which she repeatedly and publicly had a good deal of fun denying during her lifetime (including during the 1970s when such tastes became fashionable and even politically advantageous in some parts of the feminist movement),[21] was clearly a source of titillation to Sartre. His accounts of his sexual antics, and of the various special tastes of his mistresses, were just as much a source of amusement to Beauvoir. That the two intellectual comrades used other people in deeply suspicious ways is not in doubt. That their promiscuity yielded long-term friendships, and the assumption of equally long-term responsibility in terms of financial, as well as emotional, support for some of the lovers they annexed as members of their surrogate family, is equally indisputable.

Beauvoir's letters to Sartre in the late 1930s indicate a degree of sexual collusion and competition between the pair that shows them both as working out a highly ambiguous desire for joint sexual imperialism which was closely linked with their functions as teachers, and justified in terms of working out a shared life in terms of authenticity which was to remain primary, no matter what number of lovers they acquired. That Sartre and Beauvoir's 'confessions' robbed their contingent lovers of their sexual privacy, and thus, of much of their potential power, was very much to the point. Many of the lovers were treated as semi-disposable, but, when possible, retained as valued friends. Thus, a complex network of former students who had also been, or who were lovers of one, or both, of the couple, formed the basis of Sartre and Beauvoir's 'Family'. And as the ardour of their own sexual attachment cooled, their intellectual and emotional bonds were tightened by the detailed accounts of their intimate activities that the pair provided for each other.

The nature, and extent, of the pair's sexual colonization of others has only recently, with the publication of Beauvoir's letters to Sartre in

1990, become widely known, and it has prompted distressed responses from many quarters. There is, in general, little difficulty understanding the rudiments of Sartre's promiscuity. It follows familiar patterns of male desires regarding the formation of harems of attendant women. When one adds to this Sartre's deep-seated attitudes toward his mother, which heightened his fear of being abandoned for a more potent, less ugly and more adult lover, Sartre's desire to protect himself from female desertion by acquiring a range of women becomes all too understandable. Beauvoir's sexual adventurism and her acceptance of Sartre's in the most open way, as well as Sartre's willingness to share his lovers with Beauvoir, are all less typical (if consistent enough with common generalized variants of modern bohemianism through the last two centuries). But the outrage and dismay that has greeted the confirmation of these facts is connected with underlying notions which are still in place regarding the sexual double standard. The furore over the publication of Beauvoir's letters in France is an indicator that such behaviour on the part of a woman is still regarded as beyond the pale.

What remains least conventionally acceptable in all this sexual tangle is the idea that Beauvoir deliberately chose to ally herself with the most significant, amusing and intelligent male friend and companion she had discovered, rather than looking for something that at least resembled traditional sexual monogamy for women. Sartre and Beauvoir chose writing, mind and friendship as the most important indigents of their association, and they chose these factors over promises of sexual fidelity for which they substituted a code of honesty in and reportage of sexual relations with others. Their ideal was, as Beauvoir put it in a letter in 1940 to Sartre, 'our old (old but still true) idea of ethics without deserts – of grace, and the gift', an ethics reminiscent of Simone Weil's, one which the couple considered valid and matched with precision to the immediate situation of the ethical actor.[22]

However they justified their behaviour to themselves, this era of shared lovers was, in its way, remarkably productive for Sartre and Beauvoir as a couple moving out of the phase of their first infatuation but eschewing marriage. It worked in powerful and at times, perverse ways, as will be shown in the next chapter, to generate material for the production of some of their major writing, besides drawing together members of their surrogate family. It fed their mutual delight in gossip, intimate scandal, and emotional thrills. It allowed them to conceive of themselves as daring bohemian rebels rather than as sinking into the torpor of bourgeois respectability to which they feared their profession as teachers relegated them. It provided them with an entourage of intimately annexed inferiors and students who could witness and validate their own singular bond. And it identified them, further, to themselves, as two of a very special kind. They had, as Beauvoir put it, 'the identical sign on both our brows',[23] and the rules they established for their association were ones they neither recommended to others nor allowed others to judge during their lifetimes outside the closed school of the Family they thus constructed.

On 1 September 1939, Germany invaded Poland; the United Kingdom and France declared war on the 3rd; Sartre was called up on the 2nd. Beauvoir and Sartre were to be separated from the time that Sartre left Paris to join the meteorological unit of an artillery division in Alsace, near Strasbourg on 2 September 1939, until his reappearance in Paris after his incarceration as a prisoner of war in March 1941. They saw each other only three times during this period: twice during Sartre's leaves in February and April 1940, and once during a clandestine visit by Beauvoir to Sartre in Brumath in Alsace in November 1939.

Beauvoir reported that, in the early summer of 1939, she was still unwilling to face the reality of the coming war, though Sartre tried to prepare her for its inevitability. In late July, Beauvoir met Sartre and Bost, both full of foreboding, in Marseille. A few days later they happened to meet Nizan, who had left the Communist Party and was sailing for Corsica with his family. Nizan, who was killed in the war and vilified by his former fellow communists, was never seen again by them. Alarms regarding mobilization sent Sartre and Beauvoir back, after a stay at Juan-les-Pins with Madame Morel, to an eerily empty Paris, reached with difficulty via already disrupted trains. Wandering around the city, tense with anxiety about the future, escaping only temporarily into Sartre's childhood fantasy world of Hollywood westerns in the evenings, they comforted themselves with the shared conviction that the war would, at least, be short, and that it would mean the final defeat of fascism by the democratic countries of Europe. This would bring about, they hoped, a general upsurge in socialism in Europe. Construed this way, the war became imaginatively bearable.[24] And, although Beauvoir was frightened for Sartre's safety as a soldier, her major worry was about the misery of their probable separation. Sartre tried to convince her, and himself, that, as a meteorologist, he would be in little danger. On the train that took him to his first military destination at Nancy, he resolved to fraternize with his fellow soldiers, finished reading Kafka's *The Trial*, and began *In the Penal Colony* as preparation for the fully-lived surrealism of the war that was about to engulf him.[25]

Chapter 6
The Family Jewels

Besides maintaining that Sartre was her first lover, that she was monogamous and exclusively heterosexual by nature, Beauvoir insisted to the end of her days that she had no influence on Sartre's philosophy. Initially, her disclaimer merely confirmed the almost universally held belief that originating important ideas is an exclusively male prerogative, and Beauvoir was portrayed – and often still is – as serving as a mere intellectual midwife and wet nurse for the amazingly fecund Sartre. According to the legend, *all* the philosophical ideas found in Beauvoir's work originated with Sartre. Supposedly, by the late 1930s, the couple's initially symmetrical intellectual relationship had been transformed, without strife, into one of perfect asymmetry. But of all the parts of the Sartre–Beauvoir legend, this one was giving the most problems by the end of their lives. By the 1980s faith in the primacy of men's intellects no longer looked secure as a cultural certainty. A growing number of individuals, mostly women, engaged in a thoroughgoing critique of this assumption of universal masculine ownership of ideas.

In this changed cultural ambience, old assumptions about the Beauvoir–Sartre legend were questioned. It had long been known that Sartre wrote most of *Being and Nothingness* upstairs in the Café Flore with Beauvoir sitting next to him. In the 1980s questioning minds began to wonder aloud if, perhaps, Beauvoir's role in those joint sessions had not been the traditionally feminine ones of secretary, editor and moral support. But the most serious threat to the legend arose in connection with the idea of the Social Other, a concept credited to Sartre and as important to the second half of the twentieth century (through its use by liberation movements and in the analysis of social oppression) as the idea of the Unconscious was to the first. The concept of the Social Other is central to Sartre's later work, especially to his *Critique of Dialectical Reason*, and first appeared in his writing in *Saint Genet*, written between 1950 and 1952. But the concept was already to be found fully developed in 1949 in Beauvoir's *The Second Sex*, where Beauvoir used the concept of the Social Other as the mechanism that explains the social oppression of women. Furthermore, in her still earlier book, *The Ethics of Ambiguity* (1947), she can be observed seriously developing the concept.[1] Once the possibility of important ideas originating with women was no longer ruled out categorically, then the set of facts mentioned above decisively challenged the basic outlines of the Sartre–Beauvoir legend. Interviewers began to press Beauvoir on the matter, urging her to admit that she had not only influenced 'Sartre's philosophy', but had done so in a major way. Despite all the public facts to the contrary, Beauvoir stuck to her version of the legend: 'I had no philosophical influence on Sartre.'[2] She continued to deny both her influence on Sartre and her own philosophical originality even after Sartre died, and she was still denying it at the time of her death in 1986.

This is a matter that has greatly perplexed and disappointed Beauvoir's admirers. It also has remained a profound mystery. Why would Simone de Beauvoir, of all people, want a woman's central contribution to the stock of philosophical ideas credited to a man? It is now possible to answer that question. Two sets of documents, which Beauvoir left to be discovered after her death, reveal facts which provide a solution to the mystery. The Social Other, it seems, is merely the tip of an iceberg of intellectual indebtedness of Sartre to Beauvoir. This chapter and the one that follows will attempt to measure the dimensions of this colossal debt. Doing so requires close reading of key passages from *She Came To Stay* in order to chart the development of Beauvoir's philosophical views. Some of the ideas necessary to analyse this development are intrinsically difficult. But the prize is the correction of one of the great legends of the last century, one which also brings into focus a central social issue of the present one.

'You both have so many ideas in common,' said Xavière, 'I'm never sure which of you is speaking or to whom to reply.'[3]

Xavière's observation is addressed to Françoise and Pierre, the other two members of the *menage à trois* in Beauvoir's first published novel, *She Came To Stay* (1943). Because Beauvoir based Françoise on herself, Pierre on

Sartre, and Xavière on their friend, Olga, critics customarily read the novel as an approximation (Françoise murders Xavière) of the real-life trio's relations, and feelings for one another. But *She Came To Stay* is also packed with what, in a male-authored novel, would be called philosophical ideas. Consider the following scene where the trio, still in its early days, is in a night-club where Françoise calls their attention to a young woman sitting at another table:

> She was staring, as if hypnotized, at her companion. 'I've never been able to follow the rules of flirting,' she was saying. 'I can't bear being touched; it's morbid.'
>
> In another corner, a young woman with green and blue feathers in her hair was looking uncertainly at a man's huge hand that had just pounced on hers.
>
> 'This is a great meeting-place for young couples,' said Pierre.
>
> Once more a long silence ensued. Xavière had raised her arm to her lips and was gently blowing the fine down on her skin. Françoise felt she ought to think of something to say, but everything sounded false even as she was putting it into words.

And a few minutes later:

> The woman with the green and blue feathers was saying in a flat voice: '... I only rushed through it, but for a small town it's very picturesque.' She had decided to leave her bare arm on the table and as it lay there, forgotten, ignored, the man's hand was stroking a piece of flesh that no longer belonged to anyone.
>
> 'It's extraordinary, the impression it makes on you to touch your eyelashes,' said Xavière. 'You touch yourself without touching yourself. It's as if you touched yourself from some way away.'[4]

These parallel passages exhibit and contrast four ways of experiencing the human body, distinctions which were later partially echoed in Ryle's *Concept of Mind* (1949), and which provided a highly original way around the classic mind/body problem in Sartre's *Being and Nothingness*. The four-fold distinction is as follows: there is my body as part of my lived subjectivity, that is, the instrument by which I am in-the-world; there is my body as seen by others; there are the bodies of others and there are bodies construed as purely physical objects (the 'body' of Cartesian dualism). Beauvoir's night-club scene self-consciously shifts back and forth between these four philosophical points of view. The third-person narrator presents the bodies of others: the young woman staring and speaking to her companion, the woman with feathers looking at a man's hand, Xavière doing things to her arm, the feathered woman conversing, and Xavière touching and talking to herself. But Françoise's consciousness is also presented, and hence her unselfconscious experiencing of her body as her means of thinking, hearing and speaking. These two modes of experiencing the human body (as an object belonging to another subjectivity and as part of one's own subjectivity) are found in most narratives; it is Beauvoir's structured weaving of the other two modes through the scene that shows her philosophical intent. The two women coping with male flirtations are contrasted by the way they respond to the possibility of experiencing their bodies as objects of another's subjectivity. The woman with the emblematic feathers in her hair decides to experience her arm as a mere thing impersonally related to her consciousness. Similarly, the reader's attention is drawn to 'the fine down' on Xavière's skin. Beauvoir's description of touching one's own eyelashes illustrates the unbridgeable difference between experiencing one's body as the instrument of one's subjectivity and experiencing it as an object. In *Being and Nothingness*, Sartre also uses the example of touching oneself to introduce his discussion of the body and its modes of being.[5]

As well as profoundly extending ideas about the possible relationships between minds and bodies, Beauvoir's nightclub scene also illustrates the concept of bad faith, another philosophical idea fundamental to the system of thought later posited by Sartre in *Being and Nothingness*. Implicitly, the woman whose hand has been pounced upon and who has decided to pretend that her arm is an inert piece of flesh is in a quandary. Although she does not welcome the man's desire, she also, perhaps, does not wish to shatter her impression that he 'desires' her conversation. Her response is to dissociate the two sides of her human reality, which is that she is simultaneously an object and a subject. According to Beauvoir and Sartre, bad faith occurs when individuals refuse to coordinate these two dimensions of their existence. In terms of this study, Beauvoir's example of bad faith is of particular interest. No philosopher since Plato has been more successful than Sartre at providing vivid illustrations of concepts, and one of Sartre's most famous successes is his unattributed use in *Being and Nothingness* of Beauvoir's illustration of bad faith outlined above.

In the traditional reading of the Beauvoir–Sartre relationship, coincidences of ideas and imagery between their works are taken as evidence of female intellectual dependence on masculine thought. There is, however, in the present case, a problem with the orthodox interpretation, and, by any standard, it is a formidable one: Beauvoir wrote *She Came To Stay* **before** Sartre wrote *Being and Nothingness*. Although both works were published in 1943, it only became known in 1990 that five months before beginning *Being and Nothingness*, Sartre read what was over half, and very close to the final version of *She Came To Stay*. Because, as will be explained in the second half of this chapter, unreliable information was provided about how much of Beauvoir's novel existed for Sartre to read on his army leave in February 1940, some of the recently revealed facts must be stated. They come from two sources: Beauvoir's *Journal de Guerre* (1990) and her *Lettres á Sartre* (1990). Beauvoir's writing of *She Came To Stay* can be traced in both documents, but the letters are especially revealing. Between 5 October 1939 and 22 January 1940, Beauvoir commented on her progress with the novel in over 30 letters to Sartre. They show that he had previously read and discussed a draft (200 manuscript pages) of what was to be approximately the first 40 per cent of her novel. On 7 December, Beauvoir, having drafted another 300 pages, wrote to Sartre:

> Since yesterday, I've been revising the novel from the beginning. I've had enough of inventing drafts; everything's in place now and I want to write some definitive stuff. I'm enjoying it enormously, and it seems terribly – quite seductively – easy.[6]

Her letters describe, chapter by chapter, her progress with her 'final version' through December and January. By 29 December she had 60 pages in 'final draft', by 3 January, 80 pages and by 12 January, 160 pages. The revision proceeded faster than she expected, twice causing her to revise upward her promise to Sartre of how much of the final draft she could show him in February. On 17 January, she wrote: 'I really think you'll heap me with praises when you read my 250 pages (for there'll be at least 250).'[7] Beauvoir's war journal says that Sartre arrived in Paris on 4 February, spent the next morning reading *She Came To Stay*, and had as least *seven* more sessions of reading her novel before he left on 15 February.[8] The key question in noting these dates so closely relates to the material in the first half of Beauvoir's novel that must have been of special, indeed extraordinary, interest to the future father of French existentialism.

That *She Came To Stay* has not been generally recognized as a philosophical text seems due to more than just the fact it was written by a woman.[9] Firstly, unlike Sartre's fiction, its philosophical content is so deeply integrated into its narrative structure and handled with such finesse that its very existence is easily overlooked. Secondly, the novel invites and has received three other major readings: initially as a sociological study of up-market Bohemian Paris; later, after Sartre and Beauvoir became famous and it became known that the novel's major characters were based on them and their friends, as an account of their relationship; and today, with the rise of feminism, as a comparative study of three non-traditional women coping with a male-dominated world. These kinds of readings are all, in their ways, illuminating. Once, however, the novel's structural base is understood, philosophical ideas begin to leap from nearly every page. The work, in fact, articulates a philosophical system that in its basic structure differs almost not at all from the one found in *Being and Nothingness*. Through skilful orchestration of Socratic dialogues, imagery, dramatizations and third-person narration focused on characters' consciousnesses, Beauvoir had already produced a full statement of 'Sartrean' existentialism by 1940.

In the opening eight pages of *She Came To Stay*, Beauvoir, in addition to beginning the story and fleshing-out two of its major characters, blueprints much of the metaphysical architecture on which Sartre was later to build *Being and Nothingness*. Even if this philosophical edifice had been Sartre's creation, Beauvoir's presentation would deserve attention because it is so elegant, convincing and economical that an easier way into the difficult ideas found in Sartre's longer and more famous statement of the philosophy can scarcely be imagined.

The novel opens with a description of Françoise's consciousness of her surroundings as she – and this is symbolically significant – works in a deserted theatre with the Bost-like Gerbert revising a script of *Julius Caesar*.

> The typewriter was clicking, the lamp threw a rosy glow over the papers ... 'And I am here, my heart is beating.'[10]

Beauvoir's definition ('I am here, my heart is beating.') of what Sartre was to call being for-itself is packed with philosophical significance. Six points should be noted. By beginning with consciousness, Beauvoir is founding her novel's philosophy on a basis different from that of Heidegger's 'existentialism', which begins with being. Secondly, the consciousness is intentional, that is, it is of something other than itself – for example, the typewriter clicking, the rosy glow – and so, by its very nature, is connected to the world. Thirdly, the kind of consciousness represented is pre-reflective and therefore breaks with the Cartesian tradition, which begins with consciousness reflecting on itself. Fourthly, the word 'here' places the conscious individual in the physical world. Fifthly, 'I am here' indicates that the consciousness is aware of being conscious. Finally, the addition of 'my heart is beating' identifies the conscious being as a psychosomatic unity, and, in so doing, opens a new chapter for philosophy.

Having begun her ontology with individual consciousness, Beauvoir faces the problem inherent in this approach: demonstrating that an external world really exists. To succeed where others have failed she must show both that Françoise's consciousness is not reducible to its perceptions, and that the external world is not reducible to her consciousness. Beauvoir's first move is to show that Françoise has certain powers over the content of her consciousness:

> The ashtray was filled with stub-ends of Virginian cigarettes: two glasses and an empty bottle stood on a small table. Françoise looked at the walls of her little office: the rosy atmosphere was radiant with human warmth and light. Outside was the theatre, deprived of all human life and in darkness, with its deserted corridors circling a great hollow shell. Françoise put down her fountain pen.
>
> 'Wouldn't you like another drink?' she asked.
>
> 'I wouldn't say no,' said Gerbert.
>
> 'I'll go and get another bottle from Pierre's dressing-room.'[11]

The theatre is currently outside the range of Françoise's perceptions and yet the narration implies that various images of it have entered her consciousness. It is also clear that Françoise has imagined the possibility of her office as differing in one respect from how she perceives it, that is, as containing a non-empty bottle of whisky. Thus, with respect to the contents of her consciousness, Françoise's imagination gives her the power to negate her immediate perceptions. It is by such a negation that she experiences whisky as a *lack* and that the remembered bottle in Pierre's dressing-room suddenly acquires meaning as a possibility. Gerbert concurs and an action – a surpassing what-is toward what-is-not – which will further change Françoise's perceptions, is freely decided upon. With the exception of time, Beauvoir has now marked out the seven aspects of consciousness – intentionality, self-awareness, psychosomatic unity, negation, lack and possibility – which she explores at length in her novel and which Sartre later re-elaborated in *Being and Nothingness*. In addition to the empty bottle and the unfinished manuscript Beauvoir also lists a series of 'negative experiences' (later named *négatités* by Sartre), each implying a transcendence of pure perception: 'stub-ends', 'outside', 'deprived', 'in darkness', 'deserted and hollow shell', the last a recurring symbol of nothingness in her novel. Thus, in this brief passage, Beauvoir has shown that Françoise's consciousness is not merely a passive receptacle for perceptions of a material world, and is, therefore, an ontologically primitive mode of being. Furthermore, if, when Françoise leaves her office, she perceives and finds the putative theatre and whisky bottle, then Beauvoir will have gone some way toward demonstrating that a world of material things really exists. In this way Beauvoir hopes to find the elusive middle-ground between materialism and idealism.

And she does in her next paragraph.

She [Françoise] went out of the office. It was not that she had any particular desire for whisky; it was the dark corridors which were the attraction. When she was not there, the smell of dust, the half-light, and their forlorn solitude did not exist for anyone; they did not exist at all. And now she was there. The red of the carpet gleamed through the darkness like a timid nightlight. She exercised that power: her presence snatched things from their unconsciousness; she gave them their colour, their smell. She went down one floor and pushed open the door into the auditorium. It was as if she had been entrusted with a mission: she had to bring to life this forsaken theatre now in semi-darkness. The safety-curtain was down: the walls smelt of fresh paint: the red plush seats were aligned in their rows, motionless but expectant. A moment ago they had been aware of nothing, but now she was there and their arms were out-stretched. They were watching the stage hidden behind the safety-curtain: they were calling for Pierre, for the footlights and for an enraptured audience. She would have had to remain there for ever in order to perpetuate this solitude and this expectancy. But she would have had to be elsewhere as well: in the props-room, in the dressing-rooms, in the foyer; she would have had to be everywhere at the same time. She went across the proscenium and stepped up on to the stage. She opened the door to the green-room. She went on down into the yard where old stage sets lay mouldering. She alone evoked the significance of these abandoned places, of these slumbering things. She was there and they belonged to her. The world belonged to her.[12]

The smell, the half-light and the red of the carpet do not exist without Françoise, because, as appearances, their existence depends on the presence of a human consciousness. The 'mission' with which Beauvoir has been 'entrusted', and which she has delegated to Françoise, is to show that these appearances – in the present case those of a theatre – nevertheless do refer to a reality that exists independently of consciousness. Beauvoir's solution, and in the history of philosophy it is a breathtakingly original one, is to show that each appearance is part of a *series* of appearances, which for Françoise constitutes the independent reality or existence of the theatre. Rather than groping for the reality behind appearances, Beauvoir's analysis focuses on the serial nature of appearances, hoping to identify in such a series, properties from which may be inferred the existence of being independent of human consciousness. In the extract above, Beauvoir has shown three characteristics of a series of appearances. Firstly, except for the appearance of the moment, the other members of the series are absent; it is this felt absence or lack that is the lived reality of the thing. For Françoise, it is not the isolated smell of paint or the red of the carpet or the flat of the door on which she pushes that she experiences as reality, but, rather, the partially known, but always absent series of appearances, called the theatre, to which each moment's appearance belongs. Secondly, Beauvoir's paragraph shows that the unifying principle of the series of appearances constituting the theatre's reality does not depend on Françoise's whim. Beauvoir, having chosen a familiar object, invites the reader to anticipate with Françoise the series of appearances she will encounter on her walk through the theatre and, consequently, share her belief in the reality of the theatre as a being independent of her consciousness. Furthermore, the whimsical arm-stretching and calling of the empty theatre seats, inserted as it is in the otherwise objective account, calls attention to the fact that the unifying principle of the series constituting the theatre's reality does not depend on one individual's consciousness. Instead, each appearance is shown to stand in relation to *other appearances* – such as the rooms behind the doors – as well as to Françoise's consciousness. Thirdly, 'everywhere' she stands in relation to the theatre (and it would be the same for a cup or the root of a chestnut tree) offers a different appearance; so that, given the divisibility of space, 'to be everywhere' relative to something is to be in an infinite number of places. The same is true with regard to changes in light. Hence, the series of appearances comprising a thing's existence is infinitely large. From these characteristics of the series it follows that consciousness can never experience all the appearances of an object and that therefore the object's being is not reducible to consciousness of it.

In an astonishingly short space, Beauvoir's analysis shows that two regions of being, consciousness and things (or in Sartre's terminology, being-for-itself and being-in-itself) arise from appearances, but that neither is reducible to the other. Even so, the philosophical content of Beauvoir's remarkable paragraph is not yet exhausted. She has also, like Sartre in his narrative encounter with the chestnut root in *Nausea*, identified individual human beings as the source of the significance of things. But her method of doing so, and her attitude or visceral response to the fact could not be more different from Sartre's. Whereas Roquentin, *Nausea*'s 'serious' and Sartre-like protagonist, is submitted to trials which cause his language to lose its grip on reality and he, himself, to fall into painful disillusionment over the contingency of meaning, Françoise joyfully, and with complete lucidity, embraces an empty theatre, a place whose *raison d'être* is the projection of transitory meanings on itself and on the world. Mouldering stage sets speak even more forcibly of the contingency of existence than the roots of a tree, and yet Françoise is completely unperturbed by their presence, and even pleased with the knowledge that it is she who evokes the significance of places and things.

From the theatre yard, Françoise passes into a garden square to observe a view of the theatre from the outside: 'sleeping, except for a rosy glow from a single window.' Most importantly, the square provides Beauvoir with a setting to show that, through Françoise's encounter with the deserted theatre and its abandoned stage sets, she has been addressing the same nexus of philosophical problems as was Sartre in the famous chestnut tree passage in *Nausea*. Like Roquentin, Françoise 'sat down on a bench. The sky was glossy black above the chestnut trees: she might have been in the heart of some small provincial town.' Suddenly the passage becomes intensely autobiographical.

> At this moment she did not in the least regret that Pierre was not beside her: there were some joys she could not know when he was with her; all the joys of solitude. They had been lost to her for

eight years, and at times she almost felt a pang of regret on their account.[13]

When Beauvoir began *She Came To Stay*, it had been eight years since the oath-taking with Sartre in Carrousel Gardens. And even before that, when Sartre had turned up unannounced at Limousin, a fundamental, even metaphysical, difference between their characters manifested itself. Whereas Beauvoir was at ease with nature and environments relatively untouched by civilization, Sartre was not; whereas she experienced joy and excitement when confronted with the solitude of 'slumbering things', he experienced nausea and boredom. On their very first morning together in the country, he 'swept aside' Beauvoir's suggestion that they go for a walk. In her memoirs, Beauvoir notes Sartre's remarks: 'He was allergic to chlorophyll, he said, and all this lush green pasturage exhausted him. The only way he could put up with it was to forget it'.[14]

Of course, as has been seen, Sartre and Beauvoir compromised over this fundamental difference, and Beauvoir also pursued her lust for physical solitude and danger alone and later with Bost. But Beauvoir and Sartre's mismatched sensibilities on this point meant that their view of *things*, even from a city park bench, were contradictory, and this is reflected in both the tenor *and philosophical arguments* of their novels. Sartre's emotional fulminations against the contingency and superfluity of things may have been more dramatic, but Beauvoir's repose in the face of the same factors enabled her to identify the philosophically cogent points of the experience just as she had coolly picked out hand-holds on the rock faces of the mountains of the Lubéron above Marseille. The philosophical reasoning underpinning Beauvoir's paragraph on appearances meant a great deal both to Beauvoir and Sartre, as is evidenced by the fact that Sartre used his long-winded rewording of Beauvoir's argument to begin *Being and Nothingness*. There were two reasons for her argument's importance.

Sartre, in *The Transcendence of the Ego*, had committed himself to a realist position, that is, to the idea that things exist independently of consciousness of them. But, like Beauvoir, he was equally bound to a method of philosophy that, without appeal to the supernatural, proceeded from individual consciousness. This left him with a colossal and age-old problem: consciousness reveals only the appearances of things and thus cannot show that things exist when consciousness is unaware of them. Or, at least, that was the accepted wisdom. Sartre, however, dreamt of finding a solution to the problem; and *Nausea*, which began as an essay, was his attempt to do so. If he could found the belief that chestnut trees exist independently of consciousness of them, on the basis of reasoned argument true to his first principles, then and only then would the way be clear for him to construct the grand philosophical system of his adolescent fantasies. But this is precisely what Sartre did not succeed in doing in *Nausea*. He produced a literary masterpiece based on a powerful intuition of the reality of things, but the solid argument that could be admitted as evidence in the court of philosophers was conspicuously missing. The theory of appearances illustrated by Françoise's theatre walk had made his wildest dream possible for him.

Although Sartre's placement of 'his' theory of appearances in a special chapter preceding the main body of *Being and Nothingness* is expositionally nonsensical and has caused his readers many difficulties, his motivation for doing so is easily guessed. Ever since Plato conceived of the universe as divided between appearance and reality, this division has been the Achilles' heel of philosophy. In 1912, Bertrand Russell described the problem as follows:

> Thus what we directly see and feel is merely 'appearance', which we believe to be a sign of some 'reality' behind. But if the reality is not what appears, have we any means of knowing whether there is any reality at all? And if so, have we any means of finding out what it is like?[15]

For centuries, but especially in the two preceding Sartre, the 'great' philosophers directed their best and most courageous efforts toward closing the gap between appearance and reality; but none, suggested Russell, succeeded in developing a theory that was both credible and consistent. This failure is important because no one, least of all philosophers (as Popper bravely pointed out to the logical positivists), can pass beyond the first stages of knowledge without some opinions, manifest or otherwise, regarding the nature of reality. It is the philosopher's task to articulate and increase the internal coherence of these sets of opinions and occasionally – and these are the great moments in philosophy – to offer humankind a new transmutation of the basic ideas. Doing the latter means discovering in the common fund of possible starting points some fruitful arrangement that has escaped all the efforts of past philosophers. It is here that philosophy, against the odds, has achieved a measure of objectivity, in that, to be an initiate of one philosophical persuasion does not preclude an appreciation for the innovations of another, especially when those innovations pertain to philosophy's fundamental problems. The theory of appearances first set forth in *She Came To Stay* is just such a momentous innovation, and it was a sound career judgement on Sartre's part to place his restatement of Beauvoir's theory at the beginning of his *magnum opus*. It announced to those who know about such things that here was someone with a very special talent for philosophy and that the work that followed was to be read with the highest seriousness. Sartre had arrived on the stage of history with his own spotlight. All his far-fetched childhood dreams were now coming true with remarkable rapidity. But his principles and theories had already been thoroughly explored via Beauvoir's Françoise who has been left outside the theatre in the dark.

> She leaned back against the hard wood of the bench. A quick step echoed on the asphalt of the pavement; a motor lorry rumbled along the avenue. There was nothing but this passing sound, the sky, the quivering foliage of the trees, and the one rose-coloured window in a black facade. There was no Françoise any longer; no one existed any longer, anywhere.

Here Beauvoir, after having considered the worldly lacks of whisky and an unfinished manuscript, is reiterating Sartre's earlier point in *The Transcendence of the Ego*, that one's pre-reflective consciousness lacks an identity or ego. She and Sartre regarded this lack as the foundation of all lack, as that which compels individuals to project themselves into the world toward chosen possibilities. Hence:

> Françoise jumped to her feet. It was strange to become a woman once more, a woman who must hurry because pressing work awaits her, with the present moment but one in her life like all the others ... She went into Pierre's dressing-room and took the bottle of whisky from the cupboard. Then she hastened back upstairs to her office.
> 'Here you are, this will put new strength into us,' she said.[16]

Françoise and Gerbert need all the strength they can get because Beauvoir is about to use them to carry out the ultimate philosophical task. Through their dialogue, Beauvoir is going to do what, throughout history, 99 out of 100 philosophers have dared not do: engage directly with the question of the existence of other people as conscious beings. For two and a half thousand years solipsism has been Western philosophy's skeleton in the closet, and only since Descartes has it occasionally been brought out for public view. The problem is that, partisanship aside, the assumptions of neither materialism nor idealism permit the deduction of the existence of other consciousnesses, nor even an analysis of the problem of how one consciousness can act on another. The awesomeness of the difficulty inherent in this problem can be appreciated by the fact that it was not until the nineteenth century that the notion of the Other, that is, a conscious being other than oneself, was first introduced to philosophy by Hegel. But he attempted no proof of the existence of Others or justification of knowledge of them. Even so, it was a bold step forward for Hegel to even raise the issue – too bold, because, for the next hundred years, prudence prevailed over valour as other philosophers refused to rise to the challenge of extending Hegel's very sketchy ideas on this matter. Edmund Husserl was the first one of note to do so. He, like Hegel, was mute on the question of the Other's existence, but emphasized how much human thought presupposes it. Heidegger, Husserl's student, made the Other an important part of his philosophical system, but dodged the epistemological question of the Other's existence by taking a Kantian *a priori* approach. Furthermore, in anticipation of his Nazism, Heidegger's ontology subjugated the individual to a mystical collective Other, rendering concrete relations between individuals unintelligible. At the end of *The Transcendence of the Ego*, Sartre attempted his own solution to the problem of other consciousnesses, touting it as 'the only possible refutation of solipsism'.[17] But when Beauvoir wrote *She Came To Stay*, she ignored Sartre's hypothesis and substituted her own. In fact, of the three main conclusions of Sartre's essay, Beauvoir's novel totally rejected two and radically reinterpreted the third. In *Being and Nothingness*, however, Sartre has been fully converted to Beauvoir's positions. These crucial shifts in the pair's thought need careful examination.

The truly curious thing about Sartre's essay of 1937 was that it missed the radical consequences of its principal argument. If the ego was an object of consciousness, rather than a component that distorted sense data, the need for, and even the possibility of Husserl's technique of reduction or *epoché*, vis-à-vis the ego, was eliminated. If consciousness had direct access to its objects or to external reality, then the elaborate intellectual procedures of the *epoché* could be abandoned in lieu of a study of humans-in-the-world. This direct method is the hallmark of 'Sartrean' existentialism; it is also the method that Beauvoir introduced and developed in her novel. But there was an even deeper implication contained in Sartre's verdict on the ego: if consciousness is sheer activity ceaselessly transcending toward objects, then it follows that reality is divided into two distinct realms *which nevertheless are inextricably linked.* These are the realms (later baptized being-for-itself and being-in-itself by Sartre) which Beauvoir so carefully delineates in the opening pages of her novel. No mention, however, is made of these foundation concepts in *The Transcendence of the Ego.* Even more interesting is their absence from Sartre's monograph *The Emotions,* whose philosophical 'Introduction' was almost certainly not written before mid-1939. Here Sartre, still accepting the possibility of 'putting the world in parenthesis', apologizes for the present work not being one of 'pure phenomenology', and makes it clear that for him human and human-in-the-world are not equivalent categories.[18] But, by 1939, Beauvoir's novel, after a false start two years before, was well-advanced. Comparing these contemporary texts, it is difficult not to conclude that by the middle of 1939 a large gap had opened up between Sartre's and Beauvoir's philosophical development.

The gap widens even further when considering the second and third conclusions of Sartre's essay on the ego, whose externality he elevates to a kind of moral-cum-methodological imperative. The fact that one's ego is merely an object of one's consciousness raises the possibility of divesting oneself of it, like Roquentin and Françoise do on their respective benches. Solipsism, argues Sartre, is to be overcome not by affirming the subjective existence of the Other, but by also throwing into doubt one's own. The cure may seem worse than the complaint, but in any case Sartre has made a serious error: with solipsism it is not an object of consciousness that is in question but rather consciousness itself. In his final conclusion he takes his confusion a step further when he declares that given the location of the ego 'the subject-object duality ... is purely logical' and should 'definitely disappear from philosophical preoccupations'.[19] In place of interacting individuals he imagines a kind of generalized Hegelian spirit, a recipe for a totalitarian society if ever there was one.

Of course, all this is terribly un-Sartrean, which is to say, totally opposed to the theory of Others which Beauvoir, at the end of the 1930s, was setting out in great detail in *She Came To Stay.* In its opening chapter, Françoise and Gerbert, having finished with the problem of contingency, move on to solipsism.

'It's almost impossible to believe that other people are conscious beings, aware of their own inward feelings, as we ourselves are aware of our own,' said Françoise. 'To me, it's terrifying when we grasp that. We get the impression of no longer being anything but a figment of someone else's mind.'[20]

It is this experiencing of oneself as another's object that Beauvoir offers as the proof of the consciousness of *others*. In the 400 pages that follow, the ramifications that this highly unstable subject–object dichotomy has for human relations are analysed at length.

With the postulation of the Other and its ability to transform one's own consciousness, the first chapter of *She Came To Stay* has completed its sketch of the basic framework, not only of Beauvoir's philosophical universe, but also of Sartre's *Being and Nothingness*. All the philosophical matters addressed in her opening chapter, as well as additional ones, are further explored in the course of the novel. Most remarkable is the fact that her narrative, both as a whole and in its parts, is elaborately structured on the basis of her philosophical system, a fact highly significant to the question of the origin of that system and its component ideas. It shows not only that the philosophy was there in the novel from an early stage, but also that, in 1938, Beauvoir was already sufficiently fluent with its ideas to comprehensively translate them without awkwardness into a major work of fiction.

Her theory of the Other bears an especially heavy load in the novel's narrative structure, its support being crucial at three levels. Scene by scene, the relations between the characters are centred on Beauvoir's concept of the Look, which is the idea that to perceive or to imagine someone looking at oneself is to experience oneself as the other's object and hence the other as a conscious being. *She Came To Stay* persistently informs the reader who is looking at whom, a practice easily mistaken for a writer's tic but, in fact, crucial to the narrative's logic. In Beauvoir's theory there are two general modes by which two people can relate: either they can both honour each other's subjectivity, or one can play the object and the other the dominating subject. In the 1940s, Beauvoir would build an ethics based on the mode of reciprocity, but in *She Came To Stay* (as in *The Second Sex*) it was the object–subject mode of personal relations that was her primary concern. Through her characters she explores seven ways (indifference, language, love, masochism, sadism, desire and hate) by which one can enter into an object–subject relationship. In *Being and*

Nothingness, under the heading 'Concrete Relations', Sartre was to offer a condensed version of the same analysis. Beauvoir was interested, too, in what happened to these dual relations when a third party (in *Being and Nothingness* called the Third) intervened, and an overlapping series of these triangles provides a third structural level to her novel.

Before leaving *She Came To Stay* something should be said about the method Beauvoir has used in erecting the framework of her philosophy, not only because it is innovative, but also because it is the method that Sartre was to adopt in his longer and more famous statement of the same philosophical system. Beauvoir begins by observing the basic structures of consciousness: its intentionality, its pre-reflective self-awareness, its being-in-the-world and its union with a body, each having reference to concrete but universal experience and hence confirmable by the individual reader. She then shows how these structures of consciousness commit individuals to three ontologically primitive types of being, what Sartre was to call being-for-itself, being-in-itself and being-for-others. This procedure, basic to science but new to philosophy, of observing the structures of everyday experiences and then asking what macro-structures these micro-structures entail, is the methodological bedrock of the philosophy stated in Beauvoir's novel. The propensity to shift back and forth between the concrete and the abstract together with the commitment to consider things in-the-world makes her philosophical method highly congenial to presentation in the novel form. When, in *Being and Nothingness*, Sartre adapted Beauvoir's method to the essay, the difference was only a change in emphasis from the concrete to the abstract, the introduction of an extensive jargon and the imposition of a great deal of rhetoric.

Chapter 7
The 'Lost' Letters

Suppose that instead of a man and a woman, we were concerned here with two male writers, and that, like Sartre and Beauvoir, they had each explained at length the same new philosophical system, but with one publishing their presentation before the other and gaining recognition as the system's originator. In that case, it would be quite unnecessary to write this chapter. Having established that the uncredited writer had written a comprehensive statement of the philosophy that was read by the credited one before beginning to write his own would be sufficient to dislodge from academic opinion the latter in favour of the former as the primary thinker or 'true philosopher' behind the system. Of course, this conversion of opinion would not come about overnight. Reputations and territories would have been established on the basis of the false order, and, in all probability, the less principled of their holders would fight to re-obscure the facts. New books and lectures would have to be written and old ones revised. But in a decade or two – and surely it is not utopian to believe this – honour and decency among scholars would prevail with the result that the revised order of influence between the two thinkers would become accepted fact.

There is no corresponding ground for optimism in the present case. Along with most established religions, philosophy successfully continues to resist the inclusion of women in its highest echelons. Nor is this resistance limited to the philosophical establishment: the very idea of 'a great woman thinker' is probably still viewed by a majority of the public – including women – as a contradiction in terms. So one must be careful not to underestimate what is at stake here; it is infinitely more than just the relative reputations of Sartre and Beauvoir; it is more, too, than just opening up philosophy's inner sanctum to women. Ultimately the question at hand is about breaking down the bigotry that underlies the contradiction noted above. And all this underlines a great irony of the present situation. Though the origin of a philosophical system is in question, its merit and importance are not. Accepted as a male creation, after half a century the system not only continues to attract scrutiny, but has established itself as one of those extremely rare philosophical achievements whose reputation transcends the broad gulf of partisanship that separates the continental and the analytical schools of philosophy. From deep in the opposing camp, the eminent American philosopher, Arthur Danto, has written about the 'Sartrian system', by which he means mainly the one found in *Being and Nothingness*:

> The ... system, for its scope and ingenuity, its architectural daring and logical responsibility, its dialectical strengths and human relevance, and for the totality of its vision, is located in the same exalted category, the highest of its kind, with those of Plato, Descartes, Spinoza and Kant, Hegel and Russell, to cite most of his exiguous peers.[1]

It would be unfair to Sartre not to view his appropriation of Beauvoir's ideas in the context of the psychologically dire situation in which he found himself in the months following his departure for war on 2 September 1939. The previous summer Beauvoir had gone on another climbing holiday in the Alps, and, in her autobiography, she gives the adventure – which lasted several weeks – a mere 100 words, saying that she 'climbed every single peak between Chamonix and Tigne that was within the competence of an unaccompanied climber'.[2] As is so often the case, Beauvoir's account is literally true but quite misleading. She does not mention the fact that climbing every one of those peaks with her was Jacques Bost. On 27 July she wrote to Sartre that he should know:

> 1. First, that I love you dearly ...
> 2. You've been very sweet to write me such long letters ...
> 3. Something extremely agreeable has happened to me, which I didn't at all expect when I left – I slept with Little Bost three days ago. It was I who propositioned him, of course.[3]

One more contingent coupling by either Beauvoir or Sartre was of no lasting importance to their essential relationship, but a year later, as Sartre went off to war, Beauvoir's union with Bost, although he was now also romantically linked to Olga, was threatening to rise above the contingent category. If it did, it would be the first time that either Beauvoir or Sartre had broken their oath to keep theirs their only essential relationship.

Only after the 1990 publication of Beauvoir's letters to Sartre has it become possible to gauge Bost's importance to Beauvoir. Sartre's letters to her were published in 1983, and, on their basis, biographers drew conclusions (the wrong ones, it seems) regarding the nature of the famous couple's relationship at the beginning of the war. When only Sartre's half of their war correspondence is read, one is easily led to the view that he and his interests dominated the couple's relationship. His daily letters are full of demands, not only for Beauvoir's help in his double-dealing entanglements with assorted younger women (which continued by post), but also for her to read and critique his various writing projects on which he was now, despite his official status of soldier-at-war, working 12 hours a day. In contrast, he infrequently inquires about Beauvoir's writing. But a reading of her letters to him reveals that he had no need to enquire as she kept him constantly posted of her chapter-by-chapter and draft-by-draft progress with *She Came To Stay*. She even detailed for him the hours and the cafés in which she wrote each day. And, in the months leading up to Sartre's anticipated furlough in February 1940, Beauvoir repeatedly reminded him that he would be spending part of his brief freedom on reading and discussing her novel.[4] Meanwhile, she wrote him long accounts of the various love affairs she was conducting simultaneously, sometimes describing her physical intimacies at length and frequently demanding his help in manipulating and misleading her lovers. Between their letters there is, in fact, a remarkable symmetry, but with one major exception. Reading Beauvoir's, one gradually comes to realize that between September 1939 and February 1940, Bost was becoming for Beauvoir an *essential* love.

There is no evidence that Beauvoir ever contemplated giving up Sartre for Bost, but rather that henceforth she intended to have two essential loves rather than only one. Her letters show that although she violated the exclusivity of her agreement with Sartre, the transparency clause remained in force. Consequently, Private Second Class Sartre suffered a daily bombardment of illustrations of his reduced status, which began with Beauvoir's first letter after his induction. He was not yet at the Front, but she feared Bost was, and told Sartre so: 'The only painful thing is my intermittent bouts of panic concerning Bost: such violent pangs of dread for him that I feel I'm almost losing my reason. Especially in the evenings.' In her letter of the following day, 8 September, she tells Sartre how sitting at a table outside the Deux Magots 'reminded me of so many things to do with you and Bost'.[5] 'You and Bost', and later 'Bost and you', was to be the leitmotif of Beauvoir's wartime letters to Sartre.

Jacques Bost, destined to become one of France's leading journalists, was already an accomplished letter-writer, and Beauvoir placed particular emphasis on inducing Sartre to compete with him in the quantity and quality of his correspondence.[6] Thus on 11 September, she opens with, 'no letter from you today. On the other hand, I've had another two from Bost – who's very effecting.' On the 28th, Sartre scores better but apparently is still not winning: 'three letters from you, and three from Bost ... His letters are all thick and very cheerful and incredibly appealing.' On 4 October, it is 'two letters from you and two from Bost.' On the 15th, after speaking of 'my real life – my life with Bost and you – ', she says, 'I found two big letters from Bost – and also a clever little supplementary note he'd sent me. You too should send me an unexpected little note over and above your letters some time.' But it was the score card dated 1 November that Sartre must have found the most wounding.

> I called in at the poste restante: 5 letters from you, 6 from Bost – the clerk gave me an understanding smile. I bore my huge packet off to the Versailles, and for the first time read Bost's letters first.[7]

Even without the ever-growing threat of partial or total betrayal by Beauvoir, Sartre was living through an enormously difficult period. For only the second time in his life – the other being his childhood ordeal in La Rochelle – he was condemned, like other mortals, to exist indefinitely without the support of a daily chorus of adulation. Except in the disembodied form of letters, which he now feverishly sought, his life was devoid of the intellectual conversations in which he shined, of the caresses of his youthful girlfriends, of the motherliness and camaraderie of Beauvoir, of the uncritical admiration of his students, and of the increasing celebrity that had accompanied him in his Parisian café-life. In their place was a straw mattress which he shared with another Private Second Class, a tin helmet which, like his fatigues, was too big for him, and the constant living at close quarters with men whom he described as 'big guys who shit, wash themselves, snore, and smell of man'.[8] Worse still, his immediate superior, Corporal Pierre, was an authoritarian mathematics teacher who must have reminded him of his hated stepfather Mancy.[9] Sartre's defence was to withdraw from the society of his fellow soldiers into a frenzy of writing, broken only by the need to sleep, eat and launch weather balloons twice a day. In addition to his daily output of several long letters and five pages of his novel, he kept a diary that in nine months ran to 14 notebooks. This journal, whose five surviving notebooks were published posthumously as his *War Diaries*, became for him what he called his 'secret life'.[10] Meanwhile the pathological nature of his behaviour did not go unnoticed by his fellow draftees. In the French National Archives, Cohen-Solal has discovered how Sartre was perceived by the soldiers in his group. Sartre she writes, was famous among his fellow-conscripts:

> for the weeks he spends 'without taking a bath when all he had to do was cross the street and pay ten sous to have exclusive use of a bathroom in the heated building,' and for his nickname in the barracks, 'the man with the black gloves,' because his hands 'were black with dirt up to his elbows.'
>
> We also have a number of anecdotes, such as this one, provided by the corporal: 'Once I had a real fight with him while trying to stop him from burning the furniture of the house we lived in: he didn't want to waste time chopping wood when he could read or write instead.'[11]

It is perhaps significant that Sartre's diary keeping was a reversion, both in motivation and literary form, to the patterns of his early childhood writing. In writing his childish 'novel notebooks', he says, he had been 'escaping from the grownups,' and, in writing his diary, it is obvious he was escaping from the ever present soldiers. At age 9 he had 'indiscriminately poured everything [he] read, good or bad' including 'odds and ends of gloomy tales and cheery adventures, of fantastic events and encyclopedia articles' into his notebooks; at age 34 he did much the same in his diary.[12] He philosophized about the books Beauvoir sent to him (and to Bost), chronicled the absurdities and squabbles of his army life, copied out letters from friends, sketched portraits – invariably disapproving – of his associates, and shamelessly retold their stories. His childhood notebooks featured a swashbuckling hero with whom Sartre identified, but in his war notebooks Sartre has grown up to play the hero in his own name, and it is his quest to reform himself by self-examination into an ever more remarkable person, and to construct an original philosophical system that could save the world, that provides a plot for his otherwise obsessional writing. One of several surprising things about the *War Diaries* is that on the whole it is a remarkably good read. Its prose has a fresh, rough-hewn, camera-eye quality; and Sartre, who in writing about himself has not edited out the many passages that give him away as a poseur, obsessed with how the world – past, present and, most of all, the future – might perceive him. He was not yet in any mortal danger, but at any moment that could change, and if all-out war between France and Germany began, then there was the very real possibility that with his diaries he was writing his last work. On 16 September, he wrote to Beauvoir telling her that if he died, she was to publish his diaries and add 'benevolent and explanatory annotations'.[13] Meanwhile, in what was clearly either a last-ditch attempt to secure immortality as a philosopher in the event that his life should be cut short, or a repository of ideas for a major work if he should live, he tossed in among his descriptions of barracks-life and childhood remembrances every seemingly novel philosophical thought that passed through his head. But when, in January 1940, he read through what he had written, he realized that his quest for philosophical originality had been a dismal failure. On 9 January he wrote to Beauvoir about his disillusionment.

> I have reread my five notebooks, and they don't please me nearly as much as I had expected. I find them a little vague, too discreet, even the clearest ideas are little more than rehashings of Heidegger's: in the end, all I have done since September ... is only a long re-elaboration of the ten pages he devoted to the question of historicity.'[14]

Sartre's fortunes changed dramatically on the morning of 5 February 1940, in a Paris brasserie on the avenue du Maine. It was there that Sartre discovered the mother-lode of philosophical ideas that would win him worldwide fame as a philosopher. In her journal, Beauvoir recorded how, as she read his diaries, he began to read *She Came To Stay*. He was at the beginning of ten days of leave, and in the first five he had seven sessions of reading Beauvoir's novel in her presence. On his last day before departing, Beauvoir's journal says Sartre read the last chapter of her novel, which she had rewritten during his stay.[15] When on the 16th, Sartre returned to camp and his diary, he found himself, for the first (and only) time in his life, overflowing with original and major philosophical ideas. Sensing that there were more to be extracted from the lode back in Paris, Sartre's dream of becoming *known* as one of history's greatest philosophers suddenly must have looked to him like a real possibility.

On 17 February, his first full day back at his army post, Sartre began trying to put down in his diary the philosophical ideas he had unearthed in Paris. At first, it appeared that his effort would be an honourable one. He writes as follows:

> For the Beaver has taught me something new: in her novel, one sees Elisabeth complaining about being surrounded by objects she'd like to enjoy, but that she can't 'realize' ... She meant that we are surrounded by *unrealizables*. These are existing objects, that we can think from afar and describe, but never *see*.

For a thousand words Sartre continues to elaborate on Beauvoir's concept. Unfortunately, he fundamentally misremembered it: Beauvoir's system requires that the concept of unrealizables has to do with situations, not objects. By the next day, Sartre understood this, and he corrects himself in his diary.

> My comment yesterday about unrealizables could give rise to confusion. What is unrealizable is never an *object*. It is a *situation*. It's not Paris, but being-in-Paris, with respect to which the question of the unrealizable is posed.[16]

In some ways, these entries on *unrealizables* are representative of the method Sartre used to understand and transcribe parts of Beauvoir's philosophical system during the first 11 days after his leave. He takes up one element at a time, invents the terminology, and then, over several days, works towards an approximation of the underlying theory which he had briefly encountered in Beauvoir's text. However, *unrealizables* is only a minor concept in her system; it is also the only one for which Sartre in his diaries gave her credit. (When he came to write *Being and Nothingness*, even this small act of honesty was withdrawn.[17]) On 18 February 1940, having thrown his crumb of credit to Beauvoir, he moved on to laying claim to major elements of her philosophy. As the philosopher-hero of his diaries, Sartre had been slow to justify his opinion of himself through the delineation of any important new ideas. Now that he was about to articulate the philosophical ideas that would allow him to believe in his own success, he savours the moment when his childhood reveries were about to turn into something more substantial than dreams:

I feel strangely bashful about embarking on a study of temporality. Time has always struck me as a philosophical headache, and I've inadvertently gone in for a philosophy of the instant (which Koyré reproached me for one evening in June '39) – as a result of not understanding duration ... I was extremely embarrassed and put out to see myself as the sole instantaneist cast among contemporary philosophies which are all philosophies of time. I tried in *La Psyché* [a mostly unpublished work] to derive time dialectically from freedom. For me, it was a bold gesture. But all that wasn't yet ripe. And, behold, I now glimpse a theory of time! I feel intimidated before expounding it, I feel like a kid.[18]

With Bost now on leave and usurping Sartre's place with Beauvoir in Paris, it is impossible not to be reminded here of Sartre's thefts from his mother's purse in La Rochelle. The adult Sartre hopes to impress his readers with the theory of time he has glimpsed in Beauvoir's manuscript. In her novel, Beauvoir develops her theory of time incrementally, but early in the text she has Pierre, the Sartre-like character, state the bare bones of her theory. Pierre says:

'but it's also impossible to live only for the moment.'

'Why?' said Xavière. 'Why do people always have to drag so much dead weight about with them?'

'Look,' said Pierre, 'time isn't made up of a heap of little separate bits into which you can shut yourself up in turn. When you think you're living purely in the present, you're involving your future whether you like it or not.'

'I don't understand,' said Xavière.

[...]

'Let's assume you've decided to go to a concert,' said Pierre. 'Just as you're about to set out, the idea of walking or taking the metro there strikes you as unbearable. So you convince yourself that you are free as regards your previous decision, and you stay at home. That's all very well, but when ten minutes later you find yourself sitting in an arm-chair, bored stiff, you are no longer in the least free. You're simply suffering the consequences of your own act.'[19]

Here, and at other points in her novel, Beauvoir is expounding not a theory of physical time, but rather a theory of how time is experienced by human beings, that is, of temporality. It also must be emphasized that she is not moralizing, in the manner of Heidegger, about how one *should* deal with time. While her theory bears a superficial resemblance to the German's, it exists on a fundamentally different level, and Beauvoir has taken pains to drive this point home by beginning her exposition with the *assertion* that it is *impossible* to live only for the moment, in contradistinction to Heidegger's injunction that one *should* not do so.

Clearly, Beauvoir's crediting of this piece of philosophical wisdom to the fictional Sartre, Pierre, was more than the real Sartre could resist. But his first attempt in the *War Diaries* at reconstituting Beauvoir's theory of temporality, despite his fanfare introduction, degenerated quickly into pompous gibberish ['Time is the opaque limit of consciousness. It is, moreover, an indiscernible opacity in a total translucidity.'], before recovering briefly with: 'time appears to us only thanks to the *past* or the *future*: it is not given us to live in its continual flow.' The next day, however, his memory served him well as he produced the following near perfect jargonized generalization of Pierre's speech to Xavière about deciding to stay at home.

And since this immediate past is negation of a more distant past, and so on and so forth, it is by this nihilation of the total bloc of the past it *has been* that the present for-itself defines, in its presence. Thus the question cannot arise of knowing why freedom cannot escape this past, or give us another past – since, precisely, we are free *with respect to* this past.[20]

In *She Came To Stay*, Beauvoir argues that the future, no less than the past, is inextricably tied up with the present.

The day had been spent in the expectation of these hours, and now they were crumbling away, becoming, in their turn, another period of expectancy ... It was a journey without end, leading to an indefinite future, eternally shifting just as she was reaching the present.

Repeatedly, Beauvoir shows characters overcome with anxiety about their 'journey without end', who try to escape their future by denying their consciousness of the world. Sartre would have read her following example.

> If only she could fall asleep again till tomorrow – not to have to make any decisions – not to have to think. How long could she remain plunged in this merciful torpor? Make believe I'm dead – make believe I'm floating – but already it was an effort to narrow her eyes and see nothing at all.[21]

To remain listless, contends Beauvoir, is no less a projection of oneself into the future than deciding to cross town to go to a concert, and, whatever decision is made – even the decision not to decide – brings consequences (for example, of being bored or having or not having a university degree), which become part of one's present and future. *Thus past, present and future all stand in the relation of co-implication*; and conversely, the present is not even conceivable without the past and the future. The beauty of all this, which Beauvoir exploits to the utmost in her novel, is that this theory of temporality dovetails perfectly with her theory that consciousness is an emptiness (or nothingness) that ceaselessly requires filling and that, except through sleep or death, one cannot escape projecting oneself continuously toward the world. In this existential emptiness or lack, Beauvoir succeeds in grounding all the desires of her characters and, by implication, human desire in general. When Elisabeth 'looks into herself', says Beauvoir, 'all she finds is an empty shell. She had no idea that it's the common fate.'[22]

On 22 February 1940, having exhausted his stock of Beauvoirian wisdom on the past, Sartre, in his diary, moved on to 'the nature of the future' and, in particular, the way in which Beauvoir linked it to the nature of consciousness. 'The Future,' wrote Sartre, 'could exist only as complement of a lack in the present. It is the very signification of this lack.' Sartre then goes on to show that he recognized a revolutionary idea when he read one.

> It's quite astonishing that, in all philosophies and in all psychologies, it should have been possible to describe at length will, desire or passion, without being led to see the essential fact: namely, that

none of these phenomena can ever be conceived if the being which wills, suffers or desires is not gripped in its being as afflicted by an existential lack.

He also saw how this element of Beauvoir's philosophical system undermined that of her chief rival, Heidegger. After crediting Christianity with having come closest to recognizing that the human soul is 'animated' by an emptiness, Sartre continues:

> Yet it must be noted that most Christian thinkers, led astray by their monist conception of being as an *in-itself*, have confused – like Heidegger, moreover – the existential nothingness of human consciousness with its finitude. Now finitude, being an external limit of being, cannot be at the root of lack, which is found at the very heart of consciousness.'[23]

Sartre turned his attention from temporality and desire to the existence of the Other on 27 February. In December he had written, 'Love is the effort of human reality to be a foundation of itself in the Other.'[24] In *She Came To Stay* Beauvoir repeatedly makes the same point, as when she says that in loving Pierre, Françoise was 'looking upon him only as a justification of herself.'[25] Sartre and Beauvoir's observation about love is a worthy one, but of itself it is neither original nor of philosophical interest. In Beauvoir's novel, however, this pedestrian observation acquires deep philosophical resonance when it is placed in the context of a general theory of human existence vis-à-vis the Other. Just as Beauvoir's description of Françoise and Pierre's relationship appears as an exemplification of her analysis of love, so the latter appears as an exemplification of Beauvoir's more general theory of human relations. The same is true of the novel's investigations of indifference, language, masochism, sadism, desire and hatred, so that they all, including all the details of the actual behaviour of the characters, refer analytically back to each other. It is this which, in large part, accounts for the peerless philosophical unity of Beauvoir's narrative, a unity of which Sartre, as reader, would have been keenly aware, and whose basis he tried to ferret out in his diary entry of 27 February. He made some progress. One exists, he wrote, 'as a defenceless object projected onto the Other's infinite freedom,' and one's 'only way of *not-being* the Other *is* to *be-for* the Other.'[26] In a fuzzy way, he has identified the nature of the subject–object duality that underpins Beauvoir's work. But, despite going on for

89

pages, and, despite repeated fresh starts, he fails to reproduce Beauvoir's concepts of the Look and of the Third. His discussion of concrete relations is desultory and limited mainly to love and sadism, and, astonishingly, for someone who thought of himself as a philosopher, he makes no mention of solipsism. Clearly, Sartre needed more reading time with *She Came To Stay* and more tutorials with Beauvoir before being able to write the brilliant exposition of her theory of being-for-others that would appear in *Being and Nothingness*.

Fairness to Sartre requires mention of two more factors that may partially excuse his initial unacknowledged thefts from Beauvoir's philosophy. On 20 February, he received Beauvoir's letter of the 18th in which she formally announced that henceforth her relationship with Bost would be an *essential* one. Though Beauvoir scarcely had kept it a secret that things were moving in this direction, receiving her announcement must have been painful for Sartre. Bost was now with Beauvoir in Paris and, for the first two pages of her letter, she only hinted at what needed to be said: 'and though we talk non-stop from morning to night we'll never get to the end of what we have to say to one another.' In the end she put her position to Sartre straight:

> There's one thing of which I'm now sure, which is that Bost forms part of my future in an absolutely certain – even essential – way. I felt such 'remorse' because of him, that I want a postwar existence with him – and partly *for* him.[27]

Sartre's comments in old age suggest how he may have felt in the period following Beauvoir's declaration.

> Basically I didn't much care whether there was another man in an affair with any given woman. The essential was that I should come first. But the idea of a triangle in which there was me and another better-established man – that was a situation I couldn't bear.[28]

What is certain is that, after his own letter to Beauvoir of 20 February, in which he put on a brave face of indifference to Beauvoir's announcement, Sartre's behaviour in relation to her, even ignoring his diaries, became quite extraordinary. His instinct seems to have been to retaliate, but he was in a weak position to do so. His girlfriends, like Wanda (who had finally slept with him in the previous summer), had been chosen for their sexual charms rather than for their intellectual claims; none were plausible candidates for an essential relationship with him in the way that Bost was for Beauvoir.[29] Even so, it was inevitable that Wanda, with whom he had spent time while on leave, would now take on added value in his eyes (even though Sartre was willing to describe her as having 'the mental faculties of a dragonfly'), and he sought to cement their shaky relationship.[30] She, most likely sensing an opportunity, protested in a letter at the 'mysticism' of his love for Beauvoir. Sartre wrote back: 'You know very well that I'd trample on everybody (even the Beaver despite my 'mysticism') to be on good terms with you.' Or at least, in a letter to Beauvoir on the 24th, this is what Sartre said he had said. His words seem to have been aimed more at wounding Beauvoir than at placating Wanda. And it also seems that they were intended to wound himself, because immediately after writing them, his letter became abject with self-condemnation.

> I feel profoundly and sincerely that I'm a bastard. And a small-scale bastard on top of that, a kind of university sadist and a sick-making civil service Don Juan. It is necessary to change this.

For the next week Sartre continued to write to Beauvoir in this confessional, self-abasing vein, and with shrill promises of 'no more affairs for a long time', promises for which Beauvoir, in her letters, was *not* asking.[31]

Philosophical systems like the one found in *She Came To Stay* are not developed overnight nor even in a year. Yet, as is shown by Sartre's writing of 1939 and 1940, prior to his first army leave, Beauvoir had kept him almost totally in the dark concerning her philosophical theories. Indeed, she appears to have carried out the whole process of their development in secret; and this, surely, was a major violation of the couple's vow never to 'conceal anything from the other'.[32] Sartre must have seen this as a further betrayal by Beauvoir; perhaps this also mitigated his guilt for appropriating as his own the philosophy that must have been created largely without him.

The foregoing discoveries regarding the origins of Sartrean existentialism throw up a series of intriguing questions. Why did Beauvoir let Sartre get away with it? Why did Sartre not destroy his war diaries? What, if any, was the arrangement between him and Beauvoir? Did she intend for the truth to be uncovered after her death? Except for the last question, there is to date little to offer but speculation.

Understanding Beauvoir the philosopher may be helped by considering an early event in Sartre's life. When his father died, his mother whisked him straight from the burial to the train station. She then fled north with unseemly haste because if she remained near her male in-laws she risked losing possession of her child. Her worthiness as a mother was not in question; but the Sartre men were a queer lot, and being a woman meant she had no legal entitlement to the outright possession of her own child, indeed of anything, except perhaps the clothes on her back. A generation later, social morals and legal reform had changed women's position, but perhaps not nearly so much as one might think. In France, in 1938, women had still not won the vote, and, more to the point, nowhere did their right to the proprietorship of ideas exist as more than an improbable and eccentric dream. It was in this situation that Beauvoir decided what to do with her philosophical system.

The publisher's rejection of her short story collection (*When Things of the Spirit Come First*) in 1937, besides being traumatic, gave Beauvoir a valuable object lesson. Gallimard, who had published Sartre's *Nausea*, had rejected her much tamer work explicitly on the grounds that it violated society's rules as to what kind of material could be published by and about women, and told her that a particularly 'subversive' aspect of her collection was that it reflected 'what women think'.[33] So, from 1937 onwards Beauvoir knew that the criteria for publication she faced in France were radically more restrictive than those faced by Sartre, and that her best chance for becoming an author was to make her future work comply, or at least appear to comply, with the special set of rules enforced by Gallimard and others against her sex. Even today, as Sylvia Lawson notes, women are more restricted in what is regarded as fitting topics for them than it might appear. Despite the gains that the present feminist movement has brought, women continue to be plagued by narrow expectations regarding their interests, and the intellectual woman who challenges publishers by stepping 'outside what's become a comfortable feminist shopping-list of issues, is an irritant and a troublemaker still'.[34] Half a century ago Beauvoir's position was immeasurably more difficult. But this did not mean that under the social conditions of her day Beauvoir could not reasonably hope to have a philosophical text published. On the contrary, she could write an entire book on what a woman thought about philosophy if she disguised it as something else. Sartre had written and published an important philosophical text in the form of a novel; she could do the same if she did not call attention to her philosophical content.

There are strong and repeated suggestions in *She Came To Stay* that Beauvoir both intended and expected Sartre to take up her philosophy as if it were his own. In Chapter 1, as Beauvoir outlines her new version of Western philosophy, Françoise is creating a new version of *Julius Caesar* which will be identified as Pierre's production and in which he will star as Caesar. Later, attention is drawn to the fact that, in contrast to Pierre, Françoise and her typist, Gerbert, will not receive credit for their efforts; Françoise says, 'We like to do our work well; but not for any honour or glory.' At the play's first performance, when Pierre begins to deliver his lines, Françoise

> felt as if they sprang from her own will. And yet it was outside her, on the stage, that they materialized. It was agonizing. She would feel herself responsible for the slightest failure and she couldn't raise a finger to prevent it.
>
> 'It's true that we are really one,' she thought with a burst of love. Pierre was speaking, his hand was raised, but his gesture, his tone, were as much a part of Françoise's life as of his.[35]

No matter how much Beauvoir loved and admired Sartre, no matter how well she anticipated precisely his moral failings, and no matter how resigned she was to the limitations society imposed on her as a woman, it must have been 'agonizing', indeed, for her to listen quietly to Sartre as he flourished her ideas, sometimes muddling them, and always claiming them as his own.

Sartre's integrity in all this, even without the entries in his *War Diaries*, seems irredeemable. By the early 1940s, his reputation was already so well established that, if he had wished, he could have arranged to have a woman's name appear on the cover of *Being and Nothingness* along with his own. Other scenarios whereby Sartre gradually could have unveiled to the world the culturally traumatic fact that one of its greatest philosophers was a woman are easily imaginable. To be sure, once the true origins of 'Sartrean existentialism' were disclosed, it might no longer have been taken with the same seriousness, but it also might have been the case for Sartre to choose truth and a contribution to the fight for equality over the consolidation of his own reputation.

But care must be taken not to exaggerate Sartre's crime. In his formative years, Sartre was encouraged in certain proclivities – plagiarism, egomaniacal ambition and common, everyday, unreconstructed male chauvinism – which together made him highly susceptible to the temptations posed by the delights forthcoming from Beauvoir's mind. And, certainly, Sartre was encouraged in these weaknesses by Beauvoir. Her puppeteering of him and the huge deception she successfully foisted on the world also duplicated, on a grander scale, the patterns of her personal life and so must have been enormously satisfying to her own unusual appetites. Her public reputation did not come at the top of her priorities, and in any case, no matter how many ideas she gave away to Sartre, in the end there would be enough left over for her to become famous too.

Then there is the matter of Sartre's relation to Sartre. Certainly his obsessive interest in Jean Genet's life as a thief is no longer particularly puzzling. But the question remains as to whether Sartre himself was acting in bad faith about the origins of Sartrean existentialism, or did he convince himself, as he convinced the world, that he was its originator? When interviewed with Beauvoir, he often showed uncharacteristic modesty about his philosophical achievements, suggesting that, in her presence, he was, on some level, aware of his secret debt and of possible limits to Beauvoir's forbearance. But if one does not believe that Sartre wanted the truth to be discovered after he died, then his failure to destroy the incriminating entries in his war diaries is compelling evidence that he was, in the main, a 'victim' of Bad Faith.

In his maturity Sartre 'adopted' two younger women as his daughters. With one, Arlette Elkaïm, he went through legal adoption procedures so that, as he explained to John Gerassi, there would be someone after Beauvoir died to keep distributing his royalties to the five women whom he financially supported, including Elkaïm herself.[36] But, after Sartre's death, events took an unexpected turn when Elkaïm, whose legal rights prevailed over Beauvoir's moral ones, took it upon herself to decide which of Sartre's unpublished works to release. Consequently, Beauvoir, who was scarcely on speaking terms with Elkaïm, was powerless to stop the publication of Sartre's *War Diaries* in 1983. Their appearance threatened the Sartre–Beauvoir legend, which Beauvoir (although arranging for its unravelling after her death), was desperate to see preserved through her lifetime. The danger from *War Diaries* was three-fold. Firstly, Sartre's entry of 17 February 1940, where he credits Beauvoir with the concept of unrealizables, shows that he read *She Came To Stay* as a *philosophical text*. (It was this that led the present authors to do the same.) Secondly, the conspicuous cluster of original philosophical ideas in Sartre's diaries immediately after his February leave invited scholars to look for special input during his Paris fortnight, and his diaries would tell them that he had read Beauvoir's novel. So, in this way, too, the *War Diaries* could have led to a decoding of *She Came To Stay*. And thirdly, once the decoding had been effected, comparison of the philosophical contents of the novel to Sartre's diaries would reveal who really had been leading whom and, moreover, that, in writing *Being and Nothingness*, Sartre had been acting primarily in the role of interpreter and elaborator for the philosopher, Simone de Beauvoir.

From 1983 on, Beauvoir apparently regarded the discovery of the philosophical system buried in *She Came To Stay* as imminent, and against this eventuality concocted for her biographer, Deirdre Bair, an elaborate series of stories to the effect that she had scarcely begun the novel at the time of Sartre's February leave. Bair, though her strong suit was not philosophy, may have spotted Sartre's 17 February entry and confronted Beauvoir directly with what it suggested about his relation to her novel. What is certain is that Bair's lengthy description of Beauvoir's oral account of the writing of *She Came To Stay* is centred on Sartre's February leave. It is also clear that in Beauvoir's mind the crucial matter in question was which part of her novel people were to believe she had written before and after his stay in Paris. Previously, in *The Prime of Life*, Beauvoir wrote at length about the conception and writing of *She Came To Stay*, but that did not keep her from fabricating a radically different story to fend off the combined threat posed by Bair and Sartre's *War Diaries*.[37] Beauvoir's earlier account, which is consistent with the facts revealed in her letters and journals, tells how, after making a false start on the novel in October 1937, the following autumn she began it again with a new plan which included the relationships between the five major characters and everything from the appearance of Gerbert and Françoise in the first chapter to the killing of Xavière in the last.

That Beauvoir persuaded Bair that her previous account was all lies and that the new one was the truth can probably be attributed to the force of Beauvoir's personality. In any case, Bair wrote:

> Actually, by February 1940 she had written what would later

amount to less than fifty pages of the printed text, nor did she fully conceptualize it until Sartre's first leave, in that month.[38]

Beauvoir's task was complicated by the fact that the scene concerning Elizabeth and the concept of unrealizables discussed in Sartre's 17 February diary entry appears early in the second half of the novel. However, Beauvoir persuaded Bair to write that 'by the time of Sartre's February leave, she was no further along with the novel than the initial conception and the development of' Françoise and Elisabeth, and that the only parts of her 50 pages that she 'wanted Sartre to read during his leave did not concern her main character, Françoise, but rather were about Elisabeth'.[39] Since very little of the philosophical content of *She Came To Stay* is expressed through Elisabeth, this farrago of untruths, if believed, would eliminate Beauvoir's novel as the source of the philosophical ideas that appeared in Sartre's diaries immediately after returning from his February leave.

In 1983 Beauvoir published Sartre's letters, her timing perhaps inspired by hope of diverting attention from Sartre's *War Diaries*. But the letters' publication seems to have increased the awkwardness of the questions put to her by Bair, who was midway through the interviews she conducted with Beauvoir over the last six years of her life. Why, Bair asked Beauvoir, did she not publish her letters to Sartre or at least let her biographer read them? At first Beauvoir denied their existence; later, in the face of Bair's incredulity, she admitted that she did have them but that they were 'not interesting'. But Bair was very interested. 'On several occasions,' wrote Bair, 'our next meeting began with a gruff Beauvoir waving a sheaf of her letters that she had supposedly "just found in the cellar among other things", all of which supported' her claim that they contained 'nothing of any value'.[40]

To her adopted daughter, Sylvie Le Bon, Beauvoir insisted to the end that her own letters to Sartre were lost. But in a 1984 interview with a Canadian feminist magazine Beauvoir categorically stated that:

I don't feel I ought to publish letters of my own during my lifetime. When I'm dead they might perhaps be published, if they can be found.

Sylvie did find them.

One gloomy day in November 1986, while rummaging aimlessly in the depths of a cupboard at her place, I unearthed a massive packet: letters upon letters in her hand, most of them still folded in their envelopes. Addressed to 'Monsieur Sartre'. It was unexpected and moving as suddenly discovering a secret chamber in a pyramid explored countless times. She had been mistaken, her letters did exist.[41]

In fact, Beauvoir had left very little to chance. Beauvoir's 'place' was only a small studio apartment, and she knew that Sylvie, when she found them, would publish her letters which would prove to the world that the professors at the Sorbonne had been more right than they could ever have imagined when they judged that of the pair, Beauvoir, not Sartre, was the true philosopher.

PART II
SARTRE OR BEAUVOIR?

Chapter 8
A 'Preposterous' Thesis

Since the time of Kierkegaard, existentialists have used fictional characters to convey their philosophical views. Presumably their reason for doing so was the belief that the total living individual is both the subject and the object of philosophy and that *the principles of a philosophy of existence can be expressed only in a concrete setting.* (emphasis added)[1]

The American philosopher William McBride has observed that '[m]ost of the Sartre scholars in this country tend to be sympathetic to the claim that Beauvoir should be taken seriously as a philosopher, that there was a lot of exchange of ideas between the two of them.'[2] This sympathy is relatively new. Traditionally, Sartre scholars have tended to treat Beauvoir only as an eye-witness to the life (thought) of her man. In Part I of this book we have outlined and emphasized the philosophical content shared by Beauvoir's *She Came To Stay* and Sartre's *Being and Nothingness*, and called attention to the fact that Sartre's and Beauvoir's posthumously published letters and journals show that:

1 Beauvoir wrote most or all of *She Came To Stay* **before** Sartre had even begun to write *Being and Nothingness*, and,
2 Many of the philosophical ideas credited as originating with *Being and Nothingness* did not appear in Sartre's journals and other writings until **after** he had read the second draft of *She Came To Stay*.

This thesis – that at important junctures in their intellectual partnership it was Beauvoir, not Sartre, who was the originating philosophical force – is not easily swallowed by the traditionally masculinist philosophical establishment. Despite the recent weakening of psycho-cultural resistance to women-as-philosophers, for many the possibility of a gender role reversal involving one of the most acclaimed philosophers of the past century appears 'preposterous'. We therefore need to put more closely in evidence the correspondence between *Being and Nothingness* and *She Came To Stay*, including the overall philosophical indebtedness of the former to the latter.

By normal standards of scholarship, the terms on which the debate on the relative contributions of Sartre and Beauvoir is conducted are rather unorthodox. So far as we know, no evidential case has ever been made for the hypothesis that the body of ideas in dispute originated with Sartre, rather than with Beauvoir. Belief in Sartre as the source of the ideas voiced by the couple in common predates the time when the words 'woman' and 'philosopher', even less the words 'woman' and 'major philosopher', could be comfortably conjoined. Credit for these ideas accrued wholly to Sartre as part of *normal social process*. Recognition of philosophical achievement was apportioned between the two not on the basis of a determination of who contributed what, but instead, like so many things, on the basis of gender. This history of the received wisdom on the relative roles of Beauvoir and Sartre precludes direct critique. It means there exists no scholarly text purporting to establish Sartre's priority which can be invoked for scrutiny and challenge. This makes arguing Beauvoir's case like arguing against a ghost. In the absence of any serious effort to establish the legitimacy of the claims for Sartre, all one can do for the case for Beauvoir is to state it in as much detail as possible.

This chapter falls into four sections. The first and longest identifies the philosophical arguments found in *She Came To Stay* and which also appear in *Being and Nothingness*. The second considers whether these arguments originated through concrete analysis or through *a priorism*. The third examines the journal and epistolary evidence regarding the dates of authorship of *She Came To Stay* and *Being and Nothingness*. And the final section combs the same sources for evidence of which philosopher contributed what to the set of ideas shared by the two works.

The Philosophical Arguments

In order to show that our reading of *She Came to Stay* is not idiosyncratic, we are going to draw on the readings of three other authors, Maurice Merleau-Ponty, Hazel Barnes and Elizabeth Fallaize. Novel philosophical theories shared by *She Came To Stay* and *Being and Nothingness* include theories of appearances, temporality, embodiment, the division of reality between immanence and transcendence and a theory of intersubjectivity encompassing a solution to the problem of the Other, the concepts of the Third and of the Gaze or Look, and a typology of concrete relations based on a subject–object polarity.

We are going to begin with intersubjectivity or, as it is called in *Being and Nothingness*, being-for-others. There are two reasons for doing so. First, this topic takes up a third, and the most important third, of Sartre's treatise. Second, in *The Literature of Possibility: A Study in Humanistic Existentialism* (1961 [1959]) Hazel Barnes introduces Beauvoir's treatment of this material in a way that brings into focus not only the controversy with which we are concerned but also, and more importantly, the ambiguity of the developmental relations between the two works. Hazel Barnes, the English translator of *Being and Nothingness*, writes:

> For our study of bad faith in human relations we are fortunate in having both Sartre's formal analysis in *Being and Nothingness* and de Beauvoir's *She Came To Stay (L'Invitée)*, a novel which follows so closely the pattern outlined by Sartre that it serves almost as a textbook illustration.[3]

Then, following a lengthy summary of Sartre's analysis of the Other Barnes turns to Beauvoir's of the same:

> This emotional labyrinth is all faithfully illustrated for us in Simone de Beauvoir's novel, *She Came To Stay*. Although this book and *Being and Nothingness* were published in the same year (1943), the similarity between them is too striking to be coincidence. As with all of de Beauvoir's early fiction, the reader of *She Came To Stay* feels that the inspiration of the book was simply de Beauvoir's decision to show how Sartre's abstract principles could be made to work out in real life.'[4]

Barnes, however, significantly appends to this the following footnote:

> We do not at all preclude the possibility that de Beauvoir has contributed to the formation of Sartre's philosophy. We suspect that his debt to her is considerable. All we mean in the present instance is that the novel serves as documentation for the theory, regardless of who had which idea first.[5]

'[I]t is only after finishing the book,' says Barnes about Beauvoir's novel, 'that one notes with amusement its *step by step correspondence* with Sartre's description of the subject-object conflict.' [emphasis added][6] Barnes's book traces much of this correspondence, which includes an argument for the existence of others' consciousnesses. The history of this philosophical problem and Sartre's solution takes up the first of the three chapters devoted to being-for-others in *Being and Nothingness*. Whereas previously philosophy had relied on an argument from analogy – she behaves rather like me, therefore she must be conscious like me – Beauvoir and Sartre base theirs on the phenomenological event of *experiencing* oneself as the object of another's consciousness. The sudden flush of shame or pride a person experiences when made the object of another's disapproving or admiring glance provides the archetypal case. Only another consciousness, goes the argument, could cause this transformation in one's own consciousness.

But for Beauvoir and Sartre, the subject–object relation matters not so much because it answers an old philosophical question, as because they believe it structures many personal and sociological relations. In *She Came To Stay* Beauvoir identifies three fundamental procedures or attitudes which one may take up regarding the subjectivity or consciousness of the Other. A person may seek to experience herself as the Other's object; a person may seek to guard their subjectivity by making the Other their object; or a person may seek a reciprocity with the Other, whereby each treats the other as both subject and object, as equal freedoms and sources of value. Of these three fundamental attitudes to intersubjective relations, *Being and Nothingness* omits reciprocity, but devotes its third chapter on intersubjectivity to analysing the other two. For the first attitude, where one exploits one's possibilities as an object, Sartre describes two categories of concrete relations: love and masochism. For the second attitude, where one seeks to protect one's subjectivity, Sartre describes four categories: indifference, desire, hate and sadism. He closes his account of intersubjectivity by considering how the introduction of a third person (the Third or the formation of a triangle) affects the subject–object relation and gives rise to subject and object groups.

Hazel Barnes's book shows how not only Sartre's essay but also Beauvoir's novel develops all the material just outlined. Sartre's translator's reading of *She Came To Stay* identifies the correspondence at such length that here we can give only the barest outline. The novel has five important characters: Françoise, a writer through whose consciousness most of the story is told; Pierre, a young theatrical actor–director who has a long-term relationship with Françoise; Xavière, an alluring child-woman who disrupts Françoise and Pierre's relationship; Elizabeth, Pierre's sister who is an unhappy but successful painter; and Gerbert, Françoise's appealing younger assistant.

With these characters Beauvoir creates a set of shifting triangles which, through the principle of the Third, structure the work as a whole. Xavière is the apex of the first triangle, which includes Françoise and Pierre.[7] 'Relations at the beginning,' notes Barnes, 'are on the plane of indifference,' which for Sartre and Beauvoir means pretending that another person is only an object. This is how Françoise relates to Xavière when she first enters her and Pierre's life. She does not see Xavière as a self-determining subject or as an Other who might in any way affect Françoise's life. 'She is but the material for one of Françoise's projects,' explains Barnes.[8] But, notes Fallaize in *The Novels of Simone de Beauvoir*, Xavière is simply 'a representation of the implicit challenge that all other consciousnesses constitute to our own,'[9] and gradually she forces Françoise to become aware of her subjectivity.

> Xavière's emergence as a subject threatens Françoise in two ways. In the first place she forces Françoise to become aware in a new way of her self-for-others and to see her whole life in a different and dubious light ... The second threat is to Françoise's relation to Pierre. In part this is simply the Sartrean disintegration of a dual relation under the Look of a Third ... Now the difference in their [Françoise and Pierre] evaluation of Xavière makes her see Pierre as an opaque being with whom she can no longer feel an absolute unity.[10]

Beauvoir treats the physical desires that soon emerge between Xavière and Françoise and Xavière and Pierre with restraint because, says Barnes, of her 'resolve to document Sartre's statement that, whereas all human relations are implicitly sexual, they do not have sexual intercourse as their specific goal. De Beauvoir gives full weight to both parts of his theory [of desire].'[11] Later Pierre becomes the pure embodiment of the Sartrean project of love (love in bad faith, of course). In loving Xavière he wants to *be loved* by her. He wants her to choose him as the centre of her existence. Recognizing the intensity of her will to be the subject in any relationship, it will be the 'supreme conquest if she voluntarily chooses him as the limit of her freedom.'[12] Meanwhile Françoise's relation to Xavière becomes a project of love in which she is almost snared in the object-state with which she has hoped to fascinate Xavière's freedom; it is 'love on the masochistic side.'[13] 'True masochism', however, is represented by Pierre's sister, and her relationship with a married man.[14] For these and other concrete relations, Barnes's critique calls attention to the ontological structures which Beauvoir's phenomenological analyses reveal. She also shows how her novel works its way through the different categories of concrete relations as enumerated in *Being and Nothingness*. For example, Barnes writes: 'So far we have seen, in terms consistent with Sartre's analysis, exemplifications of indifference, of two projects of love, and of masochism. In Xavière we see a portrayal, in very delicate terms, of sadism.'[15]

As the plot progresses, Françoise, who for Beauvoir represents philosophy's traditional unawareness of the existence of a direct relation between human consciousnesses, experiences herself objectified in front of Xavière's consciousness with increasing frequency. Commenting on one these episodes, Barnes writes:

In this passage de Beauvoir has compressed the essence of Hegel's conflict of consciousness and of Sartre's idea that the emergence of another consciousness effects an internal hemorrhage of my world. The keyhole example soon follows.[16]

Both Beauvoir's novel and Sartre's essay use the sudden flush of embarrassment experienced by someone caught spying through a keyhole as an illustration of a subject–object reversal effected by the Other's look, from feeling oneself as wholly a subject to experiencing oneself as an object in a world organized by another consciousness.[17]

By this point in her novel Beauvoir, notes Barnes, still has not examined quite all of the philosophical implications of being-for-others. There still remains the 'exploration of hate', the last of the categories of concrete relations found in *Being and Nothingness*.[18] This is effected through Françoise's decision to kill Xavière, a 'metaphysical murder rather than a real one', and 'which is but the dramatic conclusion of a philosophical proposition.'[19]

Thus far, by focusing on Barnes's reading and with a little help from Fallaize, we have found in *She Came To Stay* all the major ideas and arguments found in two of *Being and Nothingness*'s three chapters on being-for others. The material from the third, 'The Body', is best correlated to Beauvoir's text in conjunction with the topics of temporality, bad faith and the division of reality between immanence and transcendence, or, as Sartre calls it, between being-in-itself and being-for-itself.

Merleau-Ponty identifies the hypothesis that human reality divides between immanence and transcendence as central to Beauvoir's novel. In his essay on *She Came To Stay*, 'Metaphysics and the Novel', he writes:

> Her book shows existence understood between two limits: on the one hand, there is the immediate closed tightly upon itself, beyond any word and any commitment (Xavière); and, on the other, there is an absolute confidence in language and rational decision, an existence which grows empty in the effort to transcend itself (Françoise at the beginning of the book).[20]

The novel begins with Françoise (whose metaphysical reflections we witness) acting as an experiential stand-in for two philosophical deficiencies or myths endemic to Western philosophy: that no direct relation exists between individual consciousnesses, and that consciousness can be treated as independent of body. Beauvoir sees the experience of the Other and the embodiment of consciousness as paired, and both related to the immanence/transcendence divide in human experience. Her choice of fiction as her philosophical medium permits her to analyse the two issues concurrently, while discovering their roots in the concrete. She centres the plot on Françoise's progressive disabusing of herself of the traditional philosophical views – whose foolishness becomes manifest when subjected to the context of lived experience – and the formation of new ones. Fallaize astutely brings out this dimension of Beauvoir's text.

> As happens so often in the text, the metaphysical and the psychosexual again come together here; Françoise's lack of awareness of her being-for-others, of how she appears to other people in

the world, is damaging to her awareness of herself as a sexual and gendered being. To think of herself as 'no-one', as 'a naked consciousness in front of the world'[21] is to fail to perceive herself as body and as a woman. As the crisis intensifies, and Françoise is gradually forced to recognise her existence in the world on the same terms as other people, she begins to see that 'whether she liked it or not, she too was in the world, a part of this world. She was woman among other women' (p. 146). The juxtaposition of these two statements is striking. The discovery of being-for-others, of her social existence, is a rediscovery of corporality, and hence of sexuality and gender. Françoise's illness at the end of the first part [half] of the book signals the re-emergence of her awareness that she is not pure consciousness, that she also has a corporal existence – but here she experiences the temporary preeminence of the body in passive terms as she retreats with relief into illness. [22]

Likewise, Merleau-Ponty in 'Metaphysics and the Novel' (1964 [1945]) writes as follows on Françoise's metaphysical conversion at the time of her illness and confinement to a clinic.

Henceforth, Françoise can no longer know herself from inner evidence alone. She can no longer doubt that, under the glance of that couple [Pierre and Xavière], she is truly an object, and through their eyes she sees herself from the outside for the first time. And what is she? A thirty-year-old woman, a mature woman, to whom many things are already irrevocably impossible – who, for example, will never be able to dance well. For the first time she has the feeling of being her body, when all along she had thought herself a consciousness. She has sacrificed everything to this myth.[23]

As one might expect, Merleau-Ponty also takes a keen interest in how Beauvoir's phenomenological descriptions demonstrate the wrong-headedness of mechanistic explanations of perceptual experience. The situational nature of fiction enables her to show how the body, with its organs of perception, and the subject, with its consciousness, are intertwined. The body is subjective and the subject embodied. In the real world, objects reveal themselves only to consciousnesses which are individually and materially situated. Perceptions are conditioned by variations in the state of one's embodiment and structured by the stories one tells and hears told about one's past and future. This individualized structuring extends, according to Beauvoir, Sartre and Merleau-Ponty, even to elementary space and time. Early in *She Came To Stay* Beauvoir sketches her theory of temporality through Socratic dialogues between her characters,[24] arguing that perception of time is primarily about projected futures. Later this argument emerges more fully developed from her account of the gradual demise of Françoise's world',[25] culminating with Françoise's apparent loss of Pierre to Xavière, her confinement to a hospital bed and her contemplation of existence from this new vantage point.[26] It is this exemplification on which Merleau-Ponty focuses his summary of Beauvoir's theory of temporality.

> things retreat beyond her grasp and become the strange debris of a world to which she no longer holds the key. The future ceases to be the natural extension of the present, time is fragmented, and Françoise is no more than an anonymous being, a creature without a history, a mass of chilled flesh ... There was a unique pulsation which projected before her a living present, a future, a world which animated language for her – and that pulsation has stopped.
>
> ... A feeling is the name conventionally given to a series of instants, but life, when considered lucidly, is reduced to this swarming of instants ... One can escape the crumbling of time only by an act of faith which now seems to Françoise a voluntary illusion.[27]

We want to conclude this necessarily incomplete and sketchy discussion of the philosophical material common to *She Came To Stay* and *Being and Nothingness* by looking at the way both these works begin, the 'striking and ingenious' means by which they both launch their philosophical endeavours. These projects initially faced a major obstacle. Beauvoir and Sartre wanted to take individual consciousness as their ontological starting point, while also taking up the position that things exist independently of anyone's consciousness of them. This stand presented them with a well-known problem with no known satisfactory solution: if the only access to things is their appearances to human consciousness, then how does one show that those things exist except as appearances *to* someone's consciousness. As Arthur Danto observes about Sartre's writing of *Being and Nothingness*, 'it was therefore imperative that he solve the problem of appearance in order to save his view that we are conscious of real independent things. His analysis is striking and ingenious.'[28] Roughly, that analysis goes like this. When we interrupt our usual goal-directed intercourse, we become aware of facing beyond our current field of vision a horizon of possible appearances whose number 'is, loosely speaking, infinite, or at least indeterminate.'[29] We experience each appearance as part of a series of potential appearances, a series which must be infinite given (according to our perceptions) the infinite points of view afforded by space and time. But it is impossible for a mortal human subject to be conscious of an infinity of appearances. Therefore, there must exist a world of things outside the world of human consciousness.

Being and Nothingness, in its difficult 'Introduction', begins by presenting this solution to the problem of appearances. But so too does *She Came To Stay*. Merleau-Ponty, after explaining the use of fiction as a philosophical method, begins his analysis of *She Came To Stay* with the following passage which refers to the opening of Beauvoir's novel:

> There is a perpetual uneasiness in the state of being conscious. At the moment I perceive a thing, I feel that it was there before me, outside my field of vision. *There is an infinite horizon of things to grasp surrounding the small number of things which I can grasp in fact.* The whistle of a locomotive in the night, the empty theatre which I enter, cause to appear, for a lightning instant, those things which everywhere are ready to be perceived – shows performed without an audience, shadows crowded with creatures. Even the things which surround me exceed my comprehension, provided I interrupt my usual intercourse with them and rediscover them, outside of the human or even the living world, in their role as natural things. [emphasis added][30]

Beauvoir presents her argument for the existence of things independent of consciousness by the same method she uses for her argument for the existence of other consciousnesses. We examined how Beauvoir uses Françoise's bad faith regarding the existence of the Other to demonstrate to her readers the basis of our belief in the existence of other consciousnesses. Françoise also begins the novel committed to believing, as she informs Gerbert, 'that things that don't exist for me simply do not exist at all', (Beauvoir 1984, 6) and that '[o]nly her own life was real'.[31] But of course, as Merleau-Ponty notes: '"Elsewhere" and "other" have not been eliminated; they have merely been repressed.'[32] Beauvoirian/Sartrean bad faith requires awareness of what one is denying, and it is through Françoise's perception of the reality to be repressed that we as readers are confronted at the phenomenological level with Beauvoir's theory of appearances.[33]

The novel begins: 'Françoise raised her eyes.' Interrupting her work with Gerbert on a script late at night in her theatre office, she takes in the appearances which present themselves to her there in the room. But as she non-instrumentally perceives these things she is made uneasy by the feeling that these appearances hook up to a whole series of appearances outside her field of vision. 'Outside was the theatre ... with its deserted corridors circling a great hollow shell.' She tells Gerbert that she is going to fetch some whisky, but we are told that really 'it was the dark corridors which were the attraction'.[34] Her theatre walk then reveals each appearance as part of the well-known series of appearances comprising a theatre: the corridors, the half-light, the red carpet, the auditorium, the stage, the safety curtain, the rows of seats, and the deserted theatre's solitude and sense of expectancy. And against this expanding series of appearances she notes the finitude which embodiment and temporality impose on her consciousness and hence on her capacity to perceive these appearances. 'She would have had to remain there forever in order to' exhaust this series of potential appearances which the theatre alone offered to her.[35] Furthermore, in the theatre 'she would have had to be elsewhere as well: in the props-room, in the dressing-rooms, in the foyer; *she would have had to be everywhere at the same time.*' [emphasis added][36] Beauvoir then expands the horizon of things which Françoise perceives. She steps outside the theatre where the 'houses all round the square were sleeping', a quick step echoes on the pavement, a truck rumbles along the avenue, and where she thinks of provincial towns and later of Pierre moving through the night on a train and, finally, of 'all those icy mountains and crevasses' on the moon.[37] Beauvoir uses this process of invoking the phenomenology of Françoise's lived existence, and of drawing concrete examples to repeatedly remind the reader that Françoise will 'never be able to see more than one thing at a time'[38] in an infinite or inexhaustible series of appearances. In this way Beauvoir's narrative, at its very beginning, establishes the transcendence of a realm of being vis-à-vis Françoise's and, by implication, all human consciousness. Françoise:

felt very strongly about this; the corridors, the auditorium, the stage, none of these things had vanished when she had again shut the door on them, but they existed only behind the door, at a distance. At a distance the train was moving through the silent countryside which encompassed, in the depths of the night, the warm life of her little office.[39]

This section, of course, is radically incomplete as a survey of the philosophical content of *She Came To Stay*. But my intent, rather than offering an overview of Beauvoir's early philosophical thought, has been merely to identify the book's main lines of philosophical argument paralleling those in *Being and Nothingness* and to document the fact that they have been previously identified by distinguished writers. But of these, Barnes's and Merleau-Ponty's readings of *She Came To Stay* differ in one highly significant and highly interesting respect. Unlike Barnes, Merleau-Ponty does not once suggest that Beauvoir's book might owe anything to Sartre. Why their mutual friend and colleague apportioned credit in this way will become clear when the journal and epistolary evidence is examined.

Which Came First: Analysis of the Concrete or Abstract Principles?

The three passages from Barnes's *The Literature of Possibility: A Study in Humanistic Existentialism* quoted at the beginning of the previous section brush silently against a matter of pivotal importance for understanding the 'formation' of what tradition labels 'Sartre's philosophy', and for shedding light on 'who had which idea first'. Barnes's manner of paralleling the two works suggests, but never quite makes explicit, a key question: Which comes first for Beauvoir and Sartre, the 'pattern' or 'the illustrations', the 'abstract principles' or the 'real life' cases, the 'theory' or the 'documentation' and analysis of concrete examples?

Philosophers working in philosophy's *a priori* mainstream typically begin by choosing from the common fund a set of general propositions, which they then weave together to arrive at conclusions that, finally, they may or may not exemplify with worldly examples. In this tradition, 'illustrations', 'real life cases' and 'documentation' function merely as icing for the cake. But the phenomenological/existential tradition reverses this order of procedure: it draws ontological, metaphysical and general statements from descriptions of the particular and the concrete.

In one of her first essays Beauvoir identified this method as her way of doing philosophy and explained her preference for deploying it in the context of a novel. In 'Littérature et métaphysique' (1948), which appeared in *Les Temps Modernes* in 1946, Beauvoir argues that a novel which employs 'pre-established theses is a mystification'.[40] She maintains that the basic requirement for an 'honestly written' philosophical novel such as *She Came To Stay* is that its philosophical content must not pre-date the novel itself. Rather than illustrating pre-existing philosophical ideas, the novel must be executed as a piece of original philosophical 'research' which generates (by the method described by Warnock) its philosophical content. Each of its ideas must be for the author 'a living discovery'.

So, as Elizabeth Fallaize observes, the process at work, or at least which appears to be at work, in *She Came To Stay* is 'psychological phenomena giving rise to a rationalized philosophical discourse'.[41] And for 40 years Beauvoir remained adamant that this was, indeed, the true process by which her novel developed. *She did so even in the presence of Sartre.* Sharing a platform with him in Japan in 1966, Beauvoir gave a lecture later published as 'Mon experience d'écrivain'[42] in which she explained the process by which she wrote *She Came To Stay*. She identifies a personal 'concrete psychological experience' as having led her to awareness of an ontological opposition, but which does not preclude the possibility of a reciprocity, between consciousnesses. She also describes her search for the means that would allow her 'singular story to take a universal dimension'.[43]

Briefly, we discovered something that everyone knows: the consciousness of others exists; another is a subject for himself as I am for myself; in his world I am an object which he arranges more or less as he pleases and which he may regard as hateful, unpleasant. So I had had a concrete experience and which was first of all situated on the psychological plane. But as long as one remains on the psychological plane, that is to say anecdotal, the book does not write itself. The book began to design itself in my head when I found a way of passing from this singular experience to a universal; I expressed it to myself, as I do before you, when I understood that it was the problem of others, the relationship to the consciousness of others which tormented me.[44]

Like many radical twentieth-century philosophers, Beauvoir had serious reservations about the nature of the philosophical enterprise and sought to distance herself from orthodox practice. But unlike her innovative male counterparts, this rebellion often has been turned against her as 'evidence' that she was not a 'philosopher', and, therefore, depended on Sartre for her ideas. From her earliest essays[45] to her late interviews,[46] she disdained philosophy which took the form of that lunacy known as a 'philosophical system'.[47] Noting women's insusceptibility to this madness, she reserved the word 'philosopher' for those who were – and she openly cited Sartre as an example – 'prone to obsessions of this type'.[48] But Beauvoir has paid a heavy price for this usage. Those wishing to deny the existence of Beauvoir-the-philosopher have found it rhetorically effective to quote out of context her remarks about not being a 'philosopher'.

In 1979, by which time the myth that Beauvoir was simply Sartre's philosophical handmaiden was already firmly established, Margaret Simons and Jessica Benjamin pressed Beauvoir over the origins of her theory of the Other in *She Came To Stay*.

> M.S.: Sometimes, it is difficult for me to understand correctly your relationship with Sartre, your autonomy. Your ideas of the woman's situation, and of the Other, are really your own creation. And yet sometimes, in your own statements, it sounds as though you are saying the ideas came from Sartre
> S.B.: Oh! No! Absolutely not … No, these ideas are my own, indeed … when I wrote my novels, I was never influenced by Sartre because I was writing from my lived and felt experiences.
> J.B.: So when you wrote in *L'Invitée* [*She Came To Stay*] that Françoise says what really upsets her about Xavière is that she has to confront in her another consciousness, that is not an idea that particularly came [from] Sartre?
> S.B.: It was I who thought about that! It was absolutely not Sartre!
> J.B.: But that is an idea which it seems to me appears later in *his* work.
> S.B.: Oh! Maybe! (Laughter) In any case, this problem … of the other's consciousness, it was my problem.[49]

In the final months of her life, Beauvoir was still struggling against the popular view that the philosophical thought in *She Came To Stay* was Sartre's. In an interview in September 1985, Simons, referring to the time when she started her studies with Beauvoir, remarked: 'But a lot of people told me, "Why are you working with her? Why not the man himself? She is just a follower."' Beauvoir replied:

> My books are completely personal. Sartre never interfered. *She Came To Stay*, *The Mandarins*, all of that is mine.[50]

But people do sometimes misrepresent what they have and have not done. As Hazel Barnes's remarks indicate, it does not necessarily follow that Beauvoir's novel, with its essential embeddedness in the concrete and the particular and its ostensible development of philosophical arguments from this base, is the original source of those arguments. Sartre's *Being and Nothingness* also sometimes appears to develop its arguments by the method described by Warnock. So it could have been that for 40 years Beauvoir, although Sartre never contradicted her, was adamantly falsifying her account of how she wrote *She Came To Stay*. It could have been that its philosophical discourse (or some part of it) had already been developed by Sartre, and beginning with that, Beauvoir looked around for phenomena which would illustrate it and then created the illusion – and novelists are illusionists – that the novel's philosophical insights initially emerged from the phenomena examined. This theoretical possibility of a double-barrelled deception by Beauvoir, and the deep-seated cultural tendency for women not to be believed in such matters, is why the journal and epistolary material of the two thinkers is so crucial to settling this issue of origination.

Which Book Was Written First?

In Chapters 6 and 7 we have from a biographical point of view traced the genesis and surrounding events of *She Came To Stay* and *Being and Nothingness*. Here and in the section that follows, with supporting material from Sartre scholars, we want to capsulate our findings.

Sartre's biographers divide over whether he *began* to write *Being and Nothingness* in late July 1940 or in the autumn of 1941. Contat and Rybalka, Thompson, and Beauvoir favour the later date, whereas Gerassi and Hayman say that in July and August of 1940 Sartre wrote upwards of a tenth of his essay before putting the project aside until over a year later.[51] Both these dates, however, come after Beauvoir had *finished* the first and most, if not all, of the second draft of *She Came To Stay*. Furthermore, Beauvoir had completed the final revisions to her novel several months before Sartre began or re-commenced writing *Being and Nothingness* in autumn 1941.[52] Indeed, in October 1941 Beauvoir submitted *She Came To Stay* to the publishers Gallimard.[53] In January 1942 they agreed to publish it 'as it stands'.[54]

There exists extensive, diverse and incontrovertible documentary evidence detailing Beauvoir's progress with the writing of *She Came To Stay* and also Sartre's reading of it. In *The Prime of Life*, her second volume of autobiography, Beauvoir says that after a false start on *She Came To Stay* in late 1937, she began it anew the following year and finished with the final revisions in the late spring of 1941.[55] But much more detailed and contemporaneously recorded information on the writing of her novel appears in her letters, in her war journals, and also in Sartre's letters and journals. And all of these sources tell the same story. Briefly, it is as follows.

On 2 September 1939 Sartre left Paris and Beauvoir for military service. During their separation they exchanged letters nearly every day until Sartre was taken prisoner on 21 June 1940. They also both kept journals.[56] In Sartre's absence, Beauvoir threw herself into writing her novel, and naturally in her letters to Sartre she told him about its progress. Over 30 of her letters from this period contain such references.[57] When Sartre left Paris, her novel's first draft appears to have been only about half written, but by early December she had another 300 pages. On 7 December, Beauvoir wrote to Sartre:

> Since yesterday, I've been revising the novel from the beginning. I've had enough of inventing drafts; everything's in place now and I want to write some definitive stuff. I'm enjoying it enormously, and it seems terribly – quite seductively – easy.[58]

Her letters report that of this 'new and final draft' she had 60 pages by 29 December, 80 pages by 3 January, 160 pages by 12 January, and on 17 January, anticipating Sartre's return on leave, wrote 'I really think you'll heap me with praises when you read my 250 pages (for there'll be at least 250).' Beauvoir's journal says that on 5 February, the morning after Sartre arrived on leave, he occupied himself reading *She Came To Stay*.[59] Her journal mentions seven more reading sessions that he had with her novel before he left on 15 February.[60] Sartre's first letter to Beauvoir after returning to military life concludes: '*Vous avez écrit un beau petit roman,*' suggesting that he had read more than just the revised first half of her novel (Sartre 1983, 70) And three days later, 18 February, he writes to Beauvoir about the philosophical meaning of an episode that comes near the end of *She Came To Stay* in Chapter 7 of Part II.[61] Further references to his reading of her novel follow in his letters. Meanwhile in his own journal, Sartre's entries are now replete with references to *She Came To Stay*, and these bring us to this essay's final question.

Who Thought What First?

Although it is now certain that *She Came To Stay* was written before *Being and Nothingness*, it is not *absolutely* proven that the original philosophical ideas and arguments shared by the two works did not originate with Sartre. It remains theoretically possible that these were all Sartre's ideas, which he privately communicated to Beauvoir, who then built her novel around them, and who then made up a false story about how she wrote *She Came To Stay*, to which she held for the next 40 years. To some people this possibility may appear so implausible that it does not seem worth pursuing, but the cultural bias (in which women as well as men have been socialized) against crediting the woman in such cases is so strong that even this implausible possibility must be eliminated if Beauvoir-the-philosopher is to receive her due.

Since the publication of Sartre's *War Diaries* in 1983, scholars have identified these journals, which he kept during the war prior to his capture, as the place where he first developed many of the philosophical ideas that were to form the framework of *Being and Nothingness*.[62] It is important to emphasize and document just how widespread is the agreement among Sartre scholars that his emergence as an original philosopher took place in his writing of these wartime diaries. In his introduction to the English edition of the *War Diaries*, Quinton Hoare notes that 'the prewar years seem in retrospect to have been but an apprenticeship' and the 'excitement of the notebooks' comes partly 'from the fact they represent the essential transition from that apprenticeship to the full flowering of Sartre's talents ... as an original philosopher, in *Being and Nothingness* (1943), drafts for many of whose key passages will be found here'.[63] Sartre's biographer Ronald Hayman also identifies this as the period in which 'Sartre's existentialism was beginning to take shape.'[64] Another biographer of Sartre, Kenneth A. Thompson, writes: 'It was also in these notebooks [the *War Diaries*] that he outlined his morality and drafted his philosophical reflections that were to find their definitive form in *Being and Nothingness*.'[65] Thomas Flynn observes that in these notebooks 'we discover reflections that will find their way into *Being and Nothingness*'.[66] William McBride finds in the journals 'an anticipation of some of the principal themes of *Being and Nothingness*'.[67] Likewise, for Andrew Leak the *War Diaries* 'constitute an important *avant texte* for *L'Etre et le néant*'.[68]

This 'flowering' of Sartre as a philosopher with his own ideas, however, does not manifest itself until after his leave to Paris in February 1940 and his many reading sessions with *She Came To Stay*. As Sartre himself noted in a letter to Beauvoir on 9 January 1940:

> I have reread my five notebooks, and they don't please me nearly as much as I had expected. I find them a little vague, too discreet, even the clearest ideas are little more than rehashings of Heidegger's: in the end, all I have done since September … is only a long re-elaboration of the ten pages he devoted to the question of historicity.[69]

Anna Boschetti, referring to the period just before Sartre's February leave, confirms Sartre's reading of himself. 'The philosophy we see coming to birth almost from day to day in his letters and notebooks,' she writes, 'is still much closer to a rewriting of *Being and Time* [Heidegger] than to an outline of the ethic implicit in *Being and Nothingness*.'[70] Similarly, Leo Fretz, writing of the 'confrontation between Sartre's philosophical positions from before and after 1940', speaks of 'the turnaround of 1940', when Sartre becomes 'Sartrean' in the sense that his concept of consciousness 'becomes endowed with a *personal* structure'.[71]

The simple truth seems to be that following his protracted engagement with Beauvoir's text in Paris, Sartre returned to camp metamorphosed into a dynamo of philosophical originality. For the two weeks that followed, his notebooks, offering occasional acknowledgement to Beauvoir, make the generation of philosophical ideas look as easy as picking apples from a tree.

Between 17 and 27 February, Sartre appears to have set down in his notebooks as much of the philosophical content of *She Came to Stay* as he could remember.[72] Many, but not all, of the ideas and arguments he records are the same as those that caught the attention of Merleau-Ponty,

Barnes and Fallaize. Sartre begins in good faith. He introduces the concept of *unrecognizables* (not discussed in this essay) and acknowledges that it comes from Beauvoir's novel,[73] although in *Being and Nothingness*[74] he treats it as his own. In his entry the following day, 18 February, Sartre turns to Beauvoir's theory of temporality. In retrospect, the passage which opens his exposition is one of the most shocking in twentieth-century philosophy. It shocks not because it mentions neither Beauvoir nor his recent experience of reading her novel, but because Sartre seems to be as set on deceiving himself as he is his readers. 'I feel strangely bashful about embarking on a study of temporality. Time has always struck me as a philosophical headache,' he writes before briefly reviewing his numerous past failures in this field, including in his novel *Nausea* and in his lectures. 'But all that wasn't yet ripe. And, behold, I now glimpse a theory of time! I feel intimidated before expounding it, I feel like a kid.'[75] Glimpse, indeed! What follows is pure Beauvoir, some of it little more than paraphrases of dialogues from *She Came To Stay*.[76]

Sartre continues to take possession of Beauvoir's theory of temporality on 19 February.[77] On 22 and 23 February he takes up Beauvoir's view (not discussed in this essay) of consciousness's continuous need for objects as the ultimate basis of all forms of desire. Then on 27 February, in seven impressive pages,[78] he sketches out a large part of Beauvoir's theory of intersubjectivity. Without ever quite making explicit the idea of the Gaze or Look, he makes a good job of explaining the basic subject–object polarity.[79] But he does not connect this analysis – as Beauvoir does repeatedly in her novel – with the philosophical problem of the existence of other consciousnesses. His effort's strong point is its treatment of concrete relations with the Other. He covers love,[80] sadism,[81] indifference[82] and desire,[83] but misses out masochism and hate. Nor do we find evidence that Sartre had yet taken in that concept of Beauvoir's that he later termed the Third. But this and other material from *She Came To Stay* could have been in his Notebook 13, which runs from 1 March to 5 March 1940 and was lost.

Finally, there is the matter of Merleau-Ponty's treatment of the philosophical content of *She Came To Stay* as originating with Beauvoir rather than with Sartre. This seems explained by the fact that he knew beyond doubt that Beauvoir's book was written well in advance of *Being and Nothingness*. Her letter of 23 December 1940 to Sartre begins: 'It's very cold this morning throughout Paris and particularly in the Dôme. Merleau-Ponty's here, a few steps away, busy reading my novel.'[84, 85]

Postscript

A few years ago another set of documents throwing fresh light on the relative philosophical contributions of Beauvoir and Sartre emerged to public view and is now kept in the Bibliothèque Nationale in Paris. The documents consist of a set of diaries kept by Beauvoir when she was a student between the years 1926 and 1930, almost entirely before she met Sartre. Her 1926–7 diaries have now been translated into English and published.[86] Their philosophical precociousness almost defies belief. They show that Beauvoir while still a teenage student had already settled upon her radical approach to philosophy, already committed herself to the philosopher's life, already begun to think through philosophy's big questions *for herself* and already begun to come up with original answers.

In her diaries we see her consciously developing her method, the intermingling of the personal and the philosophical. What is startling is that she links the two in the opposite direction from what is conventional. Instead of applying philosophical insight to her life, she describes her experiences at coping, or not, with life's contingencies and then, sometimes over a period of weeks or months, distils from them general philosophical questions and insights. All this is done with a logical hardheadedness that even the young Descartes or the mature Hume might have envied.

It was from one such empirical observation about her life that in 1926 Beauvoir distilled a bold and anti-Cartesian philosophical proposition. She makes an ontological distinction between 'two parts in my existence: one for others [*pour autrui*]', 'the links that unite me with all beings', and another 'part for myself [*pour moi-même*]'.[87] Here we already have two of the three primary categories of thought that formed the 'original' structure of Sartre's *Being and Nothingness*. The third she provided a year later when she introduced and discussed her notion of 'the nothingness of everything human'[88] Meanwhile she had already begun to identify and formulate what she called 'the problem of the Other'. All this when she was still a teenager and before she had set eyes on Sartre.

Indeed, how often in the history of philosophy has there been a philosopher so precocious as Beauvoir? She was only 19, but had already:

- rejected the standard notion of the self of traditional Western philosophy, as well as the one ready-made alternative (Bergson's), in favour of her own analysis;
- broadly formulated a new notion of self as an ongoing intersubjective construction;
- committed herself to pursuing the reorientation of philosophy from the study of the noumenal world to the phenomenal world;
- set about developing a new philosophical method;
- identified being and nothingness as her central theme; and
- settled upon the opposition of self and other as the primary philosophical problem that she sought to resolve.

For further reading about Beauvoir's student diaries, see this chapter's endnote 89.[89]

Chapter 9
Two Beginnings, One Philosophy

The ambiguity of language permits the construction of texts that are readable at more than one level of meaning. Showing people how to access different levels of meaning of sophisticated prose is the daily business of literature teachers. But willingness to acknowledge such sophistication in a particular text often depends on the social category to which its author belongs. This is so because social prejudices do not magically vanish when reading, teaching or writing about books. When a society withholds recognition of an existing level of meaning in a text, it imposes on that text a form of censorship. Unlike Sartre's philosophical novel *Nausea*, this has been the fate of Beauvoir's *She Came To Stay*. If for whatever reason one is so-minded, one can effect contextual censorship on a multi-level text merely by refusing to acknowledge more than one of its levels of meaning.

But in the case of *She Came To Stay* a publishing oddity has occurred which makes anyone wishing to deny that Beauvoir's novel, any less than Sartre's, is a philosophical text look either extremely foolish or intellectually corrupt. In 1979 Beauvoir's French publisher Gallimard published a 600-page collection of her minor works, either out of print or never before published, together with a year-by-year chronicle of her professional life. [*Les écrits de Simone de Beauvoir*] The collection included what originally had been the opening two chapters of *She Came To Stay*. ['Deux chapitres inédits de *L'Invitée*', pp. 275–316] Recently an English translation of these chapters has been published. ['Two Unpublished Chapters from *She Came To Stay*' in *Simone de Beauvoir: Philosophical Writings*, editor Margaret A. Simons, Chicago: University of Illinois Press, pp. 41–75.] Although the two beginnings to her novel are totally distinct in terms of the places and events described, close reading reveals a startling similarity. This chapter will explain how and why this is so.

Cultural Differences

Two cultural differences between Analytical and Continental philosophy made censoring contextually *She Came To Stay* especially easy. The first concerns the unit of work. The most famous 'Continental' philosophers have constructed 'systems' designed to encompass solutions to many of philosophy's perennial problems. Kant, Hegel, Marx, Heidegger and Sartre are examples. These system-builders took other philosophers' solutions along with some of their own and combined them in novel ways. But system-builders in the analytical tradition are virtually unknown. Here the focus of work and the basis of reputation is almost exclusively problem solution.

In the English-speaking world the Continental philosopher has been cruelly and crudely stereotyped as someone unconcerned with philosophical problems, so much so that, as Simon Critchley has observed, 'Continental philosophy has been reduced to a list of proper names'.[1] This prejudice works very strongly against the recognition of Beauvoir, who was a problem-oriented philosopher, and in favour of Sartre, who was a system-oriented philosopher. As evidenced in her student diaries,[2] Beauvoir was from the beginning self-consciously problem-oriented in her approach to philosophy. And she remained so. But Beauvoir and Sartre scholars who have been infected with the prejudice described above do not look for solutions to philosophical problems in Beauvoir's work and, if called to their attention, dismiss them as unimportant because she has not made them part of a philosophical system.

The second cultural difference facilitating the contextual censorship of *She Came To Stay* concerns phenomenological and existential philosophy in particular. Whereas rationalist philosophers begin with supposed universal truths and analytical philosophers with the presumed universal subject and then proceed to truths of diminishing generality, philosophers in the phenomenological–existential tradition begin with concrete individual experiences and then, if possible, proceed to generalizations.

This diametrical opposition of perspectives makes it easy to sabotage understanding between the two traditions. But some philosophers in the analytical tradition have worked hard to break down these barriers to cross-cultural understanding.

One of these is the Cambridge philosopher, Mary Warnock. 'The methodology of Existentialism,' she says, 'consists in a perfectly deliberate and intentional use of the *concrete* as a way of approaching the abstract, the *particular* as a way of approaching the general.'[3] And she adds:

> The existential philosopher, then, must above all *describe* the world in such a way that its meanings emerge. He cannot, obviously, describe the world as a whole. He must take examples in as much detail as he can, and from these examples his intuition of significance will become clear. It is plain how close such a method is to the methods of the novelist, the short-story writer.[4]

Close, indeed: Sartre's novel *Nausea*[5] has long occupied a central place in the phenomenological–existentialist canon. The eminent American philosopher Arthur Danto begins his book on Sartre's philosophy as follows:

> Sartre's great philosophical novel, *Nausea*, is a sustained reflection on the relationships and ultimately the discrepancies between the world and our ways of representing it.[6]

Like Warnock, Danto is an analytical philosopher, and yet he treats *Nausea* as Sartre's second most important philosophical work and devotes a fifth of his book to explicating *Nausea*'s philosophical content.

Different Stories, Same Meaning

Faced with the surfeit of evidence from Beauvoir's and Sartre's letters and diaries showing that *She Came To Stay* was written and conceived before *Being and Nothingness*, in order to save the traditional narrative regarding the development of French existentialism and to preserve Sartre's status as the sole provider of the philosophical ideas that he and Beauvoir shared, it is now imperative not to read *She Came To Stay* as a philosophical text. Obviously, given the phenomenological–existentialist philosophical tradition and *Nausea*'s status as part of its canon, this censorship appears problematic. Either henceforth *Nausea* should no longer be read as a philosophical text, or the ancient principle of a male–female double standard should be allowed to prevail once again.

But 'Two Unpublished Chapters' poses still a further threat to the traditional patriarchal exclusion of *She Came To Stay* from the phenomenological–existentialist philosophical canon. As suggested earlier, even the best teacher cannot force a reader to engage with a textual level or even to acknowledge its existence, especially when a cultural gestalt obscures a level of meaning or when self-interest would be ill-served by acknowledgement of its existence. Because the very nature of multiple levels of meaning is that they are not all easily discernible for all readers. And such circumstances create pedagogical impasses. But for the reading of *She Came To Stay*, 'Two Unpublished Chapters' comes to the rescue. It is hard to imagine how anyone who compares these two texts could thereafter *in good faith* deny that both works, no less than Sartre's *Nausea*, are philosophical texts. Let us explain.

'Two Unpublished Chapters' (*TUC*), Beauvoir's original beginning to *She Came To Stay (SCS)*, traces the childhood and adolescence of Françoise, the novel's central character. In 1938 Beauvoir abandoned these chapters after showing them to Sartre and to Brice Parain, the editor at Gallimard. Instead of beginning with an account of Françoise's childhood, Beauvoir now began her novel with Françoise as a young woman. Whereas most of the first chapter of *TUC* takes place in and around a country house, the entire first chapter of *SCS* takes place in a Paris theatre and its courtyard. Thus on the level of simple story-telling the two beginnings to Beauvoir's novel are totally dissimilar. Nevertheless when one compares the two texts one is struck by the fact that large parts of both are centred on very similar, but otherwise highly idiosyncratic, descriptions. Some examples, all drawn from the opening pages of the two beginnings to the novel, will show what we mean.

> *TUC*: 'there was a scent of scrub, there were pine needles, a taste of apple ... and Françoise no longer existed anywhere.'[7]
> *TUC*: 'She spent a long time lying there, her mind blank. She no longer even felt her body: she could feel the warm air, she could smell the scent of the grass; in the valley wrapped in mist, two red spots shone. Suddenly, Françoise was no more than this mist, these bright spots, and there was nothing else left in the world.'[8]
> *SCS*: 'She leaned back against the hard wood of the bench. A quick step echoed on the asphalt of the pavement; a motor lorry rumbled

along the avenue. There was nothing but this passing sound, the sky, the quivering foliage of the trees, and the one rose-coloured window in a black façade. There was no Françoise any longer, no one existed any longer, anywhere.'[9]

TUC: 'she ... had the mission to make as many, as beautiful and varied things as possible come into existence'.[10]
SCS: 'It was as if she had been entrusted with a mission: she had to bring life to this forsaken theatre.'[11]
SCS: 'but for me this square exists and that moving train ... all Paris, and all the world'.[12]

TUC: 'if she looked away it had no more existence for anyone'.[13]
SCS: 'When she was not there, ... [they] did not exist for anyone; they did not exist at all.'[14]

TUC: 'Until today, nobody smelt the scent of charcoal and scrub; nobody knew that these white rocks and the black bare remains of the trees existed; they did not know it themselves; it was as if they had not existed at all. But now, I am here.'[15]
SCS: 'When she was not there [in 'the dark corridors'], the smell of dust, the half-light, and their forlorn solitude did not exist for anyone; they did not exist at all. And now she was there.'[16]

TUC: 'in her absence, the scents, the light were plunged in a torpor that could not be conceived of: one might as well try and imagine oneself dead.'[17]
SCS: She exercised that power: her presence snatched things from their unconsciousness; she gave them their colour, their smell.'[18]

TUC: 'Françoise's heart swelled: the people on the street, the people in the houses, all the people needed her; when she abandoned them, their movements and their faces disintegrated like a deserted landscape.'[19]
SCS: 'I feel that things that don't exist for me simply do not exist at all.'[20]

TUC: 'when she stood up to leave, she felt as if she was committing a betrayal ... From the moment she pushed open the stained-glass door, the shadows and the scents were swallowed in impassive night.'[21]

SCS: 'She put her hand on the door-knob, then turned back with a qualm of conscience. This was desertion, an act of treason. The night would once more swallow the small provincial square.'[22]

TUC: 'she felt she was the center of the world'.[23]
SCS: 'wherever I may go, the rest of the world will move with me'.[24]

TUC: 'A brief anguish wrenched her heart: she could not be everywhere at once.'[25]
SCS: 'she would have had to be everywhere at the same time'.[26]

TUC: 'Françoise knew perfectly well who she was; sometimes at night, she could hear her parents talk about her when they thought that she was asleep.'[27]
SCS: 'We get the impression of no longer being anything but a figment of someone else's mind.'[28]

Clearly then – and this is not a difficult matter to see – in these two beginnings to her novel, Beauvoir is telling us more than just, in the one, about a child's mundane experiences in the woods and, in the other, about a 30-year-old woman's mundane experiences in a theatre. It is also abundantly clear that this something extra, this other stream of meaning which Beauvoir delivers to us, is approximately the same in both texts. She has constructed these otherwise dissimilar narratives as vehicles for introducing the same or similar sets of philosophical ideas. Both narratives serve Beauvoir-the-philosopher as means to an end. The philosophical and argumentative shape of the novel as a whole required her to introduce certain ideas and positions at or near the beginning. She especially wants to settle at the outset some basic ontological questions, that is, what kinds of being exist and the broad nature of the relations between them. Being a phenomenologist, she can do this through her characters' perceptions. Indeed, for Beauvoir only phenomenological evidence, not abstract reason, is admissible.

A distinctive thesis of Beauvoir is that consciousness is not just the desire to be, but also the desire to reveal being, of taking delight in the pure witnessing of the world around oneself, of confronting the mere existence of the world in pure and selfless and, sometimes, joyous wonderment. The first seven groups of quotations above catch Françoise in this mode of intentionality. The eighth relates to Beauvoir's concept of embodiment (that a person's experiential world is centred on their body moving in physical space), the ninth to her theory of appearances by which she demonstrates phenomenologically the existence of a world independent of consciousness, and the tenth to her theory of the Other.

But the important thing for us here is not so much the ideas themselves, but rather that the two texts, despite their dissimilarity on the level of simple story-telling, convey similar content on another level of meaning, namely, that of phenomenological philosophy. The only rational explanation for this similarity is that Beauvoir's 'Two Unpublished Chapters' and *She Came To Stay*, no less than Sartre's *Nausea* and *Being and Nothingness* are philosophical texts.

Chapter 10
Whose Ethics?

Simone de Beauvoir and Jean-Paul Sartre's ethics is distinguished by two key propositions. One is notorious, the other highly distinctive among ethical systems. Their joint denial that there exist objective values (objective in the sense that they transcend human freedom) continues to scandalize. And their principle that human freedom is the ultimate and primary value, remains one of the landmarks in the twentieth-century history of ideas. These two famous propositions point to two distinct but interrelated orders of ethical problems: how should one treat one's own freedom, and, moving more obviously onto the classical terrain of ethics, how should one treat others, especially in terms of their freedom.

There is no doubt that the ethics first forged by the two French existentialists immediately before, during and after the Second World War, remains a theoretical edifice of continuing philosophical interest. What we wish to examine in this chapter is the ascription of the design of this ethical system to Sartre. It will be our contention that this system is more accurately described as originating with Beauvoir. Our method will be to examine the writings of the two philosophers in the light of the development of the arguments which contributed to the construction of their shared ethical theory. It is probably important to stress here that in this chapter we are not concerned with scrutinizing the ethics voiced by either philosopher. Rather, we are concerned with the question of which of them developed the *philosophical* arguments from which their ethics was made.

In this chapter we wish to sketch a few major points of the background to what we believe deserves to be called Beauvoirian ethics, and then, again briefly, to state and note the initial appearances of the various philosophical arguments that comprise it.

Methods of Expropriating Beauvoir's Philosophical Theories on Behalf of Sartre

The usual account of the development of the ethics espoused by Beauvoir and Sartre is singularly one-sided. It credits the invention of the ethics to Sartre, who had indeed promised such a system at the end of *Being and Nothingness* (1943).[1] But the methodology by which various scholars have arrived at the conclusion that this ethics was Sartre's creation rather than Beauvoir's, or even both of theirs, is extremely curious.[2] At the heart of the matter is the need to find the arguments – and there are a handful of them – which distinguish Sartre's and Beauvoir's ethical viewpoints from mere opinion and raise them to the level of philosophy. Such arguments are, in the main, conspicuously lacking in Sartre's philosophy of the 1940s. These absent arguments tend to receive peculiar treatment from Sartre scholars, who generally either fail to note the logical hiatuses which signal these omissions or else cite relevant works by Beauvoir to fill the most obvious gaps. In this, Beauvoir tends to be treated simply as Sartre's mouthpiece. Further, there are many occasions when parts of the argument which do appear in Sartre's work are treated anachronistically, with Sartrean commentators not noting that the arguments appeared first, and usually more fully, in Beauvoir's writing.[3]

A variant of these traditional methods of expropriating Beauvoir's philosophical theories on behalf of Sartre is to note briefly that there may have existed between the pair a mutual philosophical influence. But, since the couple were forever discussing their philosophical ideas, no one can say whether the ideas expressed first in Beauvoir's writings were not dictated to her by Sartre. This kind of manoeuvre is usually accompanied by an unspoken elision which simply, and traditionally, ascribes Beauvoir's ideas to Sartre. Meanwhile, except for the proviso that Sartre may not have been philosophically uninfluenced by Beauvoir, it is business as usual: 'Sartrean' is the operative philosophical adjective, not 'Beauvoirean'. Even joint ascriptions are declined. The apparent presumption of this method, that those now demanding recognition for philosophical contributions made by women will be satisfied with token concessions, may be both radically misjudged and historically flawed.

Background

It is ironic that the system of ethics whose origins are here in dispute grew out of a fundamental philosophical divergence between Beauvoir and Sartre. This seems to have occurred as early as April 1940, when, as Beauvoir later recalled in the second volume of her memoirs, *The Prime of Life* (1960), she and Sartre discovered that they no longer agreed on the nature of freedom. Sartre was on leave from the army, and the heightened nature of their interaction during this time encompassed their philosophical discussions. Beauvoir says:

> During the days that followed we discussed certain specific problems, in particular the relationship between 'situation' and freedom. I maintained that from the angle of freedom as Sartre defined it – that is, an active transcendence of some given context rather than mere stoic resignation – not every situation was equally valid: what sort of transcendence could a woman shut up in a harem achieve? Sartre replied that even such a cloistered existence could be lived in several quite different ways. I stuck to my point for a long time, and in the end made only a token submission. Basically I was right. But to defend my attitude I should have had to abandon the plane of individual, and therefore idealistic, morality on which we had set ourselves. (Beauvoir 1969, p. 434)

Despite her prudential 'submission', Beauvoir, independently of Sartre, began to develop an ethics which differed fundamentally from the purely individualist one she previously had shared with her companion. This new theory, together with its main supporting arguments, was fully developed by 1946 and outlined by Beauvoir in a number of works including *The Ethics of Ambiguity* (1946–7). Beginning in the mid-1940s, Sartre gradually adopted Beauvoir's ethical theory which subsequently has been treated as his. Beauvoir differs from Sartre in her primary ontological orientation, particularly in her fundamental account of freedom, and of the possible relationships between the self and others. And Beauvoir's starting point allows her to develop a fully coherent social ethics in ways that always remained intensely problematic for Sartre.

Ontological Problems

The greatest obstacle to deriving an ethics of any kind from the ontology of Sartre's *Being and Nothingness* has long been well understood. His *magnum opus* asserts the existence of two kinds of freedom. One he calls 'the empirical and popular concept of 'freedom', which pertains to 'the ability to obtain the ends chosen'. The other he calls his 'philosophical concept of freedom', and for which he emphasizes 'success is not important' (Sartre 1956, p. 483). In contradistinction to this Sartrean dualism, Beauvoir argued that freedom is univocal, but bi-dimensional, that is, that *all* freedom, by its nature, is simultaneously ontologically given and concretely situated.

Early in *The Ethics of Ambiguity* Beauvoir signals her understanding of the problems thrown up by Sartre's ontology for the construction of an ethics. She introduces Sartre's fundamental concept of freedom by noting that Sartre declares that every man is free, that there is no way of his not being free' (Beauvoir 1948, p. 24). She immediately points out the difficulty this idea poses for an ethics of freedom:

Does not this presence of a so to speak natural freedom contradict the notion of ethical freedom? What meaning can there be in the words *to will oneself* free, since at the beginning we *are* free? It is contradictory to set freedom up as something conquered if at first it is something given. (*ibid.*, p. 24)

To counter this glaring inconsistency, Beauvoir, rather ruthlessly, remarks that Sartre's concept of freedom lacks meaning because freedom, rather than being 'a quality naturally attached to a thing' (p. 25) is something which 'merges with the very movement of this ambiguous reality which is called existence' (p. 25). Freedom, she insists, always and only exists in the context of a situation, and 'always projects itself toward something' (p. 25). What Sartre described in *Being and Nothingness* was not freedom itself, but 'only the subjective and formal aspect of this freedom' (p. 26). For Beauvoir, freedom is always bi-dimensional: its ontological dimension does indeed exist, and it exists as it is described by Sartre in *Being and Nothingness*, but there is also, and always, its position in the world.

In the end, Beauvoir is categorical in her rejection of Sartre's concept of freedom in favour of her own. Alluding to Sartre's remarks about a slave being as free as his master, Beauvoir writes:

If a door refuses to open, let us accept not opening it and there we are free. But by doing that, one manages only to save an abstract notion of freedom. It is emptied of all content and all truth. (Beauvoir 1948, p. 29)

'Emptied of all content and all truth': a more complete divergence between Beauvoir and Sartre on this central issue is not possible.

Sartre's theory, or, to be more accurate, his truncated version of Beauvoir's theory of interpersonal relations, also posed an insuperable obstacle to the creation of an ethics. In *Being and Nothingness*, he portrays all human relationships as inherently conflictive. Either, he argued, we consent to be another's object, or we struggle to make the other our object. After each encounter with another person, writes Sartre, 'nothing remains for the for-itself except to re-enter the circle and allow itself to be indefinitely tossed from one to the other of the two fundamental attitudes' (Sartre 1956, p. 412). This ontological position has, as Mary Warnock and others pointed out, dire and obvious consequences for the construction of an ethics. If one person's freedom is the other's obstacle, and if we are ontologically caught in this circle of conflict, then it makes no sense to argue that one should make the freedom of others one's own goal.

This subject–object conflict, however, is only a part of the theory of interpersonal relations which Beauvoir set out at length in *She Came To Stay* (1943), before Sartre had begun to compile his notes for writing *Being and Nothingness*. In her novel, Beauvoir, in addition to offering an extended analysis of subject–object conflict, stresses the possibility of reciprocity between pairs of subjects, that is, relations wherein both individuals cultivate the subjectivity or freedom of the other. This dimension of inter-subjectivity was further emphasized in her play of 1945, *Who Shall Die?* Sartre, on the other hand, did not show definite signs of embracing this part of Beauvoir's theory until 1952 in *Saint Genet*.

The Problem of Justification

Beauvoir and Sartre were, however, always in complete agreement about the non-existence of objective or transcendent values. They both characterized belief in such values as a form of bad faith. This subjectivist position poses enormous difficulties for the construction of an ethics. It seems to make ethical values purely a matter of personal preference, thereby destroying the very notions of 'right' and 'wrong', and making any appeal to any generalized value self-contradictory. Of the many obstacles which stood between Beauvoir and Sartre and their goal of creating an ethics grounded in their existentialism, this was the most severe. The precept that human freedom is, or should be, considered the supreme value was, as Sartre discovered with the enthusiastic response to his famous Club Maintenant lecture of October 1945, enormously appealing. But without a philosophical argument consistent with, or, preferably, deriving from their existentialist ontology, Beauvoir and Sartre's principle of freedom only carried weight as opinion. Sartre seems to have been content to leave this crucial point on this personal level. In his essay, *Existentialism and Humanism* (1946), a revision of his Club Maintenant lecture, as well as in subsequent works, Sartre fails to provide the missing philosophical arguments. Peter Caws echoes the general disappointment of Sartre scholars when he notes that Sartre's attempt at 'moral generalization is a matter more of evangelistic rhetoric than of philosophical reasoning' (Caws 1984, p. 120).

The necessary arguments to fill this very real gap in Sartre's and Beauvoir's ethics, however, are not missing, but located elsewhere – in texts by Beauvoir. Whereas Sartre famously expresses his *sentiments* about freedom in *Existentialism and Humanism* (1946), the *philosophical* arguments needed to ground these ideas are found in Beauvoir's earlier, and more substantial, *Pyrrhus and Cinéas*. This philosophical essay, begun in 1942 and finished in July the following year, was rushed into print the month after the Liberation in 1944. As Claude Francis and Fernande Gontier note, it introduced existentialism to the French public and 'aroused enormous curiosity' (Francis and Gontier 1987, p. 210). The essay stresses Beauvoir's concept of situated freedom. Indeed, the essay arose directly out of Beauvoir's continuing disagreement with Sartre over the ontological nature of freedom, and in it are found the beginnings of her philosophical arguments for justifying freedom as a universal value (Bair 1990, pp. 270–1, 639). It is this essay, together with *The Ethics of Ambiguity*, written by Beauvoir in early 1946 while Sartre was in America, that scholars of Sartrean ethics usually cite when they wish to supplement Sartre's stirring rhetoric with philosophical reasoning. In these works Beauvoir offers sets of arguments for freedom as a universal value at two levels: that of one's own freedom, and – closer to the traditional field of ethics – that of the freedom of others.

One's Own Freedom

Beauvoir's primary argument for valuing one's own freedom begins with a premise obtained by a subtle but profound shift of the ontology of *Being and Nothingness*. There, Sartre argued that the reflective apprehension of the self as contingent freedom, that is, an existence without external justification and meaning, gives rise to extreme anguish which all seek to escape though various forms of bad faith, and which he characterized as the project to be God. However, in the final two pages of his treatise, Sartre, without warning, hedged his bets by asking if it might be possible for one to escape this project of bad faith. The crucial point for an understanding of these anomalous pages, is that a draft of *Pyrrhus and Cinéas*, was already extant (Bair 1990, pp. 270–1, 639; Beauvoir 1969, pp. 547–50). There, Beauvoir agrees with Sartre that the fundamental human project is to escape from or diminish the contingency or gratuitousness of existence. But she rejects his thesis, which is more assumed than argued in his essay, that this project must take the form of bad faith and the project to be God. In opposition to Sartre, Beauvoir, in her essay, develops the case for pursuing the fundamental project not through bad faith, but rather by embracing freedom, which, in good faith or bad, is the only source of values offering justification and meaning.

This further departure from Sartre's ontology gives Beauvoir her primary argument for valuing one's freedom. It is both elegant and clear: everyone's fundamental project is the justification of their existence. Freedom is the only source of justification. Therefore, everyone should choose freedom as their ultimate value (Beauvoir 1960, pp. 95–6; 1948, pp. 24–32).

The Freedom of Others

Beauvoir's argument for valuing one's own freedom provides no moral criteria for judging between free acts on the interpersonal and social planes. For this, additional grounding was needed, and once again Beauvoir, not Sartre, provided it. 'Respect for the liberty of others,' she writes in *Pyrrhus and Cinéas*, 'is no abstract rule; it is a prime condition for the success of my efforts.' This is an appeal to self-interest, as defined by her ethics of authenticity, and, in this context, Beauvoir offers two reasons to value the freedom of others.

The first is an argument that appears repeatedly in her work, nowhere so forcefully as in her play, *Who Shall Die?*[4] A medieval town is under siege and without enough food to see it through to spring, when an ally has promised to come to its rescue. The all-male and previously enlightened town council has decided to conserve food by expelling from the town walls and to certain death everyone except able-bodied men. At the eleventh hour, the decision is reconsidered, and a new council member speaks as follows:

> You have declared: the old men, the sick are simply useless mouths to feed. Why should not a tyrant decide that your liberty is useless and your lives a burden to the city? If one single man can be considered as refuse, one hundred thousand men put together are but a heap of trash. (Beauvoir 1983, p. 61)

And another councillor, referring to the shared nature of human life, adds: 'There is a covenant between all of us. If we break it, the whole community turns to ashes' (p. 61). This was a timely argument for Beauvoir's French audience which was still emerging from Nazi occupation. It is also one which any society forgets at its peril.

But it is Beauvoir's second argument for valuing the freedom of others which, because it emerges directly from her ontology, is most philosophically interesting. She argues that success at justifying one's existence is maximized through relations with free and equal individuals. 'A man alone,' says Beauvoir in *Pyrrhus and Cinéas*, 'would be paralysed by the manifest vanity of all his goals' (p. 65). To reduce and make bearable the contingency of one's existence requires the validation by others of one's projects. But such valorisation is truly valued, argues Beauvoir, only if it comes by the free choice of one's peers. This principle holds obvious and often radical implications for personal relations.

But Beauvoir develops this ethic much further. By linking it to her concept of situated freedom, she both extends its compass to the broader social context and fills it with empirical content. In the project of justifying one's existence, the social dimension offers a means of surpassing one's finitude. In *Pyrrhus and Cinéas*, Beauvoir argues:

> The freedom of others can do nothing for me unless my own goals can serve as his point of departure; it is by using the tool which I have invented that others prolong its existence; the scholar can only talk with men who have arrived at the same level of knowledge as himself ... I must therefore endeavour to create for all

men situations which enable them to accompany and surpass my transcendence; I need their freedom to be available to use me, to preserve me in surpassing me. I require for men health, knowledge, well being, leisure, so that their freedom does not consume itself in fighting sickness, ignorance, misery. (Beauvoir 1960, pp. 114–15)

This passage, written in 1943 or earlier, sums up the social aspect of the ethical theory which Sartre, some years later, incorporated into his own writing. That it continues to bear his name, rather than Beauvoir's, seems decidedly wrong.

Chapter 11
The *Absence* of Beauvoir

The *Absence* of Sartre

Despite the vicissitudes of intellectual fashions there can be no question that Jean-Paul Sartre and Simone de Beauvoir were, without doubt, two of the most internationally significant intellectual figures of the twentieth century. Whatever else might be said about them, their achievements, both jointly and separately, are of the highest magnitude. In terms of that achievement, and at the moment we are especially concerned with Sartre's, it is more than interesting to consider the publication in 1994 of a standard reference book titled *A Companion to the Philosophy of Mind* (Guttenplan 1994). This compendious volume includes fascinating and sophisticated essay-length entries on topics such as 'consciousness', 'content' of consciousness, 'desire', 'emotion', 'imagination', 'intentionality', 'perception', 'perceptual content', 'psychology and philosophy', 'the self', 'self-deception' and 'subjectivity'. The volume's title uses the word 'philosophy' without qualification or modification, suggesting, by inference, that it provides a general and thorough overview of the major contributions to the various philosophical fields and topics it discusses. But something rather curious happens when the volume is checked for the range of philosophers and the range of ideas it treats. A good illustration of what we have in mind can be seen by noting the philosophers mentioned in essays surveying topics of central interest to Sartre scholars. Under 'consciousness', T. H. Huxley, Daniel Dennett, Thomas Nagel, A. Goldman and John Searle all feature, along with a score of others with whom we confess unfamiliarity. Under 'desire', Socrates, Plato, Spinoza,

Hume and Mill, and Robert C. Stalnaker, P. Geach, Dennis W. Stampe and Fred Dretske are all cited. Under 'emotion', the philosophers drawn upon include Plato, Aristotle, Spinoza, Descartes, Hobbes, Hume and William James, and, alongside them, M. Scheler, J. Panksepp, H. Fingarette, P. D. MacLean and a dozen others. Under 'perception', Aristotle, Descartes, Wittgenstein and Strawson are all mentioned. 'Perceptual content' treats Strawson, Fred Dretske, T. M. Crane, D. M. Armstrong, C.A.B. Peacocke and others. Under 'psychology and philosophy', Chomsky, Searle and Dennett are featured along with Goldman, Putnam, T. Burge and many others. The section entitled 'the self' draws on Descartes, Locke, Hume, Kant, Wittgenstein, Strawson, Evans, Lewis, McDowell, Parfit, Perry, etc. Finally, in the entry on 'self-deception', only Pears, Fingarette and Davidson figure as individually identified referents.

What is more than peculiar when noting the often repeated presence of all these philosophers, is the striking *absence* of Sartre, who must be counted in the handful of the most important and influential twentieth-century contributors to the philosophical discussion of all these topics and areas. However, given the range of philosophers who do feature in the volume, Sartre's exclusion is not, really, so very surprising. The politics of this situation are well understood. The volume, for all its massive, 642 pages and closely printed double-columned format, and its promise of inclusiveness, is a product of seriously partisan and exclusionary intellectual politics. It is a reference work for a particular kind of discourse on intellectual – specifically philosophical – history from which Sartre and numerous other important thinkers are deliberately excluded. As is well known, beginning roughly a century ago, Western philosophers split into two camps: with the Continental camp amorphous and quarrelsome, and the Anglo-American camp well-organized and rigidly disciplined. Rather than co-existing peacefully, the two sides, especially the Anglo-American, have worked to limit the rival philosophical camp's credibility. It is a sorry state of affairs (although there are now signs of the beginning of a rapprochement), with students of one or the other of the great branches of twentieth-century philosophy often being trained in something approaching ignorance of the alternate tradition. The excision of modern continental philosophers from pertinent entries in Blackwell's otherwise admirable volume represents just one example of the intellectual politics of absence which can so sorrily skew the records of intellectual history. However, the erasure of various philosophers' names, and the failure to register proper credit for their work is quite a different matter from banning their ideas. One of the noteworthy aspects of Blackwell's *Companion to the Philosophy of Mind* is the presence in it, especially in passages covering recent works, of ideas which most of us would credit to Sartre. The point here is really a very simple one: philosophers, dispossessed of their official identity, are easily dispossessed, as well, of credit for their ideas.

The 'Absence' of Beauvoir from Sartrean Studies

One of the admirable qualities of Sartrean scholarship is its tradition of placing Sartre's philosophy in the context of his antecedent and contemporary philosophers. Of course, Sartre himself encouraged this practice through his example in *Being and Nothingness* with its expositions on the similarities and divergences of his ideas with those of his philosophical forebears. By doing so, Sartre reminds his readers of how philosophy is intrinsically a collaborative process, even if one's collaborators are long dead, and that new philosophical ideas rarely, if ever, appear without a more or less distinguished genealogy of intellectual precedents behind them. This fine and honest tradition of placing Sartre's ideas and their development within the context of a community of interacting thinkers is especially well-served by *The Cambridge Companion to Sartre*, edited by Christina Howells. This work, which runs to 400 pages, is particularly strong in tracing the interrelationships between Sartre's thought and that of thinkers with whom Sartre's life was roughly contemporary. Writers covered in this way (and in this case it is both welcome and noticeable that the net has been cast so wide as even to encompass a number of Analytical philosophers), include the following: Adorno, Althusser, Aron, Barthes, Baudrillard, Carnap, Cassirer, Deluze, Derrida, Foucault, Freud, Gandillac, Genet, Gide, Stuart Hampshire, R. M. Hare, Heidegger, Husserl, Hyppolite, Jaspers, Kojève, Lacan, Christopher Lash, Lefèbvre, Lévi-Strauss, Lyotard, Mauss, Merleau-Ponty, Popper, Thomas Nagel, Paul Nizan, Ricoeur, Rorty, Ryle, Strawson and Wittgenstein.

However, for all its wide range and overt generosity, the *Cambridge Companion to Sartre* also displays another vivid case of *absence*, one which, unfortunately, characterizes Sartre studies generally. In fact, the absent individual does receive one mention in the book in question, but – and again this is characteristic – in the role of the great man's biographer. In terms of historical, factual and ethical importance, this absence, compared to the presence of the 37 male writers rightly linked with Sartre, far outweighs the previously noted absence of Sartre in the *Companion to the Philosophy of Mind*. In the *Companion to Sartre* only one deeply significant figure is excluded from the reckoning, and that person is both the most important person in the relevant intellectual history, and a woman. The excluded one, so eloquent in her absence, is, of course, Simone de Beauvoir.

The tradition in Sartrean scholarship of more or less completely ignoring the presence of Beauvoir in the formation of 'Sartrean philosophy' is, again, of course, part of a much larger historical tradition of positioning women at the margins of intellectual history. Here, rather than exploring that tradition and the particular form it takes in the study of Sartre and Beauvoir, we merely note its prevalence. But there is another factor which contributes to the absence of Beauvoir, and, like Sartre's absence from one version of the philosophical canon, it concerns the use of language.

The Third Method

The barrier between Continental and Analytical philosophy is founded not so much on ideas, as it is on attitudes to language in philosophical discourse. What began as a reaction to the self-entangled verbiage of turn-of-the-century neo-Hegelianism – a reaction which few people would dismiss as unnecessary, has led to institutionalized extremes of the opposite kind. The standard Analytical philosophical essay displays a highly stylized literary form, which takes the mathematician's use of language as its ideal. It is difference of opinion over the worthiness of this ideal which, more than content, often divides the two philosophical traditions.

Within the Continental tradition itself, there are also two self-consciously different approaches to the use of language in philosophical investigation. But here the co-existence of these two methodologies is intended to be complementary rather than oppositional. One method takes the familiar form of the essay. The other is one which we will now consider. In his 1945 essay 'Metaphysics and the Novel', Merleau-Ponty, writing with special reference to Beauvoir's *She Came To Stay*, commented on the symbiotic relationship between these two philosophical methods. Merleau-Ponty begins his essay by noting that, since the end of the nineteenth century, the boundaries between literature and Continental philosophy had dissolved and that 'hybrid modes of expression' had developed in response to the opening up of what he calls 'a new dimension of investigation' (Merleau-Ponty 1964, p. 27).

In his essay, Merleau-Ponty is especially concerned to analyse the impulse behind Beauvoir's success at using fiction as a philosophical medium in *She Came To Stay*. He distinguishes between two kinds of metaphysics. 'Classical metaphysics,' he writes, 'could pass for a speciality with which literature had nothing to do because metaphysics operated on the basis of uncontested rationalism, convinced it could make the world and human life understood by an arrangement of concepts' (1964, p. 27). Even philosophers who begin on the experiential level, tend to end by explaining the world on the basis of abstractions. But Merleau-Ponty continues:

> Everything changes when a phenomenological or existential philosophy assigns itself the task, not of explaining the world or of discovering its 'conditions of possibility,' but rather of formulating an experience of the world, a contact with the world which precedes all thought *about* the world. After this, whatever is metaphysical in man cannot be credited to something outside his empirical being – to God, to Consciousness. Man is metaphysical in his very being, in his loves, in his hates, in his individual and collective history. (1964, pp. 27–8)

'From now on,' concludes Merleau-Ponty, 'the tasks of literature and philosophy can no longer be separated.'

In 1946 Beauvoir published her essay, 'Literature and Metaphysics', which expands on Merleau-Ponty's thesis. Like Merleau-Ponty, she divides philosophy and philosophers roughly into two camps. One includes Aristotle, Leibniz, Spinoza and Kant, and holds that philosophical truth exists only in a 'timeless and objective' sense. These philosophers, says Beauvoir, regard 'as negligible the subjectivity and historicity of experience' (Beauvoir 1948, p. 116).[1] They deny the philosophical relevance of the individual and the concrete, and, in so doing, implicitly presume that they, as philosophers, are capable of taking a universal rather than merely an individual point of view toward the metaphysical reality they seek to explain. Beauvoir, however, notes Eleanore Holveck, 'argues that philosophers pretend to explain all things universally, but in fact these universals are based in the consciousness of some individual thinker who claims knowledge of the universal, a claim that must be justified' (Holveck 1995,

p. 70). For Beauvoir, the universalist presumption is an egomaniacal delusion fostered by masculine privilege (Beauvoir 1965, p. 221; 1948, pp. 16–17). Earlier in 1944, in *Pyrrhus and Cinéas*, she writes: 'Man cannot escape from his own presence nor from the singular world that his presence reveals around him; even his effort to uproot himself from the earth makes him dig a hole for himself. Spinozism defines Spinoza, and Hegelianism Hegel' (Beauvoir 1944, pp. 34–5).[2] In the same essay she writes:

> The universal mind is without voice, and every man who claims to speak in its name only gives to it his own voice. How can he claim the point of view of the universal, since he *is* not the universal? One can not know a point of view other than one's own. (1944, p. 58)

In other words, Beauvoir regarded truth, including metaphysical truth, as always relative to a knowing subject. '[C]oncrete experience,' she writes, 'envelops at once the subject and object' (Beauvoir 1952). Beauvoir regards, notes Margaret Simons, any 'attempt to describe reality without reference to the experiencing subject ... as distorting as trying to describe the subject without reference to the context of circumstances' (Simons 1994). Beauvoir understood, like Merleau-Ponty, like Sartre, although perhaps not always in the same way, that foreswearing the philosopher's traditional universalist pretension carries with it strong methodological implications.

In 'Literature and Metaphysics', Beauvoir outlines a philosophical method founded on her anti-universalism. If it is only possible to view the world from a particular point of view, then philosophical activity must start by looking at particular and concrete descriptions of subjects' relations with the world and with other consciousnesses. Beauvoir called her chosen philosophical territory 'the metaphysical dimension' of human reality, that is, 'one's presence in the world, for example, one's abandonment in the world, one's freedom, the opacity of things, the resistance of foreign consciousnesses'. 'To make' philosophy, she argues, is 'to be' philosophical in the sense of sensitizing oneself to these individual metaphysical experiences, and then describing them (1948, p. 114). It is only on the basis of these particular statements that Beauvoir believes that general philosophical statements can legitimately be constructed. (1948, p. 119)

Beauvoir's distinctive philosophical achievement, notes Eleanore Holveck, was 'to ground her abstract philosophical positions in the real world of lived experience, a lived experience she created imaginatively in ordinary language that was more concrete, more rich than any abstract philosophical language' (1955, p. 72). Beauvoir's rejection of *a priorism* and of a universal point of view, makes the starting point of a good philosophical argument the description of a particular individual's metaphysical relations with the world, a description which the reader can then compare to her or his own. Beauvoir identifies fiction as the medium most naturally suited to this end. She explains that although the essay can give 'to the reader an intellectual reconstruction of their experience, it is this experience itself, such that it presents itself before any elucidation, that the novelist claims to reproduce on an imaginary plane' (1948, p. 105). Beauvoir continues:

> In the real world the sense of an object is not a concept knowable by pure understanding: it is the object in as much that it unveils itself to us in the global relation that we maintain with it and that is action, emotion, sentiment; one asks of the novelists to evoke this presence of flesh and bone whose complexity, singular and infinite richness, overflows all subjective interpretation. (1948, pp. 105–6)

Beauvoir's essay on method also attacks what she sees as philosophy's traditional authoritarianism and mystification. Against the tradition of the philosophical messiah, whom she calls 'the theoretician', she identifies a kind of reader who is willing to accept other people's philosophical propositions only after

> a movement of his whole being before forming judgements that he pulls from himself without someone having had the presumption of dictating them to him. It is this which is the value of a good novel. It is capable of inducing imaginary experiences as complete, as disquieting as lived experiences. The reader interrogates, doubts, he takes sides and this hesitant elaboration of his thought is for him an enrichment that no doctrinal teaching could replace. (1948, pp. 106–7)

Beauvoir identifies philosophical fiction which appeals in this way to the reader's liberty as a valuable form of philosophical research. Because of its grounding in the concrete and its implicit appeal to the reader's critical judgement, fiction's approach to the use of language facilitates advancement beyond the traditional dogmatic abstraction of philosophy and philosophers. Speculative philosophical essays are then free to draw upon the results of the concrete inquiries of philosophical fiction in the same way that in science, theoretical papers draw upon the results of empirical research.

For Beauvoir, and in the main for Sartre as well, all real description of the world takes place from the point of view of an individual-in-the-world. In lieu of the abstract and free-wheeling impersonality traditional to philosophy, Beauvoir's essay describes a philosophical process whereby the essay draws from and builds on the concrete analysis of fiction, a symbiotic relationship which she sees as similar to that which exists in science between theory and experiment (1948, pp. 118–20).

This symbiotic relationship is one form that Sartre and Beauvoir's joint philosophical production took. There are dozens of examples of ideas whose development can be traced to this type of interchange between the two philosophers. Because the theme of this chapter is *absence*, we will examine the origins of this concept as a case in point.

The Theory of Absence as a Case History

Explanation of and comments on the concept of absence

'Absence' is an important sub-category of concrete nothings or, as Sartre calls them, *négatités*. It is important to note the part they play in his philosophical universe. His task in *Being and Nothingness* is to describe phenomenologically how the individual conscious being, or *pour-soi*, engages with the non-conscious being, *en-soi*. As Sartre notes, to accomplish this he needs, in the first instance, 'to establish a connection between the two regions of being' (Sartre 1956, p. 3). Given his method of reasoning from the concrete and the particular to the abstract and the general, this means identifying some definite human activity that epitomizes the relation being-in-the-world. For this he identifies the 'attitude of interrogation'. 'In every question,' he writes, 'we stand before a being which we are questioning ... this being which we question, we question *about* something. That *about* which I question the being participates in the transcendence of being' (1956, p. 4). By 'the transcendence of being' Sartre means being which is external to consciousness. He continues:

> I question being about its ways of being or about its being. From this point of view the question is a kind of expectation: I expect

a reply from the being questioned. That is, on the basis of a pre-interrogative familiarity with being, I expect from this being a revelation of its being or of its way of being. The reply will be a 'yes' or a 'no'. (pp. 4–5)

But consider a 'no' answer to a questioning of being, such as 'Peg is not here.' This is a concrete negation, an instance of what Sartre calls non-being. His problem – and it must be recalled that the title of Part One of *Being and Nothingness* is 'The Problem of Nothingness' – is to demonstrate that a non-being such as 'Peg is not here' is what he calls a 'component of the real', that is, something which is external to consciousness rather than merely a psychological or linguistic construct. His methodology commits him to carry out this demonstration by direct appeal to the concrete and the particular, rather than the traditional *a priori*. Therefore, Sartre builds the general concept of nothingness on the basis of phenomenological demonstrations which show the real existence of types of concrete nothings, that is, of instances of non-being. It is in this strategic context – of demonstrating that human consciousness reveals not only being, but also non-being – that the idea of absence first appears in *Being and Nothingness*.

War Diaries

On 1 February 1940, Sartre wrote a few pages in his diary on the concept of *absence*. The date of this entry is significant, as it indicates that he was considering this topic two days **before** he left for his week-and-a-half leave in Paris that we described in Chapters 6 and 7. His analysis takes as its concrete basis the consideration of a husband, Pierre, and his wife. Sartre asserts, *a priori*, that there is a fundamental or ontological difference between Pierre's absence from his wife and his 'simply "being away from", in the sense in which one might say that two towns are 20 kilometres away, or distant, from each other'. Sartre says that 'being away' and 'distance' exist as relations only in so far as they are established by consciousness. He goes on to note in his journal: 'But absence belongs to the very heart of things: being absent is a particular quality of an object. In vain will one seek to reduce this quality to a purely mental perspective'. His task is to show concretely that absence is not merely a mental attitude or act, but rather 'that there exists something like absence'. To this end, he declares: 'absence is a certain relationship between my being and the

Other's being. It is a certain way I have of being given to the Other' (Sartre 1984, p. 187). His concrete argument for this hypothesis is as follows:

> There can be *absence* of Pierre only in relation to his wife, for example, because here Pierre's existence alters the very being of his wife's for-herself – and in an essential manner. Pierre's presence is constitutive of the *being* of his wife as for-herself, and vice-versa. It is only against the background of this prior unity of being that absence can be given between Pierre and his wife ... It's a *new* mode of connection between Pierre and his wife, which appears against the original background of presence. That original background of presence is *lifted* and denied by absence – yet it's what makes the latter possible. (Sartre 1984, p. 188)

Sartre concludes that lived absence 'can be understood **only** as a concrete relation between two existents against a basic background of unity of contact. Pierre's wife is immediately given to Pierre as *not being there*' (p. 188).

Before considering Beauvoir's roughly contemporaneous writing on absence, two aspects of Sartre's notebook entry on *absence* should be mentioned. First, he has merely asserted the possibility of the existence of absence between two people: he has not offered any phenomenological description which permits him to argue from the concrete and the particular to the abstract and the general. In fact, at no point does he attempt to describe an absence from the point of view of a person perceiving an absence. In other words, he is still working on the level of the *a priori*. Secondly, at this point, Sartre's abstract concept of absence is surprisingly narrow. Not only is it limited to relations between people, but also to between pairs of people for whom the absence of one alters the being of the other 'in an essential manner.' We want to emphasize that we do not raise these points as criticisms of Sartre. What we are doing here is tracing the development of an idea.

Before examining Sartre's handling of absence in *Being and Nothingness*, we want to consider Beauvoir's treatment of the same in *She Came To Stay*. Sartre's letter to Beauvoir of 15 February 1940 – his first full letter to her since his return from Paris – ends with the paragraph: 'You've written a beautiful novel' (Sartre 1993, p. 55). His letter to Beauvoir on 18 February includes the following, where the passage to which he refers comes near the end of *She Came To Stay* in Chapter 7 of Part II (Beauvoir 1984, pp. 354–5).

> I've got plenty to do, which makes me happy: I'm beginning to see glimmers of a theory of time. This evening I began to write it. It's thanks to you, do you realize that? Thanks to Françoise's obsession: that when Pierre is in Xavière's room, there's an object living all by itself without a consciousness to see it. I'm not sure if I'll have the patience to wait for you to see it when someone takes you my notebooks. On that subject, my love, you haven't had the time to tell me what you thought of my theory on *contact* and *absence*. Do tell me. (Sartre 1993, p. 61)

Beauvoir could not help but be interested in Sartre's comments on absence, because the notion of absence is central to several passages in *She Came To Stay*, including the one to which Sartre's letter refers. But it is a description of absence that comes much earlier in the novel that proved especially significant to Sartre and Beauvoir's joint development of this idea.

She Came To Stay

Before considering this passage, several points must be noted regarding this novel's structure. The character, Françoise, provides the narrative point of view for most of the text. But through the novel's first half, Beauvoir also uses Françoise to personify two philosophical positions: a form of solipsism, and philosophy's traditional and stubborn denial of the body's philosophical relevance. The latter posed an expository dilemma for Beauvoir. She could not offer vivid illustrations of Françoise's embodiment through Françoise's consciousness without that character ceasing to represent the position against which Beauvoir is arguing. Beauvoir finds her way out of this difficulty by using another character, Elisabeth, who has a highly developed awareness of her and others' bodies, as the narrative focus of a chapter early in the novel.

The brief scene from Beauvoir's novel which we are about to examine shows off the dexterity and suppleness of her philosophical method, and her ability to apply it simultaneously to more than one philosophical idea. Elisabeth, Françoise's friend and rival, enters Françoise's room, knowing she is not there. Chairs are strewn with Françoise's clothes, and her desk piled with books and papers.

Elisabeth looked at the couch, at the mirror-wardrobe, at the bust of Napoleon on the mantelpiece beside a bottle of eau-de-Cologne, at some brushes and several pairs of stockings. She closed her eyes once more, and then opened them again. It was impossible to make this room her own: it was only too unalterably evident that it remained an alien room.

Elisabeth went over to the looking-glass in which the face of Françoise had so often been reflected and saw her own face. (Beauvoir 1984, pp. 64–5)

Then Elisabeth sits down at Françoise's desk.

A volume of Shakespeare's plays lay open at the page Françoise had been reading when she had suddenly pushed back her chair. She had thrown her dressing-gown on the bed and it still bore, in its disordered folds, the impress of her careless gesture; the sleeves were puffed out as if they still enclosed phantom arms. These discarded objects gave a more unbearable picture of Françoise than would her real presence ...

Elisabeth pulled towards her some sheets of paper which were covered with notes, rough drafts, ink-stained sketches. Thus scratched out and badly written, Françoise's thoughts lost their definiteness; but the writing itself and the erasures made by Françoise's hand still bore witness to Françoise's indestructible existence. (p. 65)

With the very important exception of the bust of Napoleon, all the objects at which Elisabeth looks have an instrumental relation to Françoise's body – the couch, the chair, the eau-de-Cologne, the brushes, the looking-glass, the clothes, the sheets of paper, the books. Similarly, all the observed spatial relations (the chair pushed back, the clothes strewn about, the folds in the dressing gown, the puffed out sleeves, the piles of books and papers, the book left opened, the handwriting), have been defined by Françoise's body. The entire room is haunted by Françoise, who is elsewhere. The room's contents, including their spatial arrangements, refer to Françoise's body which is not there. The reference point of the room's spatiality, which Elisabeth knows to be Françoise, is missing. Elisabeth perceives this *absence*, this non-being, this concrete nothingness. That she does so is an objective fact, not an abstract negation, not a negative judgement, not a mental construct. The bust of Napoleon looks on to prove the point. Besides Françoise, there is an infinity of people who are not there in the room. Napoleon and Shakespeare are two of them, but their not being there is devoid of reference. Only Françoise's body is missing from the room's spatiality. Only Françoise is perceived as an absence.

This passage from Beauvoir's novel is exactly the sort of required phenomenological account of a perceived absence which is missing from Sartre's entry on absence in his diary. It also, and this is a paradoxical aspect of the concrete phenomenological approach, describes an absence which implies a category or family of absences much larger than the one which Sartre defined *a priori* with his abstractions. The perception of Françoise's absence is independent of any significant alteration of Elisabeth's being.

Being and Nothingness

The presentation of the phenomenon of absence in *Being and Nothingness* is one of Sartre's most wonderfully virtuoso and inimitable philosophical performances. In terms of depth of explanation, it surpasses by a long way anything Beauvoir wrote on the subject. But Sartre's account also shows itself profoundly influenced by and indebted to Beauvoir's exploration of absence in *She Came To Stay*. First, there is the general point that he no longer holds the view that absence can occur only between two people for whom the absence of the one alters the being of the other 'in an essential manner'. Secondly (and more interestingly), Sartre has incorporated into his two examples of absence certain key and idiosyncratic elements of the description by Beauvoir which has just been considered.

Sartre's two accounts of absence in *Being and Nothingness* are separated by several hundred pages. The first, the better known of the two, comes in Part One, Chapter 1 where Sartre builds up the general concept of nothingness on the basis of phenomenological demonstrations of the existence of types of concrete nothings, of instances of non-being. These include questioning, fragility and destruction, but it is Sartre's account of absence which is most frequently cited, and which has most captured the philosophical imagination. Sartre imagines himself entering a café late for an appointment with Pierre. He surveys the room and its occupants and says to himself, 'He is not here.' Sartre takes as his task the demonstration that this negation arises in some sense from an intuition or perception, and not purely from a judgement or a linguistic construction. His method of achieving this differs considerably from Beauvoir's. Rather than trying to pull his reader directly into the experience of entering a café and finding Pierre not there, he offers a meta-description of the experience. Whereas Beauvoir describes Elisabeth's experience of absence in all its parts *from the point of view of Elisabeth who is caught up in the experience*, Sartre, for the most part, describes the perceived absence of Pierre from an analytical distance mediated by explications of various concepts. For example, Sartre appeals openly to a non-sensationalist theory of perception, whereas in Beauvoir's description it remains implicit. Sartre writes:

> But we must observe that in perception there is always the construction of a figure on a ground. No one object, no group of objects is especially designed to be organized as specifically either ground or figure; all depends on the direction of my attention. When I enter this café to search for Pierre, there is formed a synthetic organization of all the objects in the café, on the ground of which Pierre is given as about to appear. (1956, p. 9)

This principle of perception is identical to the one which Beauvoir uses to structure her phenomenological description of Elisabeth's experience of absence, that is, where all the objects in Françoise's room form a synthetic background against which her absence is perceived.

When it comes to demonstrating the cardinal point that the non-being, the 'flickering of nothingness', which Pierre perceives upon entering the café, is no mere linguistic or mental negation, Sartre draws directly upon Beauvoir's account. Sartre, only thinly and jokingly disguising the source of what became one of his most famous examples, turns Napoleon into Wellington and Shakespeare into Valéry.

> Pierre absent haunts this café and is the condition of its self-nihilating organization as ground. By contrast, judgments which I can make subsequently to amuse myself, such as, 'Wellington is not in this café, Paul Valéry is no longer here, etc.' – these have a purely abstract meaning, they are pure applications of the principle of negation without real or efficacious foundation, and they never succeed in establishing a real relation between the café and Wellington or Valéry. Here the relation 'is not' is merely thought. This example is sufficient to show that non-being does not come to things by a negative judgement; it is the negative

judgment, on the contrary, which is conditioned and supported by non-being. (pp. 10–11)

Sartre's second account of *absence*, which comes in his chapter on the body and its section 'The Body-For-Others,' is more directly based on Beauvoir's phenomenological description of Elisabeth in Françoise's room. This time Sartre describes himself waiting for Pierre in Pierre's room.

> This room in which I wait for the master of the house reveals to me in its totality the body of its owner: this easy chair is a chair-where-he-sits, this desk is a desk-at-which-he-writes, this window is a window through which there enters the light-which-illuminates-the-objects-which-he-sees. Thus it is an outline complete with all its parts, and this outline is an outline with content. But still the master of the house 'is not there.' He is *elsewhere*; he is *absent*.
>
> Now we have seen that absence is a structure of *being-there*. To be absent is to-be-elsewhere-in-my-world. (pp. 341–2)

Sartre's next paragraph draws on and elucidates another section of *She Came To Stay* which touches on the phenomenon of absence, this time in terms of its relation to presence. In Beauvoir's novel, Françoise, seriously ill and confined to her private room in a nursing home, thinks about her friends, Xavière and Pierre. 'Wherever her eyes fell, they caught only absences.' A few minutes later she hears them climbing the stairs.

> They were coming from the station, from Paris, from the center of their life; it was a portion of this life that they would spend here. The steps halted outside the door.
>
> 'May we come in?' said Pierre, as he opened the door. There he was, and Xavière was with him. The transition from their absence to their presence had, as always, been imperceptible. (Beauvoir 1984, p. 199)

Sartre elaborates on this imperceptibility and then on the difference between a portion of a life spent elsewhere and spent in one's presence.

> the presence or absence of the Other changes nothing.
>
> But look! Now Pierre appears. He is entering my room. This

appearance changes nothing in the fundamental structure of my relation to him; it is contingency but so was his absence contingency. Objects indicate him to me: the door which he pushes indicates a human presence when it opens before him ...

But the objects did not cease to indicate him during his absence ... Yet there is something new. This is the fact that he appears at present on the ground of the world as a *this* which I can look at, apprehend, and utilize directly. (1956, p. 342)

Taken together, all these passages on absence illustrate the collaborative and intertextual process that went into the making of *Being and Nothingness*.

Beauvoir Retrieving Beauvoir

In the course of preparing this chapter, we located a textual borrowing which undermines – but only partially – the symmetrical reciprocity which we saw as characterizing Sartre's and Beauvoir's philosophical efforts on *absence*. It seems that, like Sartre's accounts of absence in *Being and Nothingness*, Beauvoir's description of Elisabeth's perception of absence in *She Came To Stay* draws heavily on a prior piece of writing. The second of the original opening two chapters of *She Came To Stay*, which Beauvoir wrote between 1937 and mid-1938 and then discarded and which we discussed in Chapter 9, contains a scene in which a much younger Françoise is let into *Elisabeth's* room to wait for her (Beauvoir 1979, pp. 306–7). The descriptions of the two rooms in the two works are essentially the same. In Elisabeth's room a pair of stockings, some brushes and a bottle of eau-de-Cologne are on the mantelpiece. A jacket lays across the bed where Elisabeth has thrown it. A book of plays by a famous playwright – this time Sophocles – is open at where Elisabeth had been reading it. Her chair has been left pushed back from her desk. There are various papers covered with her handwriting and embodying her thoughts. But some of the telling touches of the later version are missing or incompletely conceived. For example, Françoise imagines the room's missing inhabitant looking at a Van Gogh print rather than at herself in a mirror. More importantly, the bust of Napoleon is missing from the mantelpiece. And, perhaps most importantly of all, the passage lacks the precise philosophical focus of the corresponding one in *She Came To Stay*.

In conclusion, it merits repeating that the concept of absence lies at the heart of Sartre's ontological project. His, like Beauvoir's, conception of human action balances on the interface between being and non-being, between what is and what is not but might be. Both philosophers worked to reveal the essential (in the sense of no dependence on personal differences) structure of reality *from the point of view* of the individual human existent. Through phenomenological descriptions of boundary situations between being and non-being, and most notably Beauvoir's descriptions of absence, Sartre identifies an objective and fundamental structure of human reality – rather like seventeenth-century epistemologists distinguished between primary and secondary qualities in order to identify objective structures of material reality.

Obviously, all the similarities between Sartre's and Beauvoir's various texts concerned with the topic of *absence* do not tell the whole story. Like the puffed-out sleeves of Françoise's dressing gown, these textual correspondences themselves point to an absence. For Sartre and Beauvoir, the formative period of their thought on the question of absence lasted at least five years, during which *absence* must have figured repeatedly as a topic in their conversation. But it also must have been the case that absence was only one of many such topics in their joint and ongoing explorations of philosophical issues. It is this, the detailed exploration of this profoundly collaborative and cross-textual process between the two philosophers generally, that half-century of intellectual partnership between equals, which is an absence which should be a fundamental presence in the study of both Beauvoir and Sartre.

Chapter 12
Beauvoir in the Intellectual Marketplace

A recent visit to one of London's largest and most comprehensive academic bookshops disclosed some interesting (and, we think, telling) information on the reception of Simone de Beauvoir's work. Her writing is still significantly in demand, at least among her English-speaking readers, over 20 years after her death, and over 60 years after some of that writing's first publication. Equally, it looks as if Beauvoir is not only holding her place as an icon, as 'the emblematic intellectual woman of the twentieth century',[1] as Toril Moi puts it in her excellent study of Beauvoir, but more importantly she is still widely read (at least in England, at least in translation). Booksellers and publishers have registered her purely economic value for what is now half a century. A selection of her writing has been continuously in print since it first appeared, and there exists as well a significant and still growing secondary body of commentary on this work from literary critics, biographers, writers of memoirs, feminist theorists, cultural historians and straightforward enthusiasts. Despite Michèle Le Doeuff's melancholy (and somewhat frustrated) admission that, with the exception of her own fine analysis and that of a few Beauvoirian colleagues, interest in Beauvoir in France is currently moribund, at least among dominant feminist intellectuals, Beauvoir is still very much functioning in the marketplace.[2] She shifts units; and continues, in the shape of posthumously published letters and journals and new additions and translations, to deliver product.

What we are interested in is this split: Beauvoir's retention of a wide readership (with largely popular but also professional components), and her peculiarly ambivalent reception by the international intellectual community, where she seems to be treated largely either with a kind of uncritical and unanalysed affection as a classic modern icon or else dismissed as a source of ideas, with the attitudes toward her work by those who reject it displaying a range of response which runs from indifference to hostility. We have two chief concerns here: the first has to do with *which* Beauvoir is visible in the general marketplace, the second with her place in the less tangible, but ultimately equally ferocious intellectual marketplace of the dominant ideas of the post-Second World War period. These two markets are, of course, not only co-existent but joined: both encompass various economic and social factors (sales, salaries, prestige and at least limited power of many kinds) as well as more intangible factors such as loyalty to variant ideas and the development of operative worldviews.

To begin to address our first question, we want to go back to our London bookshop. There were roughly 80 books (covering roughly 20 titles) by or about Beauvoir on the shelves, though they weren't in one place. Hunting for the scattered parts of her corpus became a rather amusing treasure hunt. There was a cache of Beauvoirs in the Fiction section: five of her texts were available there. The Biography section contained a real trove of material: all her memoirs, several volumes of letters and three separate biographies of Beauvoir were on the shelves. The former Women's Studies section (with its new, more fluidly transgressive and less womanish title of 'Gender Studies') contained several volumes on her work as well as copies of *The Second Sex*. We found more *Second Sex*es as well as *Old Age* in an area devoted to general social commentary and popular sociology. The Literary Criticism section threw up a number of monographs on her novels and short stories. Most interesting for our purposes, however, was where Beauvoir was not. As on all our sporadic visits to the same bookshop over the past 25 years the Philosophy section offered nothing whatsoever on Beauvoir: in this category she has had, and, it seems, continues to have, no existence whatsoever. This is not simply a case of the passing of the intense interest in mid-century French existentialism: Merleau-Ponty still figured on the shelves. There were, in addition, roughly 15 titles either by or about Sartre (including, ironically, our own study of the Beauvoir–Sartre partnership, *Simone de Beauvoir and Jean-Paul Sartre: The Remaking of a Twentieth-Century Legend*,[3] which, despite Beauvoir's being the lead name in the title and the book's major concern to question the reception of Beauvoir as a philosopher, still wound up captive in the shelving territory of her much-beloved lifelong companion, while the space which could have, indeed, should have, been hers remains, as usual, empty).

That this should be the case, that the marketplace should have no place for Beauvoir the philosopher, while it retains a good deal of space for Beauvoir the novelist, the essayist, the feminist and the cultural icon is perhaps not surprising. Beauvoir's major philosophical works are not, and have never been readily available for the English-language reader. *The Ethics of Ambiguity*, her main traditional philosophical production, published in 1947 and translated by Bernard Frechtman in 1948 is only intermittently in print. Another essay on ethics, *Pyrrhus and Cinéas* from 1944, Beauvoir's second published work, which came out in the wake of her deeply philosophical novel, *She Came To Stay* in 1943, did not appear in its entirety in English translation until 2004, though selections from it appeared in translation in *Partisan Review* in 1946.[4] *L'Existentialisme et la sagesse des nations* (1948) which contains major essays on ethical idealism and realism in politics, on literature and metaphysics, and on justice was never, to our knowledge, translated at all, in whole or in part, until the publication in 2004 of *Simone de Beauvoir: Philosophical Writings*. From Beauvoir's collection of essays, *Privilèges* (1955), only 'Must We Burn Sade?' has been, again, intermittently available, while 'La pensée de droite aujourd'hui' and 'Merleau-Ponty et le pseudo-sartrisme' remain inaccessible. Beauvoir's additional essays written for *Les Temps Modernes*, her and Sartre's famous journal of which she was, in fact, the chief editor for many years, have never been collected, much less translated. It is, we think, highly curious that the most purely intellectual part of the body of work by 'the emblematic intellectual woman of the twentieth century' does not, in fact, have a place in the market, and might just as well, in fact, not exist.

That such a curious case should, indeed, *be* the case is perhaps, in many ways, not overly surprising. 'Philosopher', again, as Michèle Le Doeuff (among others) points out with blinding obviousness, is not a category which easily admits that awkward category, 'women'. Equally, and even more curiously, Beauvoir herself took great pains to dissociate herself from her own philosophical production and her own philosophical originality. Her reasons had to do with her experience of the intellectual market-place, though the accounts she gave of her rejection of the appellation 'philosopher' have their own fascinating edge. That Beauvoir *was*, in fact, a philosopher, and one of major importance is something of which there can be no doubt; that Beauvoir herself regarded being a philosopher as her most scandalous personal secret in a life whose last half was lived very much in public is even more interesting. The 'philosophical' was a category from which she insisted she be excluded during her lifetime, and that she should do so is, we think, a matter of extraordinary interest.

In *The Prime of Life*, the second volume of her memoirs published in 1960, Beauvoir looked back on herself in 1935 and gave the following account of her decision not to devote herself to philosophy, despite her clear talent as a philosopher. Margaret A. Simons provides a new translation of this crucial aspect of Beauvoir's autobiographical self-presentation:

'Why not try my hand at philosophy?' she asks herself in 1935. 'Sartre says that I understand philosophical doctrines, Husserl's among others, more quickly and more exactly than he ... In brief, I have ... a developed critical sense, and philosophy is for me a living reality. I'll never tire of its satisfactions.'

'However, I don't consider myself a philosopher. I know very well that my ease in entering into a text comes precisely from my lack of inventiveness. In this domain, the truly creative spirits are so rare that it is idle of me to ask why I cannot join their ranks. It's necessary rather to explain how certain individuals are capable of pulling off this concerted delirium which is a system, and whence comes the stubbornness which gives to their insights that value of universal keys. I have said already that the feminine condition does not dispose one to this kind of obstinacy.'[5]

Throughout her public career, Beauvoir took pains to separate herself from the title of 'philosopher'. The statement just quoted is one of many such denials. Her readers have tended to take her at her word, without noting the idiosyncratic definition she uses for this term. A clue is given in her comment, just noted, on philosophy consisting of a 'concerted delirium which is a system'. Another clue is contained in her remarks in an interview with Margaret Simons in 1985, where the topic of discussion was the omission of much of the philosophical apparatus from H. M. Parshley's translation of *The Second Sex*:

'Well, I think it's very bad to suppress the philosophical aspect because while I say that I'm not a philosopher in the sense that I'm not the creator of a system, I'm still a philosopher in the sense that I've studied a lot of philosophy, I have a degree in philosophy, I've taught philosophy, I'm infused with philosophy, and when I put philosophy into my books it's because that's a way for me to view the world and I can't allow them to eliminate that way of viewing the world, that dimension of my approach to women, as Mr. Parshley has done. I'm altogether against the principle of gaps, omissions, condensations which have the effect, among other things of suppressing the whole philosophical aspect of the book.'[6]

'Philosopher', it should be clear by now, is a term which Beauvoir uses with extraordinary precision (and the shelves of the Philosophy section in the bookshop would be thinly stocked indeed if this definition was generally operative. We could, for instance, start by clearing the Wittgenstein material and carry on backwards through the alphabet from there). We want to cite one more statement by Beauvoir to make it utterly clear what she was doing when she rejected this term for herself. In another interview with Simons, this time in 1979, after insisting that her 'field is literature' and that she has never 'created a philosophical work', she explains further to Simons who mentions *The Ethics of Ambiguity* as an indubitably philosophical production, that:

'For me it is not philosophy; it is an essay. For me, a philosopher is someone like Spinoza, Hegel, or Sartre; someone who has built a great system, and not simply someone who likes philosophy, who can teach it, understand it, and who can make use of it in essays. *A philosopher is somebody who truly builds a philosophical system.* And that, I did not do. When I was young, I decided that it was not what I wanted to do.'[7] (emphasis added)

After this clarification, we think one can safely say that, using Beauvoir's terms, the bookshop Philosophy shelves would have to be stripped almost bare. With Beauvoir, we are dealing with a very special and strikingly limited definition of philosophy. (And we must, as an aside, note how utterly charmed we are by the confidence, indeed arrogance of Beauvoir's rejection of her place among those who had surrendered to the 'concerted delirium' of abstract systems building to whom she alone grants the title of 'philosopher': 'I decided,' she says, 'that it was not what I wanted to do.' Without a shred of doubt about her ability to have constructed her own systemic edifice, Beauvoir sees herself, rather splendidly, as having simply chosen not to do it.)

While it does not take much thought to realize why the general reading public has not clamoured, en masse, to recognize Beauvoir as a significant philosophical force (and we think we need only nod here to the still unusual idea of the 'female philosopher' to make the point), Beauvoir's consistent rejection of the classification (and her equally consistent appeal to a most unusual definition of the term) demands further comment. A clue to her dormancy in this matter must be linked to her own first forays into the marketplace as well as to her already noted statement that 'the female condition does not dispose one to this kind of obstinacy', that is, to the 'concerted delirium' of philosophical systems building.

For it would be wrong ever to underestimate Beauvoir's shrewd understanding of her own place in the intellectual market. She was always a woman with her living to make and her first attempts to break into publication carried lessons which she never forgot. In *Memoirs of a Dutiful Daughter* (1958) and *The Prime of Life* (1960), the first two volumes of her autobiography, Beauvoir repeatedly underscores her commitment to the literary life which, indeed, had been hers for over 15 years by the time she began writing her memoirs in the mid-1950s. But the woman who had published three novels, *The Second Sex*, *The Ethics of Ambiguity* and a great deal of journalism as well as a moderately successful play in the 1940s, who had won the Prix concourt in 1954 for *The Mandarins*, and who had been at the centre of the international existentialist craze for over a decade, was in a very different position than she had been in the late 1930s as an unpublished author. In 1938, as a 30-year-old secondary schoolteacher, desperate to break into print, Beauvoir failed abjectly in her initial attempt to publish. The publication in question was her first serious fiction, a collection of short stories later entitled *When Things of the Spirit Come First*, which did not appear until over 40 years later, in 1979. In the mid-1930s, during the two years she worked on the stories, Beauvoir said she 'was sustained by the hope that a publisher would accept them'.[8] Sartre had books of psychology published in 1936 and 1937, *Nausea* had been accepted by Gallimard and was about to appear to instant acclaim. The couple were desperate for success for their writing, success which would lift them out of their lives as schoolteachers with which Beauvoir was now bored, and which looked to her too enclosed. Those 'past nine years began to look rather threadbare', she explained; she wanted, she said, 'something to happen to me from the outside, as it were, something new and different.'[9] In *The Prime of Life*, Beauvoir treats the rejection of her volume of stories by two publishers offhandedly: the book, she said, 'was defective', her 'didactic and satirical aims were laboured far too heavily', it was a typical case of a beginner believing she had been original when she had been nothing of the kind.[10] Beauvoir's autobiography blurs the disappointment which the rejection of *Things of the Spirit* caused. She had been so certain of publication that she had told her family and friends of the imminent appearance of the book.[11] And the rather anodyne account given in *The Prime of Life* for the stories' rejection takes on quite a different light when supplemented by the comments she made to her biographer Deirdre Bair:

> 'Sartre told me that [Brice Parain (the editor at Gallimard) said] it really had nothing to do with me or the quality of my writing, but that the house of Gallimard did not understand books written by women which were about the lives of women of my generation and background; that modern France and French publishing were not yet ready to deal with what women thought and felt and wanted; that to publish such a book would brand them a subversive publishing house and they couldn't risk offending all sorts of patrons and critics ... and he told me not to say anything negative about Gallimard, because they were so powerful and he needed them and perhaps with my next novel I would, too. So I kept my mouth shut and swallowed the hurt and told everyone the book was poorly written and because it dealt with silly girls it would probably not have sold anyway.'[12]

Anyone who has received their first rejection after venturing into the marketplace can imagine Beauvoir's reactions. And the comments received in such vulnerable circumstances tend to influence their recipients in a way that no later criticism, made after any degree of success, can ever do. Sartre's mercenary, but realistic warnings were an additional, difficult factor for Beauvoir. His pleas were also prescient. Beauvoir did, in the end, need Gallimard, who became the publisher of most of her books, including, with wonderful irony, *The Second Sex*, Beauvoir's most subversive treatise on the condition of women. Despite a bout of depression, Beauvoir let Sartre take her stories to another publisher, Grasset. The book was turned down again: she then refused to submit it elsewhere, despite Sartre's continued encouragement. In 1982, and looking back on this initial defeat just before the English translation of the collection appeared, Beauvoir admitted just how hard she took these failures:

'Two rejections were enough insult, enough humiliation. I was so naive then! If I had only known how many great writers are hurt by repeated rejection of their work, then I might have had the courage to try again with another publisher, but at the time I only believed that my work was inferior, undeserving of public attention. I saw myself as a failure and for a long time viewed myself as unworthy.'[13]

If the market would not accept what one of the publishers' readers called her 'description of post-war young women influenced by the intellectual currents of their day' in stories laced through with 'intelligence' and 'the ability both to observe and to analyse' and which gave accounts of 'certain contemporary milieus' which were 'extremely accurate',[14] clearly, there would be no place for a woman who wished to take her place among the handful of thinkers over the centuries, who spent their lives constructing philosophical systems. The ambitious writerly neophyte who was Beauvoir at the end of the 1930s listened carefully to the voice of the market. She would tell her stories of intelligent women in the certain intellectual milieus she best knew, but from now on, she would give the market what it wanted as well. The door to success in philosophy, even if it had been the one against which she most wanted to push, must have looked utterly closed to this humiliated schoolteacher.

If this young woman, 'infused with philosophy', had good reason to believe that the market did not want what she had to give in terms of textual treatment of either women or philosophy, she nevertheless was outstandingly successful in finding ways to write her way into the market in ways that allowed her to exercise her philosophical drive and to report on the condition of the women of her generation. And she found her way through the closed doors remarkably quickly. *She Came To Stay*, the novel on which she was working while the rejections for *When Things of the Spirit Come First* were received, is deeply informed with a profoundly original treatment of the problem of the Other, which found a way out of the impasse of Hegel's master/slave dialectic onto the open ground of situated existential reciprocity as well as offering exactly the kind of commentary on the problems faced by twentieth-century intellectual women which had so disturbed Gallimard in Beauvoir's first manuscript. The novel marked Beauvoir's first secure entry into the market, and the fiction was received as the kind of sex, scandal and confessional commodity with which the market has rarely had problems. For the most part, these are still, overwhelmingly, the terms within which it is read. As we noted above, it is unwise to underestimate Beauvoir's shrewdness with regard to the market once any particular lesson had been learned.

Beauvoir's personal disavowal of the title 'philosopher' (and one might add here that she tended to be wary of all labels, a good example is her refusal of the 'feminist' tag until late in her life), however, goes only a small way toward explaining her absence from the philosophy shelves. To understand this, we think it is necessary to look at the trajectory of postwar French thought and at its influence on English-speaking readers. We're dealing here with trails of intellectual fashions and, while it seems to us to be too simple to invoke the double clichés of Anglophone empiricism versus Francophile abstraction, and French intellectuals' tendency often to adopt German philosophies as their points of departure, we think there is enough truth in these received views to map the territory we want to cover. (For example, Tom Rockmore, in his excellent study *Heidegger and French Philosophy: Humanism, Antihumanism and Being* mentions Nietzsche, Heidegger, Marx and Freud as the German thinkers who most significantly underpin postwar French thought. We think it's difficult to argue with this observation, though like Rockmore, we think it is only fair to add two more German thinkers, Husserl and Hegel, to the list).[15] What is of crucial interest in the case of Beauvoir are the ways in which the French intellectuals' postwar swerve to varieties of neo-Heideggerianism has served to obscure her work as a philosopher, and the ways in which this direction has occluded her thought even for those who might be judged most receptive to it.

It strikes us as continuingly bizarre that for the past 25 years one can scarcely move in the study of literature in England or America without tripping over some (usually partially assimilated) variety of neo-Heideggerian thought. Derrida, Lacan, Foucault, Gadamer, Lyotard, Irigaray: the Heideggerian line of irrationalist writers are, and have been, the power-names to invoke in order to signal intellectual depth and currency. Neither deconstruction nor the Lyotardian version of postmodernism are conceivable as intellectual formations without their Heideggerian roots. The attacks on (and often simply sneers at) rationality and humanism which are now so commonplace in literary studies as to have become orthodox are also directly attributable to the influence of this intellectual lineage (though the strong presence of Nietzsche filtered through both Heidegger and neo-Heideggerians must also be mentioned as important to these developments). Convinced as we are of the (at the very least) compatibility between Heidegger's philosophy and Heidegger's Nazism, it is scarcely surprising that we belong to the group who regards this development with more than regret.[16] However, that is another (very large) argument. What we are interested in here is the intellectual market's investment in the Heideggerian topics of Being and Dasein, in his attempt to find a way out of the Cartesian philosophical line, and in the ways in which, as Richard Rorty remarks, for neo-Heideggerians, '"Language" [has] become the latest substitute for "God" or "Mind" – something mysterious, incapable of being described in the same terms in which we describe tables, trees, and atoms.'[17] These dominant ideas, which seem to us to constitute a faithfully Heideggerian attempt to reinstate the ineffable as a respectable category in non-theological European imagination, (whether this is identified by the Heideggerian name of 'Thinking' or some other term, and which seems to comprise a curious attempt to move to a postmetaphysical position by the invocation of the utterly unknowable), have affected the continuing lack of space in the intellectual market for Beauvoir as a philosopher.

Some of the factors which have blocked serious consideration of the philosopher Beauvoir are outlined succinctly by Rockmore, who intelligently follows the work of Pierre Bourdieu on the sociology of knowledge in France. For example, the French tradition of the philosophical 'master-thinker' presented a role which Sartre filled only too well in the immediate aftermath of the Second World War and the early 1950s. In some ways, there was no getting past him during his lifetime and the strong interest in Sartrean existentialism which was a feature of English and American intellectual life in the 1950s and 1960s represented part of the international response to this peculiarly French phenomenon. We think it is useful to note certain continuities here: Bergson had a similar effect in English-speaking countries during the modernist period; Derrida, Lacan and Foucault (with Heidegger in the background as the meta-master-thinker) seem to have shared this role more recently. It seems as necessary for the functioning of French intellectual life to overthrow master-thinkers as to establish them, and the eclipse of Sartre, after the waning of his period of most profound influence, bears a distinct similarity to the treatment of Bergson's reputation earlier in the century (and the current, minor Bergson revival of the moment is interesting in this light). The turning away from Sartre to Heidegger outside of France, however, presents another kind of case. There are good historical reasons why the

Heideggerian line, which ultimately privileges the self as sovereign, and which allows no grounds for discussion of ethics, of the good, should have become so widespread from the 1970s to the present in English-speaking countries, but that, too, is another argument. There are many reasons why the political right should be quite satisfied with this circumstance: it is more puzzling why neo-Heideggerianism should find such favour with the political left, though here one can cite factors such as a generous tendency to conflate the new with the avant-garde and the avant-garde with the progressive, and a willingness to interpret some descriptions of repression as attacks on it.

One minor factor in the rise of Heideggerian anti-humanism has to do with Beauvoir and Sartre's own strong misreading of Heidegger. Their interpretation of Heidegger left their existential humanism (which is so important for Beauvoir's treatment of the problem of the Other, and therefore, for her treatment of women, the old, the oppressed) relatively undefended against neo-Heideggerian attacks. Sartre's misreading of Heidegger, was signalled early, and very publicly, in his wildly successful popular lecture of 1945, 'Existentialism is a Humanism', which builds on Beauvoir's notions of reciprocity and his own work on authenticity and which stresses the importance of action. Sartre's ideas were savaged by Heidegger in his 'Letter on Humanism' of 1947, which became the main text through which French intellectuals had access to Heidegger.[18] Heidegger proposes a postmetaphysical 'humanism', related not to the biological or to the anthropological or, indeed, to any material activities of suffering existents, but rather to the thought of being, the forgetfulness of which has led, in Heidegger's view, to the 'homelessness' and alienation of 'modern man'.[19]

This philosophy of the ineffable seems so far from the notions of engagement espoused by Sartre and reciprocity espoused by Beauvoir that it is most curious that both French philosophers believed themselves to be working the same philosophical ground as Heidegger. For example, in *The Second Sex*, Beauvoir, in explaining her discussion of the body as a situation as opposed to a thing, writes that this must be seen in terms of the 'perspective [she is] adopting – that of Heidegger, Sartre, and Merleau-Ponty'.[20] These fellow-philosophers are claimed as members of her own, coherent group of thinkers. Discussing the need for a new translation of *The Second Sex* in 1982 and in 1985, the year before her death, Beauvoir lamented H. M. Parshley's mistranslation of 'la réalité humaine' as 'human nature' in the English edition of the book:

'you tell me that [Parshley] speaks of human nature whereas I have never believed – nor Sartre either, and on this point I am his disciple – we never believed in human nature. So it's a serious mistake to speak of "human nature" instead of "human reality," which is a Heideggerian term. I was infused with Heidegger's philosophy and when I speak about human reality that is, about man's presence in the world, I'm not speaking about human nature, it's completely different.'[21]

This is a fascinating response as 'réalité humaine' is itself a highly problematic French translation of Heidegger's 'Dasein', which suggests the inclusion in the Heideggerian category of the particular, social ways in which human beings exist and have existed, which are exactly what Heidegger wants to exclude from his ontology, and exactly where he locates the corruption of being which his thought is designed to purify.[22]

The 'réalité humaine' which exercised Beauvoir, as one of the key ethical philosophers of her age, had nothing to do with an ontology which severs itself from experience, and everything to do with questions of agency, freedom, rights and justice, in short, with the identifiably modern project which Charles Taylor describes in terms of a historically modern identity which implicates us 'in a sense of self defined by the powers of disengaged reason as well as in the creative imagination, in the characteristically modern understandings of freedom and dignity and rights, in the ideals of self-fulfilment and expression, and in the demands of universal benevolence and justice'.[23] Heidegger himself found the idea of the modern encapsulated by these terms entirely bankrupt, and it was precisely to avoid the poison of modernity that he asserted the need to take thought back to the notions of the Pre-Socratics, which erase, among other things, the modern notion of the subject. This unease with the subject, with agency, with freedom, is a standard marker of the current intellectual marketplace. The neo-Heideggerian projects which, again as Taylor remarks, are grounded on a view of the 'subject who is enfolded in language which he can neither oversee nor escape' or locked in transmu-tations of paradigms of psychological or social and political power which simply play themselves out as self-governing systems, which 'disclaim any notion of the good'[24] are antithetical to the entirety of the Beauvoirian project. Beauvoir's absence from the philosophy shelves begins to look overdetermined, especially as major lines of feminist work (which have been instrumental in keeping her work alive, and which still provide the major forum for discussion of Beauvoir) become more deeply immersed in the neo-Heideggerian stream, and move away from a defining interest in justice and onto the blurred terrain of gender as performance. The intellectual marketplace has for a quarter of a century not been a friendly place for Beauvoir the philosopher, with her passion for justice, her insistence on responsibility, her obsession with freedom, her attention to material conditions and her ethics of reciprocity. But the neo-Heideggerian era has passed into its twilight, and the place that is undeniably Beauvoir's on the Philosophy shelves in the London bookshop is unlikely to remain empty forever.

PART III
BEAUVOIR AND BEAUVOIR

Chapter 13
Gender and Method

Philosophy's Literary Forms

In this chapter we want to examine a category error, which is common in studies of Beauvoir, in which her fiction and her philosophy are treated as mutually exclusive and separate categories. The underlying problem at work in contributing to this mistake is that of the conflation of a writerly form with the type of subject matter addressed in it. Falling into this confusion is particularly misleading for readers of Beauvoir because one of the most significant and fascinating aspects of her methodology lies in her explicit rejection of any formalist division between literature and philosophy. This is an intriguing aspect of her work which places it in an honourable and innovative philosophical position. It is not often enough noted that one part of the Western philosophical tradition – a part which is especially admirable – is the diversity of writerly forms that have proved useful to its major practitioners. The dialogues of Plato and Hume, the fables of the Enlightenment philosophers, the dramatic narratives of Kierkegaard, the parables and aphorisms of Nietzsche, as well as the essays of Kant and Sartre are all part of that heritage. Equally, the mathematician's 'paper' used by Tarski and Russell, and the scientific paper adapted and made so fashionable by the logical positivists, and that strange literary form devised by Wittgenstein, so eccentric that it apparently remains without a name and yet has its antecedent in Spinoza's *Ethics*, all form part of the major lineage of ways in which philosophy has been successfully written.

As the above list suggests, no one writerly form can be designated as the only one properly used for the most sophisticated philosophical investigation. And it must be noted that modern philosophy, from the mid-nineteenth century on, has been particularly interested in choosing, adapting and, in some cases, inventing literary forms to fit the particular philosophical subject matter under investigation. Simone de Beauvoir is one of the most interesting contributors to the modern development of the diversity of forms of philosophical writing. The significance of this aspect of her work was recognized by some of her contemporary philosophical associates, most particularly by Maurice Merleau-Ponty. In what follows we want to consider briefly the nature and ramifications of Beauvoir's originality in terms of philosophy's tradition of methodological diversity.

The waters surrounding Beauvoir's contribution to philosophical method are somewhat muddied because the literary forms she used innovatively for philosophy – the novel and the short story – have (unlike the literary forms of Wittgenstein) resulted in writing which has been chiefly esteemed largely as works of *literature*. In fact, many of Beauvoir's compositions rest simultaneously in two categories, literature and philosophy. This sometimes confuses readers who value these works as important instances of achievement in one of the categories while remaining unaware of their significance in the other. It helps, we think, to remember that Beauvoir was by intellectual and personal temperament a chronic transgressor of boundaries of all kinds. In her conflation of literature and philosophy she demonstrates one of her most brilliant instances of this tendency.

In the mid-1940s, first Merleau-Ponty and then Beauvoir herself wrote lucid essays explaining her unorthodox but not entirely unprecedented philosophical methodology.[1] These essays not only illuminate Beauvoir's method, but also explain it in terms of the philosophical ideas which inspired it. The reasoning behind Beauvoir's method is fascinating. And to begin to understand it, it is helpful to begin with one of Beauvoir's foundational ideas – one she adopted very early – that is, the notion that the universal point of view is not available to the philosopher.

Gender and the Philosopher's Point of View

Adoption of new or neglected literary forms by philosophers is usually linked to decided views of what are and are not the proper substantive concerns of philosophy. The logical positivists' imitation of the compositional forms of science, for example, grew from their position that philosophy should limit itself to being the handmaiden of science. Similarly, Beauvoir's practice, as well as her advocacy of using writerly forms usually associated only with purely literary work for philosophy is tied to her strong views about what kind of philosophical knowledge is possible. She sets out these views very clearly in her essay 'Littérature et métaphysique' which appeared in *Les Temps Modernes* in 1946, and which, it must be noted, treats the terms 'metaphysics' and 'philosophy' almost synonymously. Beauvoir begins her essay by dividing philosophy and philosophers roughly into two camps. The first camp, which includes Aristotle, Leibniz, Spinoza and Kant, holds that philosophical truth exists only in a 'timeless and objective' sense, and thereby regards 'as negligible the subjectivity and historicity of experience'.[2] In denying the philosophical relevance of the individual and the concrete, this school implicitly presumes that a philosopher is capable of taking a universal rather than merely an individual point of view toward the metaphysical reality he or she seeks to explain. Beauvoir regards this view as seriously deluded. As Eleanore Holveck notes, Beauvoir 'argues that philosophers pretend to explain all things universally, but in fact these "universals" are based in the consciousness of some individual thinker who claims knowledge of the universal, a claim that must be justified'.[3] Beauvoir rejects this universalist presumption as largely delusory, egomaniacal and only apparently tenable. She diagnoses it as a position which only a man, working from a position of masculine privilege could possibly accept.[4] It is crucial to note Beauvoir's insistence on the masculinist basis of this philosophical error. It is a point to which she returns in her writing throughout her career. For example, very early, in *Pyrrhus and Cinéas*, Beauvoir argues that personal arrogance formed the sole foundation of Hegel's declaration that individuality is only a moment of a universal future. She writes: 'Man cannot escape from his own presence nor from the singular world that his presence reveals around him; even his effort to uproot himself from the earth makes him dig a hole for himself. Spinozism defines Spinoza, and Hegelianism Hegel.'[5]

Against these universalist delusions, Beauvoir juxtaposes the orientation of thinkers who, like herself, insist upon the philosophical relevance of individual human experience. She believes (and this is where her anti-universalist principles accord with and feed into the thought of the philosophical postmodernists) that a fundamental characteristic of human reality is that no one, including all of history's great male philosophers, can take a universal or God-like point of view, whatever they may claim to the contrary. This point is essential for Beauvoir and she states her position clearly in *Pyrrhus and Cinéas* in 1944. Her attitude toward the universalist standpoint of most traditional philosophy is one of intellectual and moral contempt, a contempt she announced vehemently:

> The universal mind is without voice, and every man who claims to speak in its name only gives to it his own voice. How can he claim the point of view of the universal, since he *is* not the universal? One can not know a point of view other than one's own.[6]

Beauvoir's own position with regard to the universalist philosophical perspective was, in fact, settled in the 1930s, a fact that her fiction of that decade demonstrates and which Merleau-Ponty shows he understands well in his essay on her work. For Beauvoir, truth, including metaphysical truth, is always relative to a knowing subject. She believed, as she noted succinctly in her preface to *America Day by Day* in 1948: 'concrete experience envelops at once the subject and object'.[7] As Margaret Simons, one of the most sensitive readers of Beauvoir's philosophy remarks, Beauvoir always regarded any 'attempt to describe reality without reference to the experiencing subject ... as distorting as trying to describe the subject without reference to the context of circumstances'.[8] But if, for Beauvoir, no member of the human race is granted a detached Archimedean point of view of their fellow (and inferior) human beings; if pure thought and the contemplation of equally pure existence are impossible; and if, in addition, the pretence of being able to do so is abandoned, then strong methodological implications follow for philosophy.

Merleau-Ponty on Beauvoir

Merleau-Ponty understood (and accepted) Beauvoir's anti-universalist arguments. Further, he understood the techniques she employed in her fiction as one way of practising the new philosophical methodology demanded by acceptance of her argument. The year before the appearance of Beauvoir's essay, Merleau-Ponty had already begun the public explication of her philosophical method. His essay, 'Metaphysics and the Novel', explained the importance of *She Came To Stay* as a philosophical text. Merleau-Ponty begins by noting that, since the end of the nineteenth century, the boundaries between literature and philosophy had dissolved and that 'hybrid modes of expression' had developed in response to the opening up of what he calls 'a new dimension of investigation'[9] This new dimension grew from the apprehension that all intellectual works are 'concerned with establishing a certain attitude toward the world, of which literature and philosophy ... are just different expressions.'[10]

It is this concern with 'establishing a certain attitude toward the world' which Merleau-Ponty identifies as the impulse behind Beauvoir's success at using fiction as a philosophical medium. He, like Beauvoir, distinguishes between two kinds of metaphysics. 'Classical metaphysics', he writes, 'could pass for a speciality with which literature had nothing to do because metaphysics operated on the basis of uncontested rationalism, convinced it could make the world and human life understood by an arrangement of concepts'.[11] Furthermore, even philosophers who begin on the experiential level, end by explaining the world on the basis of abstractions. But Merleau-Ponty continues:

Everything changes when a phenomenological or existential philosophy assigns itself the task, not of explaining the world or of discovering its 'conditions of possibility,' but rather of formulating an experience of the world, a contact with the world which precedes all thought *about* the world. After this, whatever is metaphysical in man cannot be credited to something outside his empirical being – to God, to Consciousness. Man is metaphysical in his very being, in his loves, in his hates, in his individual and collective history.[12]

'From now on', concludes Merleau-Ponty, 'the tasks of literature and philosophy can no longer be separated.' He reaches this conclusion, because, like the philosopher/novelist he is writing about, he is committed to approaching philosophical questions from the point of view of the individual, a point of view traditionally adopted by the novel and the short story.

Beauvoir's Philosophical Domain

It should be noted that in narrowing the domain to which philosophy is seen as properly addressed, Beauvoir and Merleau-Ponty are following a well-travelled definitional path. They prescribe methods of doing philosophy which match their chosen philosophical interests and proscribe others. In 'Literature and Metaphysics', Beauvoir, at her subversive best, outlines a philosophical method that inverts the philosopher's traditional universalist presumption. If the world, as she insists, can be viewed only from a particular point of view, then the philosophical enterprise must begin with particular and concrete descriptions of subjects' relations with the world and with other consciousnesses. Beauvoir's chosen philosophical domain is what she calls 'the metaphysical dimension' of human reality, that is, 'one's presence in the world, for example, one's abandonment in the world, one's freedom, the opacity of things, the resistance of foreign consciousnesses'. 'To make' philosophy, she says, is 'to be' philosophical in the sense of sensitizing oneself to these individual metaphysical experiences, and then describing them.[13] If these particular statements are recognized by others as true for them, they can then be used to construct general statements about 'the essence at the heart of existence'.[14]

Beauvoir 'was able', argues Eleanore Holveck, 'to ground her abstract philosophical positions in the real world of lived experience, a lived experience she created imaginatively in ordinary language that was more concrete, more rich than any abstract philosophical language'.[15] With Beauvoir's rejection of *a priorism* and of a universal point of view, a good *philosophical argument* becomes, for Beauvoir, a description of a particular individual's metaphysical relations with the world which the reader recognizes as characterizing his or her own experience. Beauvoir identifies fiction as a medium especially well suited to this end and she takes care to explain what she means by this in 'Literature and Metaphysics'. Although she notes that philosophers may use the essay to give 'to the reader an intellectual reconstruction of their experience, it is this experience itself, such that it presents itself before any elucidation, that the novelist claims to reproduce on an imaginary plane'.[16] Beauvoir continues:

> In the real world the sense of an object is not a concept knowable by pure understanding: it is the object in as much that it unveils itself to us in the global relation that we maintain with it and that is action, emotion, sentiment; one asks of the novelists to evoke this

presence of flesh and bone whose complexity, singular and infinite richness, overflows all subjective interpretation.[17]

Despite the remarks at the beginning of this section which point out philosophers' tendency to define philosophy in terms of their own most pressing interests, it is important not to underestimate the seriousness with which Beauvoir proposes, as does Merleau-Ponty, the world of the concrete as the correct field of a major philosophical research programme. It was not just Beauvoir's distaste for the male presumption behind the universal point of view which led her in this direction. She believed passionately in the exploration of the individual and in the concrete as the route to true philosophical understanding. She believed – and from an early age acted on her belief – that close observance of one's relations in-the-world could bring new illumination to old philosophical problems, like the existence of other consciousnesses.

The Freedom of the Reader

Beauvoir's famous concern with the consciousness of others powerfully shapes her philosophical method. It underwrites one of two ethical issues which she, never far from the ethical plane, weaves through her essay on methodology. Beauvoir wants to guard against what she sees as philosophy's traditional authoritarianism and mystification, whereby what she calls 'the theoretician'[18] presents concepts as articles of faith to passive readers. Instead, she identifies a constituency of readers who are out of sympathy with the tradition of the philosophical messiah, who 'want to guard the freedom of their thought', who 'find repugnant this intellectual docility' demanded of them.[19] This kind of reader, says Beauvoir, is only willing to accept others' propositions after

> a movement of his whole being before forming judgements that he pulls from himself without someone having had the presumption of dictating them to him. It is this which is the value of a good novel. It is capable of inducing imaginary experiences as complete, as disquieting as lived experiences. The reader interrogates, doubts, he takes sides and this hesitant elaboration of his thought is for him an enrichment that no doctrinal teaching could replace.[20]

It is not surprising that this radical vision which Beauvoir spelled out in 1946 for the full enfranchisement of the reader continues to meet incomprehension and dogged resistance. It violates all traditions of received philosophical authority and automatic respect for intellectual hierarchies. It remains, when fully comprehended (as Beauvoir fully realized and intended), something of a philosophical scandal.

The Ethics of Philosophical Research

Beauvoir's concern for the reader's freedom interconnects with her essay's second ethical dimension. She envisions novels which appeal directly to the reader's liberty as serving as a valuable form of philosophical research. This research role, she argues, imposes an ethical obligation of reciprocity on the philosopher-novelist. It

> demands that the novelist himself participates in this research to which he admits his reader: if he foresees in advance the conclusions which the reader must reach, if he indiscreetly places pressure on him to give up his adherence to pre-established theses, if he grants him only one degree of freedom, then the novelistic work is only an incongruous mystification; the novel takes on value and dignity only if it constitutes for the author as for the reader a living discovery.[21]

It is notable that Beauvoir invokes the prestigious word 'research' to characterize her ideas in this matter which, again, is crucially one of ethics. The ethical principle which Beauvoir demands of philosopher-novelists, namely that the results of their research should not be predetermined, is, indeed, cognate with the professional code of the laboratory scientist. By linking the codes of experimental science and those of the philosopher-novelist, Beauvoir underscores both the precision of her demand and its intellectual and social value.

Beauvoir considers her analogy between philosophical fiction and experimental science so apt that she pursues it further. The validity of a scientific law is based on the series of experiments which have established it and which it summarizes. Beauvoir insists that, in a similar manner, the collection of singular experiences examined by the philosopher-novelist and/or philosopher-essayist is the only legitimate foundation for metaphysical truth. Moreover, just as the ethically rigorous sciences continue to confront established laws with new and more sophisticated empirical data, so too the philosopher must continue to appraise her general philosophical propositions against the results of fresh applications to concrete existence. The novel, because of its grounding in the concrete, facilitates this movement beyond the traditional dogmatic (and unacceptable) abstraction of philosophy and philosophers. But the literary-philosophical method, warns Beauvoir, only works if the author remains willing to reflect on the problems and unforeseen developments which the philosophical novel, like the scientific experiment, may throw up.

Conclusion

Beauvoir's pursuit of the abstract and the general via the concrete and the particular is, as previously noted, the common currency of existentialism. Beauvoir's methodological contribution, realized in *She Came To Stay* and explained and historicized in Merleau-Ponty's 'Metaphysics and the Novel' and in her own 'Literature and Metaphysics', merged, in the existential/ phenomenological context, the methods of the philosopher and the fiction writer. We have seen how Beauvoir explains her choice of the novel as a literary form in which to do philosophy is motivated by several key ideas. She rejects the universal point of view as a sham; she chooses the individual and the concrete as her domain of philosophical inquiry; she enacts her ethical regard for the reader's freedom; and she announces her stance regarding ethical practice in philosophical research.

In retrospect, the last point appears starkly significant. In laying down for the philosopher-novelist the requirements for a novel 'honestly written', she is, in the typically understated way by which she carves a path for herself as a philosopher, telling us something very important about her own novels, especially about the one which inspired her and Merleau-Ponty's essays on philosophical method. And surely as ethically responsible readers we are obliged to listen to Beauvoir on this point. It is worth repeating, as her essay does, that she views a novel as merely a 'mystification' if it employs 'pre-established theses', if it does not constitute for the author 'a living discovery'. A novel's philosophical content, she insists, must not pre-date the novel itself, but instead must be the result of the philosophical research of which the novel consists. This is the basic requirement for an 'honestly written' metaphysical novel.[22] Given that the title of Beauvoir's essay's alludes directly to Merleau-Ponty's 'Metaphysics and the Novel', which hails her *She Came To Stay* as a philosophical text, it is, by implication, to her own novel to which her essay points as an example of one honestly written.

Chapter 14
Gender and Ethics

Between 1942 and 1946 Beauvoir wrote two book-length essays on ethics. The first, *Pyrrhus and Cinéas*, was rushed into print following the Liberation of Paris in 1944, becoming a major vehicle for the introduction of 'Existentialism' to the French reading public.[1] Two years later, Beauvoir published the more developed *The Ethics of Ambiguity*. In this same period she wrote and published numerous other works focused on ethical problems, including the essays 'Idéalisme moral et réalisme politique' and 'Eye for Eye', the novels, *The Blood of Others* and *All Men Are Mortal*, and the play, *Who Shall Die?*[2] These works are all closely related, and all provide examples of Beauvoir's fully-formed ethical thought.

Beauvoirian ethics has been highly influential in providing philosophical ballast for liberation movements, whose success is a salient feature of the decades following the Second World War. Her ethical theory also is remarkable philosophically for the extent to which it emerges, not from a basis of categorical premises or ad hoc position-taking, but rather as a logically coherent outgrowth of her ontology. Indeed, most of the facets of Beauvoir's philosophy examined in the preceding chapters form part of the derivation of her ethics. From her theory of consciousness she accounts for the origin of value. From her theories of embodiment and intersubjectivity she establishes the situational and social nature of freedom. And on the basis of these results, together with her theory of consciousness, including its two modes of intentionality, she develops her theory of social ethics. This chapter will examine these three sets of arguments.

The Origin of Value

In *Ethics: Inventing Right and Wrong*, J. L. Mackie notes the importance to modern ethics of 'the question whether values are or are not part of the fabric of the world'.[3] Philosophers who answer yes to this question are called 'cognitivists' because they attribute truth or falsity to judgements about values. Conversely, 'noncognitivists' hold that ethical terms are not descriptive, and that the propositions which contain them are therefore neither true nor false.[4] For the noncognitivists – and, like their opposite numbers they are an extremely diverse group – moral judgements are only recommendations or prescriptions or evocations or personal preferences or expressions of social conditioning. Beauvoir's ethics is distinguished by being situated in between these two positions. She locates this middle ground and the ethics which she builds on it directly in the fundamental categories of her ontology.

In *Pyrrhus and Cinéas*, when Beauvoir asserts that no values exist in the world of non-conscious being prior to consciousness putting them there, she is adopting, in part, the noncognitivist position. But the way she arrives at this view is very much her own. In the following passage, she considers what it would be like to be a non-conscious being:

> If I was only a thing myself, indeed nothing would concern me; if I shut myself in, the other is also shut off to me; the inert existence of things is separation and solitude. There exists no ready-made attachment between the world and me. And in so far as I am within nature a simple given, nothing is mine.[5]

Without consciousness there can be no concern, and therefore no value. How then do values come into existence through consciousness?

In *Pyrrhus and Cinéas* Beauvoir argues that values, like transcendence, are inevitable consequences of consciousness's intentionality. Consciousness, as a binary relation projected from a human body, requires objects, other beings, for its other term. Without something to be conscious *of*, consciousness does not exist. It is in this sense that every act of consciousness is said to begin as a *lack* of being, and every 'transcendence of the given' as 'defining the present as a lack'.[6] Beauvoir identifies this lack, including a lack of justification for one's existence, as the ultimate basis of desire: consciousness emerges continuously as the project of overcoming its lack, of obtaining being. Beauvoir's hypothesis is that this goal-directed, justification-seeking spontaneity universally characterizes consciousness. The objects of consciousness and the concrete goals comprising a person's project of being, however, are a matter of their individual situation and choice. Within the limits of its worldly situation, a consciousness is intrinsically free, and this freedom requires continuous choices between alternative objects and goals. Beauvoir's ethical starting point is that it is on the basis of such choices, born of the situated freedom of consciousnesses, that all values, including self-justification, emerge in the world.

Beauvoir describes the human 'project' and the lack that haunts it as follows:

> Because my subjectivity is not inertia, not a falling back upon itself, nor a separation, but on the contrary a movement towards the other [being], the indifference between the other and myself is abolished and I can call the other mine; the link that unites me to the other can only be created by me; I create it by the fact that I am not a thing but a project of myself towards the other, a transcendence ... I am not first a thing, but a spontaneity which desires, loves, wants, acts.[7]

This view of desire and value begs to be compared, (and Beauvoir herself makes this comparison), to the one which underpins the stylized notion of rationality, tendentiously called 'rational choice theory'. Although indigenous to economics, in recent decades this doctrine has colonized large parts of the social sciences and – as it is usually deployed – is a major sub-species of methodological individualism. On two separate accounts, Beauvoir's conception of desire and value reverses this currently influential mini-system of metaphysics. The latter conceives of the individual as possessed of an ordered set of desires or values, called 'preferences', and it labels an individual 'rational' or 'irrational' if her or his choices confirm or disconfirm this presumed ordering. Under this metaphysic, 'rational consumer choice', for example, is a euphemism for a kind of obedience to one's supposed essence, so that a person who takes this 'rational' approach to their self is an example of someone caught up in the bad faith of immanence. Beauvoir's view of humankind does not admit a distinction between preferences and choices. One can be 'irrational' in the sense of not choosing what people in authority would like other people to choose, or in the sense of miscalculating or misremembering the most efficient way to a goal, or in the sense of exercising one's freedom to make different choices at different points in time, but not in the sense of not choosing what one prefers. For Beauvoir, the last is both an ontological impossibility and a contradiction in terms.

Beauvoir's view of the nature of individual desires also reverses that of rational choice theory. The latter conceives of human beings primarily as objects, as receptors of sensations. Men and women are inclined to rise above this passive state only in so far as they hope to increase their pleasurable sensations and decrease their painful ones. In consequence, the universal goal is 'to have everything one wants', to exist in a state where every desire is satisfied, to abide in contented, heaven-like repose. Beauvoir takes the opposite view. She conceives of the human as active, as a spontaneity engaged ceaselessly in a project, as a being whose consciousness endlessly casts itself into the world toward something, as 'a transcendence which throws itself toward the future'. The sensations of pleasure are not experienced separately from a person's projected existence. Persons do not become radically different kinds of being when they experience enjoyment. For Beauvoir, 'All pleasure is project.'[8] She illustrates this principle as follows:

> the pause is relaxation after the fatiguing exercise; from the summit of the hill I view the path travelled and it is present in its entirety in the joy of my success, it is the walk which gives value to this rest, and my thirst which gives value to this glass of water.[9]

This argument leads to a more general point: it is not possible 'to separate the end from the project that defines it and recognize in it an inherent value'.[10] Against conventional belief, in her analysis of the structure of human consciousness, Beauvoir finds that: 'It is desire which creates the desirable, and the project which sets up the end.'[11] She accuses those who pretend that values exist in the world before and without human beings, as if values were there to be gathered like pebbles on the beach, of the bad faith of immanence, of being guilty of a 'false objectivity'. Similarly, she labels the opposite practice of trying 'to separate the project from the end and reduce it to a simple game' as 'false subjectivity'.[12]

Beauvoir emphasizes the significance her theory of desire holds for the conduct of political affairs, where the separation of ends from means, as postulated, for example, by the economist's sensationalist theory of desire, provides the rationalization in whose name most modern crimes against humanity have been and continue to be committed. In 'Idéalisme moral et réalisme politique', an essay from 1945, Beauvoir writes:

> that which it is necessary to understand is that end and means form an indissoluble totality; the end is defined by the means which receive from it their meaning, an action is a significant whole which deploys itself through the world, through time, and of which the unity can not be broken. It is this singular totality that it is a matter at each instant of constructing and choosing.[13]

For Beauvoir, although the projective nature of the human being is ontologically determined, the form the project takes is not. The goals and sub-goals by which lack of being is to be filled are neither given nor fixed. Out of consciousness's freedom, people create and choose their goals minute after minute, and it is through these choices, Beauvoir argues, that values are injected into the world. They are generated inexorably by the intentional structure of consciousness, by the way consciousness engages with the world, so that, in this sense, values are, like the lack or non-being which gives rise to them, objective and ever-present. Values are not an optional extra to be added to human existence. They are as much a part of the fabric of the world *one lives in* as the sun and the earth. This is the 'ambiguity' of the human condition: we exist simultaneously in the objective and the subjective, the one inseparable from the other.

'Freedom,' Beauvoir writes in *The Ethics of Ambiguity*, 'is the source from which all significations and all values spring. It is the original condition of all justification of existence.' By crediting human freedom as the source of all value, Beauvoir remarks that, in one sense, she 'carries on the ethical tradition of Kant, Fitche, and Hegel.' But she also notes that, in another sense, her analysis of freedom and value differs radically from that of her precursors. In setting out her ethics, she, unlike the philosophers she has listed, makes no false appeal to the universal. She remains faithful to her self-imposed injunction not to feign access to a universal point of view. Likewise, she reminds her reader that: 'Universal, absolute man exists nowhere.' In her ethics, she writes, 'it is not impersonal universal man who is the source of values, but the plurality of concrete, particular men [and women] projecting themselves toward their ends on the basis of situations whose particularity is as radical and as irreducible as subjectivity itself.'[14] Elizabeth Fallaize notes that in these circumstances,

'"Humanity" consists not of a totality aspiring to the same aim ... but of a mass of individuals each with his or her own freedom and aspirations.'[15] This generative structure for value is homologous to Beauvoir's theories of temporality and spaciality. We have noted Beauvoir's explanation of how human bodies engaged in projects act as shifting reference points around which physical space is organized. Here her argument is that an individual's engagement with the world also leads her or him to create ever-shifting fields of value.

In common with other existentialists, Beauvoir identifies the subject's non-self identity as giving rise to anxiety and, in turn, to the seeking of justification for their existence. This means establishing and embracing values. But, given that these values do not exist independently of human consciousness, it is Beauvoir's thesis that values come into being only through the projects which a person freely chooses. A freely adopted goal is itself a declaration of the existence of a value. This makes a person's values and, thereby, justification of their existence, ultimately dependent on their freedom. Beauvoir gives this as the reason why a person might choose to embrace their freedom rather than the bad faith of immanence. In any case, if freedom is the source of all values, and if a person values anything, then it follows that she values her freedom.

The Structure of Freedom

'Freedom' is a notoriously slippery word, especially in the hands of philosophers. Beauvoir embarked on a hazardous path when she developed an ethics in which freedom was the concept around which everything turns. That she succeeded in inventing an ethics of freedom which both triumphs over philosophical banality (and confusion) and finds wide relevance in human affairs, owes much to the care she took in theorizing its central concept. Three aspects of that theory need careful treatment here: freedom's situational nature; situations as more or less freedom enhancing; and the interdependence of consciousnesses.

From the early 1940s onward, Beauvoir emphasized the distinction between 'an abstract notion of freedom', one 'emptied of all content and all truth', and her concept of *freedom in situation*.[16] 'A man,' she writes in *Pyrrhus and Cinéas*, 'is simultaneously freedom and facticity; he is free, but not in the sense of that abstract freedom expounded by the Stoics; he is free in situation.'[17] This view that freedom, like physical area, is a two-dimensional phenomenon is central to Beauvoir's ethical and social thought.

On the one hand, everyone is originally free, in the sense that they always project themselves spontaneously into the world toward something through the intentionality of their consciousness. This is what Beauvoir calls 'the subjective and formal aspect' of freedom, because it follows from what she identified as the fundamental structure of consciousness.[18] But the Beauvoirian individual also is situated in a world of givens, including her own immanence. Her situation includes her past, her physical, historical and social place, her economic circumstances, her body and her objectification by others, both as a unique individual and as a member of various recognized categories. On one hand, it is *against* these givens that imagined ends are intended by a consciousness (for example, eating a piece of chocolate cake which is now on the plate) and, on the other, it is *by* these givens that ends are realized (for example, cutting and lifting a piece of the cake with a fork). It is this ability to change the given situation (getting the cake from the plate into one's mouth), rather than merely being able to dream of doing so, that Beauvoir means by 'freedom'.

The conception of the human being as project, as perpetual transcendence, is refreshingly immune to the excesses of utopianism. In terms of the Beauvoirian vision, a situation in which all desires are satisfied, in which all conditions are ideally perfect, is consistent only with death. Life requires dissatisfaction; success requires resistance. 'The resistance of the thing sustains the action of man as air sustains the flight of the dove.' Freedom becomes manifest as 'a movement of liberation' beyond something judged as limiting freedom itself.[19] Beauvoir's best state of affairs is not the apathy of contentment, or the perfection of paradise, but rather the exhilaration that comes when situations yield to wilful exertions of freedom, and when goals which have been reached appear as points of departure for new acts of surpassing and for new values:

> The creator leans upon anterior creations in order to create the possibility of new creations. His present project embraces the past and places confidence in the freedom to come, a confidence which is never disappointed. It discloses being at the end of a further disclosure. At each moment freedom is confirmed through all creation.[20]

By way of contrast Beauvoir considers the case of someone who persists in beating their fist against a stone wall. Here the individual's 'freedom exhausts itself in this useless gesture without succeeding in giving itself a content. It debases itself in a vain contingency.' The given situation, the stone wall, fails to destruct, so the person's project, with its chosen value and attempt at self-justification, collapses in on itself. This person would be well advised to choose a different goal. However, it is not uncommon for people to find themselves surrounded by stone walls, real and metaphorical, which have been erected by other people and which do not leave them the option of choosing other goals. Beauvoir considers their plight:

> In case his transcendence is cut off from his goal or there is no longer any hold on objects which might give it a valid content, his spontaneity is dissipated without founding anything. Then he may not justify his existence positively and he feels its contingency with wretched disgust.

Obviously, human situations vary greatly in terms of their congeniality to freedom in Beauvoir's sense. She calls a situation 'privileged' if it tends to permit a person to realize their goals indefinitely, and a situation one of 'oppression' if it cuts a person off from their goals.[21]

Beauvoir is especially interested in the part intersubjectivity plays in creating and sustaining situations of oppression between social groups. And her analysis of this aspect of intersubjectivity informs her work on women in *The Second Sex*, on the aged in *Old Age*, on race in *America Day by Day*, as well as major elements in her fiction. She identifies the subject–object relation between consciousnesses as the ontological foundation and generative basis of many socially asymmetrical situations. Members of oppressed object groups tend to internalize subject groups' negative objectification of them. But the intersubjective worlds conceived and described by Beauvoir which affect ethics extend much wider than this. Preconstituted spheres of intersubjectivity exist, where one finds 'realities which resist consciousness and possess their own laws'.[22] People are thrown into these worlds of *collective intentionality*, wherein social habits and social hierarchies have assigned values and meanings to various objects and groups of people. Beginning as a child, one 'emerges in a world filled with meanings which impose themselves'. Each value and each individual's values take on their meaning within these cultural fields of values. In this way, says Beauvoir, her 'situation is defined through its relation to the society to which I belong'.[23] Collective intentionality even extends to specifying what kinds of characteristics do and do not count in defining and evaluating an individual. And, whatever the criteria, an individual is defined by herself and by others in relation to other individuals whose identities also are determined relative to others.[24] We each exist, in part, as the ongoing product of this interdependence of subjectivities.

The Ethics of Ambiguity identifies an extreme but not uncommon situation of intersubjective oppression where collective intentionality has succeeded in 'mystifying' the member of the oppressed group to such a degree that 'his situation does not seem to him to be imposed by men, but to be immediately given by nature, by the gods, by the powers against whom revolt has no meaning'.[25] As Sonia Kruks explains, because the Beauvoirian subject is 'intrinsically intersubjective', this kind of 'oppression can permeate subjectivity to the point where consciousness itself becomes no more that a product of the oppressive situation', and, in this way, 'situations can become conditions that impose their meaning on the subject'.[26]

But Beauvoir's vision of intersubjectivity has an alternative side. We have been considering its less optimistic side, whereby individuals and groups, engaged as terms of the subject–object relation, struggle with one another for or concede subjective domination. This is the mode of *subjection* in intersubjective relations. But the reversibility of the subject–object relation's asymmetry entails the possibility of a second mode, one where the parties to the relation choose to treat each other and themselves both as subject and object, as equal freedoms which are simultaneously original sources of value and of meaning. Beauvoir calls this second mode of intersubjectivity, where the parties agree to alternate in serving as the subject and object terms, that of *reciprocity*. In *The Second Sex* she identifies 'exact reciprocity' as a situation where 'each is at once subject and object'.[27] Reciprocity pertains not only between individuals, and between groups (collective reciprocity), but also, as will be explained in the next section, between the individual and society and between groups and society (civic reciprocity). This second mode of intersubjectivity is a natural complement to Beauvoir's conception of freedom as situated and it assumes a central role in her social and ethical thought.

Historically, as Bob Stone notes in considering Beauvoir's ethics, it has been standard practice to view freedom as 'a sort of property or possession, that is, something I can *have* in isolation from everyone else'. Stone continues:

But for Beauvoir I am not related to my freedom as a thing is to its properties since I am not a thing; rather, I *exist* my freedom as my own constant self-transcendence of my 'properties.' Indeed it is this perpetual intentionality within and toward the world and others that decides what 'self' and 'other' are to be. Thus understood, freedom is inherently opened onto other people.[28]

Linda Singer also notes the importance and originality of Beauvoir's 'sense of a freedom which realizes itself in engagement with and for others'. Commenting on the tradition of treating freedom 'as a quality or attribute of persons, rather than relationships', she says that Beauvoir's 'rewriting has the effect of shifting the locus of freedom from that of isolated autonomous individuals to freedom emergent from a situation of relatedness and affinity'.[29]

Social Ethics

The traditional map of moral philosophy is as ordered as a French formal garden. The map neatly splits between deontological theories, which hold that certain formal rules of conduct should be followed regardless of their consequences, and teleological theories, which hold that the moral worth of an act must be judged by its consequences. Beauvoir's disbelief in the existence of universal categoricals would seem to place her with the teleologists, who come in two varieties, the egoists and the universalists, or, as they usually are called, the utilitarians. The egoists hold that one should always do what will promote one's own greatest good, whereas the universalists believe that one should obey those moral rules which will bring the greatest good to the greatest number of people. Both groups contain many and diverse notions of what constitutes 'good' or the moral end. Popular foundational notions of the good include that of the greatest balance of pleasurable sensations over painful ones, that of self-realization, that of knowledge or power, as well as various assortments of these.

What is so noteworthy about moral philosophy's traditional landscape is that there is no room in it for Beauvoirian ethics. That there is no place for a woman's ethics in a design laid out exclusively by men and produced by patriarchal societies scarcely qualifies as surprising. Yet the manner in which Beauvoir's ethical theory differs from those of her male counterparts is, although profound, not immediately obvious. When considering philosophical ethics, thinkers formed within patriarchy ethics, are conditioned to think of all human relations as originating in social solipsism or in the mode of subjection of intersubjectivity. Beauvoir's innovation was to develop an ethical discourse *founded* on the mode of reciprocity. One effect of this shift is to establish for ethics a domain free of the is/ought dichotomy. Beauvoir offers four arguments in support of respecting and promoting other people's freedom. Her arguments need to be explained on their own ground, to show how the ethical landscape they project differs from the traditional one.

The central thrust of Beauvoir's social ethics is that success in justifying and finding meaning for one's existence and in disclosing being is maximized in a world of free and equal individuals. 'Man can find a justification of his own existence only in the existence of other men.' Underpinning the whole of her case is her intersubjective hypothesis: 'The me–others relationship is as indissoluble as the subject–object relationship.'[30] The bare bones of her argument are as follows: we all rely on others for this justification and meaning and for the creation of cultural being; others can serve us in this way only to the extent that they are free; therefore, it is in our self-interest to guard and to promote the freedom of others. Beauvoir develops this case through the explication of four ways in which people's freedoms are reciprocal, that is, positively interdependent.

'A man alone in the world,' says Beauvoir in *Pyrrhus and Cinéas*, 'would be paralysed by the manifest vanity of all his goals.' To reduce and make bearable the contingency of one's existence requires the validation by others of one's projects. 'Only the freedom of others can make necessary my being. My essential need is therefore to have free men facing me.' Because the other person's freedom is the source of that valuation, one must value the other person's freedom in order for her valuations to be seen as significant. To deny the value of someone's freedom is to deny oneself the validation which that freedom might otherwise provide.[31]

Beauvoir carries this argument further and develops it into one for equality. She notes that we value the valuations of our peers more than the valuations of those who are not our peers. It is only one's equals who can truly appreciate and understand one's existence:

> Others can accompany my transcendence only if they are at the same point on the road as I. In order that our appeals [for justification] are not lost in the void, it is necessary to have near me men prepared to hear me; these men must be my peers.[32]

Therefore, it is in a person's self-interest to promote equality, to have free and equal subjects to valorize their existence. This principle not only holds obvious and radical implications for personal relations, but also extends, by way of the idea of the general interdependence of subjectivities, into the broadest social realms. For example, in denying women equal rights and opportunities, societies also deny most men the opportunity of sharing their lives with women whom they see as their equals. 'He would be liberated himself in their liberation,' notes Beauvoir of men in relation to women's freedom in *The Second Sex*, a work full of empirical detail regarding the material and social conditions which pertain to the project of obtaining freedom and equality for women. Similarly, Beauvoir's earlier *Pyrrhus and Cinéas* gives empirical content to her more general arguments for freedom and equality, especially by linking them with needs. 'For people I ask for health, knowledge, well-being, leisure so that their freedom is not consumed in fighting illness, ignorance, misery.' Similarly, doing violence to a person deprives us of their peership and, thereby, 'possibilities for expansion of our being'. Beauvoir's essay 'Eye for Eye' (1946) explores further the relation between violence and her ethical theory.[33]

Individuals also, argues Beauvoir, require the freedom of others if they are not to be devitalized by awareness of their individual finitude. A logical consequence of consciousness's intentionality is that the 'fact of transcendence precedes any end, any justification'. This is an elemental structure of human temporality which makes the justification of projects, beyond the satisfaction of basic biological needs, inherently problematic. If a project has no justification beyond itself, then its realization abolishes its justification. In 'the light of reflection, any human project seems absurd, because it only exists through the limits it assigns to itself.' For this reason 'A man alone in the world would be paralysed by the self-evident vanity of all his goals; he could not bear to live.'[34] Twentieth-century literature has made the negative existential consequences of this structure of consciousness one of its central themes. (*The Stranger* (1942), by Beauvoir's friend and sometime colleague, Albert Camus, is one celebrated example). Beauvoir, however, argues that the malaise which Camus and others document is allayed by an interlinking of the projects of free individuals across space and time. Women and men, she writes:

> are free and I am thrown into the world among these strange freedoms. I need them, because once I have surpassed my own

goals, my acts will fall back upon themselves inert, useless, if they are not carried by new projects towards a new future ... The movement of my transcendence appears vain to me as soon as I have transcended it; but if through others my transcendence prolongs itself always further than the project I presently form, I will never be able to surpass it. [35]

Beauvoir notes that a person's need for others to join them in their projects has practical implications.[36]

The other's freedom can do nothing for me unless my own goals can serve as his point of departure; it is by using the tool which I have invented that the other prolongs its existence; the scholar can only talk with men who have arrived at the same level of knowledge as himself ... I must therefore endeavour to create for all men situations which will enable them to accompany and surpass my transcendence. I need their freedom to be available to use me, to preserve me in surpassing me.[37]

Sonia Kruks notes that in *The Second Sex* Beauvoir extends her argument for the need for the interlinking of human projects to 'the perpetuation of the species', without which all linkage would cease. In this way Beauvoir sees 'the phenomenon of reproduction as ontologically founded'.[38]

Beauvoir identifies a reciprocity between the individual and civil society as another basis of personal freedom. In order for collective undertakings to have meaning, society must affirm at every opportunity the importance and even sacred character of its individual citizens, the dignity of each man, woman and child, taken one by one. 'This is what democratic societies understand,' writes Beauvoir, 'they strive to confirm citizens in the feeling of their individual value; the whole ceremonious apparatus of baptism, marriage, and burial is the collectivity's homage to the individual; and the rites of justice seek to manifest society's respect for each of its members considered in his particularity.' In return for being validated as 'a unique and irreducible value',[39] for having personal relations honoured, and for providing a framework in which freedom is secured, enhanced and celebrated, the individual offers reciprocation, ranging from extreme sacrifices in times of collective crises, to the daily consideration given to the well-being of one's immediate civic environment.

Having experienced the onslaught of fascism and watched the rise and spread of communist states, Beauvoir was especially sensitive to the perils of breaking the civic covenant between individuals and of the allure of the rhetoric of holistic union. Her play, *Who Shall Die?* (1945), addresses the question of what happens when people fail to observe civic reciprocity.

In Chapter 9 we noted that for Beauvoir the intentionality of consciousness has two modes: the desire to be and the desire to disclose being. The present chapter has considered three ways in which people's freedoms are reciprocal, that is, positively interdependent: first, through mutual validation; secondly, through the interlinking of projects; and thirdly, through civil society. Each of these pertains primarily to the mode of intentionality of the desire-to-be. But the fourth category of reciprocity relates fundamentally to the desire for disclosure of being. In *The Ethics of Ambiguity* Beauvoir identifies this mode of intentionality as our 'original type of attachment to being', but argues that in the confusion of life, the desire for disclosure is subsumed in the desire to be.[40] Or, as Debra Bergoffen usefully puts it, it is 'contextualized' in terms of the projects of the desire to be.[41] Beauvoir says that wanting freedom and desiring being 'are two aspects of a single reality. And whichever be the one under consideration, they both imply the bond of each man with all others'. Why? Because in a civilized world this being which consciousness desires is mostly humanly made. This is the case not just in a material or economic sense, but, more importantly, in cultural and interpersonal ones. We all live in worlds in which each object, even the moon and the stars, 'is penetrated with human meanings. It is a speaking world from which solicitations and appeals rise up'. One's own freedom, properly informed, wants freedom for others so that they can join in the creation of the being which consciousness desires. 'To will that there be being is also to will that there be men by and for whom the world is endowed with human significations. One can reveal the world only on a basis revealed by other men.' As Bergoffen notes, the 'desire of disclosure is also the ethical will of liberation'. As Beauvoir stresses, 'To want existence, to want to disclose the world, and to want men to be free are one and the same will.'[42]

In patriarchal societies men seek the domination of women. Such societies, by definition, make the mode of subjection of intersubjectivity their archetypal mode of human relations, that is, the one not only demanded between men and women, but also favoured generally. (The same point would hold, in principle, for matriarchal societies.) It seems wholly natural, therefore, that such a society's systems of and discourses on ethics should be predicated on the mode of subjection in human affairs. Indeed, it would be most unexpected for such societies to promote awareness of the nonessentiality upon which their ethical discourse was predicated, as this would call directly into question the fundamental relation upon which those societies depend for their continued existence. It is for these very plain reasons, that ethics, in Western philosophy, has consisted primarily of declaring limits to or rationalizing the subjection of one's fellow human beings.

Philosophical ethics is traditionally pursued as the study of systems of restraints on conduct. This negative outlook is well captured by J. L. Mackie, when after having surveyed 'the object of morality' as manifested by philosophers through the ages, he sums up his findings as follows:

> Protagoras, Hobbes, Hume and Warnock [G. L.] are all at least broadly in agreement about *the problem that morality is needed to solve*: limited resources and limited sympathies together generate both competition leading to conflict and an absence of what would be mutually beneficial cooperation.[43]

Of course, resources are limited. But, by itself, this fact generates competition neither more nor less than it does cooperation. No one contends that historically, as resources have become more generally plentiful, cooperation has superseded competition. The balance between these two responses to the existence of Others surely depends not on the quantity of resources, but rather on the relative emphasis which the society, including its philosophers, places on the two modes of intersubjectivity. How can sympathies between a society's members and factions not be in short supply if that society is founded on the mode of subjection in human relations?

Beauvoir disagrees fundamentally with her precursors 'about the problem that morality is needed to solve'. Without denying the need for restraints in patriarchal societies, she sees the ethical problem primarily as one of overcoming a particular kind of ignorance, one encouraged and protected by philosophers and teachers of philosophy who present the problem of morality only within the context of the mode of subjection or the subject–object mode of intersubjectivity. It is in this restricted context that ethical discourse meets the is/ought dichotomy – the logical impossibility of deriving an 'ought' or normative statement from a statement

199

of facts, or a fact from a normative statement. By calling attention to the possibility of the mode of reciprocity, Beauvoir, rather than saying that one 'should' behave in certain ways, seeks to show why it *is in fact* in one's self-interest to act in ways which are generally thought to be altruistic. 'The respect of the liberty of others is not an abstract rule: it is the first condition of the success of my effort.'[44] As Linda Singer notes, 'Freedom, on this view, finds in others not only obstacles, but also its sites of realization and recognition.'[45] It should be clear, by now, why Beauvoir's ethics have scarcely been recognized. The ethics of reciprocity are not to be found on 'official' maps of moral philosophy. Beauvoir's ethics have been excluded from the record not just because it is the invention of a woman, but also because it is a dangerous ethics, dangerous not only to several thousand years of philosophical tradition, but also to society as presently constituted. Just how much this is the case can be seen in the programmes for change she proposed in her two major works of applied ethics, *The Second Sex* and *Old Age*, and in her critiques of the ethical status quo which structure her late fiction.

Chapter 15
The Second Sex

With her passionate commitment to the principle that philosophy and experience were of a piece, Beauvoir was exceptionally well placed to provide ethical analysis of major human abuses which depended on fallacious deployment of the notions of subject and object, of embodiment, and of intersubjectivity. After the more general orientation of *Pyrrhus and Cinéas* and *The Ethics of Ambiguity*, Beauvoir put her philosophical discoveries to more practical use than any philosopher since the age of revolutions when the thought of Locke and Rousseau served as foundational sources for the rise of modern democracies. In this chapter we are going to examine the ways in which Beauvoir put her philosophy to work in the service of women.

The second sentence of *The Second Sex*, the twentieth century's classic and pivotal analysis of women's condition, consists of a prescient statement of just how annoying its contents were likely to be.[1] 'For a long time I have hesitated to write a book on women,' writes Beauvoir by way of introduction. 'The subject is irritating, especially to women, and it is not new.'[2] With these deft words, and with her characteristic lucidity, Beauvoir embarks on her monumental project of irritation on behalf of women, noting her own hesitant attitude at the prospect of her undertaking, and signalling her historical place in a debate which she is joining rather than initiating. It is also clear that the first reader to be irritated by what follows in the substance of the book is Beauvoir herself, whose disgust at the levels of imbecility and injustice her research into the condition of women throughout human history unearthed both tried her patience and prompted from her a philosophical and cultural response of such complexity that its intricacies are still not fully mapped. As Jo-Ann Pilardi demonstrates in her excellent recent study of the history of *The Second Sex*'s reception, Beauvoir's text is so rich and multifaceted that it has provoked a range of partial and variant responses, each in tune with the characteristic interests of its time. There is no reason to believe that this process has been completed. It is, quite obviously, one of those rare classic statements on the human condition whose power only grows as its many dimensions are discovered and interrogated. *The Second Sex* was received as a major publication from the first, and early responses to it ranged from personal attacks on Beauvoir for her unwomanliness to praise for its seriousness and stylistic excellence. Beauvoir's forthrightness about maternity as a cultural practice rather than a solely biological fact attracted particular attention amid the simplistic psychologizing of the anti-feminists of the 1950s. The obsession with sexual behaviour of the 1960s cited Beauvoir's book alongside *The Kinsey Report* as evidence on sexual practices. With the re-emergence of liberal feminism in the United States in the late 1960s and early 1970s, *The Second Sex* was claimed as a foundational text by key activist writers such as Kate Millett and Shulamith Firestone. In the 1980s and 1990s, the book has attracted distinguished philosophical commentators such as Michèle Le Doeuff, Monique Wittig and Judith Butler, who build on Beauvoir's work in significant ways, but also serious criticism by the new wave of feminist critics who have attacked the text for its reliance on Sartrean existentialist ideas, for its rational 'masculine' orientation (which is linked to its failure to glorify maternity in particular and feminine gender difference in general), for its insensitivity to class and cultural diversity, for its lack of celebration of the female body, and for a universalism unacceptable to those allied with postmodernist theory. *The Second Sex* has and continues to attract the kind of ferocious, productive debate which only characterizes texts of the utmost importance.[3]

The Second Sex needs to be read in the light of Beauvoir's literary-philosophical method. As ever, Beauvoir's philosophical arguments are grounded in lived experience: the distinction between the subjective and the objective is not simply elided, but rejected. And, given Beauvoir's strong conviction that history forms the central constituent element in the construction of experience, the historical research which so massively informs the project should be read as the collective voice of the culture which shapes possibilities for those individuals it assigns to the category of 'woman'. The point here is that the scholarship behind Beauvoir's writing, and her great care in recording the voices of the past in relation to women should be read somewhat differently than historical evidence is usually treated. For Beauvoir, history's voice is not dead but living. It produces effects which tend to allow or disallow given ethical and ontological possibilities. The philosophical effects of the dominant historical voice within a culture carry meanings which must be understood before they can be questioned.

The Second Sex is full of such voices speaking at, about and to women. Beauvoir orchestrates this historical and contemporary cacophony by means of a philosophical plan which pulls together arguments from the deep and repeatedly forgotten history of feminist thought and from elements in the work of Merleau-Ponty, Sartre, Lévi-Strauss, Husserl, Kierkegaard, and, especially, her revisionary view of Hegel, which support her own theories of situation, intersubjectivity and the Social Other. Before looking in some detail at the philosophical structure of the work, the complex personal genealogy which led Beauvoir to its composition demands consideration.

It is altogether fitting that the philosopher of ambiguity should give mixed accounts of the effects of her own experience as a woman. On one hand, in the Introduction to *The Second Sex*, she notes that 'if I wish to define myself, I must first of all say: "I am a woman"; on this truth must be based all further discussion.'[4] One recalls the importance of her gender position to the young Beauvoir: the need to find a career as an alternative to the socially propitious marriage her family could not secure; the importance of previous women philosophers to her ability to imagine herself in that role; the wish to be a female pioneer in a discipline which seemed to be the almost exclusive preserve of men. On the other hand, Beauvoir often makes statements in her autobiographies and interviews about the negligible effect of her sex on her life. A few examples of this tendency, which has attracted considerable criticism, and, at times, dismay among Beauvoir's most sympathetic readers, indicate her purpose in making these remarks. Beauvoir wrote all the volumes of her memoirs and gave most of her interviews *after* the publication of *The Second Sex*. When she writes or speaks of herself in these later contexts, which form part of the larger project of constructing a philosophy which is simultaneously a witnessing of experience, she does so with the arguments of *The Second Sex* fully formed as a strong portion of her intellectual background. Remarks on the lack of the impact of her sex on her life sometimes serve as illustrations of her own previous blindness to the obvious, sometimes glossed further by Beauvoir as indications of the subtle forms gender oppression may take.

One exchange of this type in an interview with Alice Schwarzer serves as an example of the strategies Beauvoir employs in analysing her own position while locking it into ideas regarding the position of women in general and the impact of history on women's possibilities. The question Schwarzer asks is a familiar one:

'You said in a commentary on *The Second Sex* that the problem of femininity had not touched you personally, and that you felt you were in a "highly impartial position." Did you mean that a woman can, as an individual, escape her feminine condition? On the professional level and in her relations with others?'

Beauvoir responds:

'Escape her condition as a woman? No! But actually I've been very lucky. I've escaped most of woman's bondages: maternity, the life of a housewife. Also in my day there were fewer women who pursued advanced studies. To have a postgraduate degree in philosophy was to be in a privileged position as a woman. I received immediate recognition from men – they were ready to accept friendship with a woman who had succeeded on their own level, because it was so exceptional. Now that many women are advanced students, men are afraid of losing their own status.'[5]

Beauvoir's answer to Schwarzer's question, one often put to her in various forms, centres on the way she slipped through a historical net, gaining her degree in philosophy when her token status as a pioneering woman was not yet felt as threatening by her male colleagues, and avoiding what she feels remain the unreconstructed aspects of feminine roles. This is not so much a statement of *personal* exceptionalism, as an account of being the fortunate beneficiary of particular *historical* circumstances which she, as an individual, embraced. This intense awareness of herself (and all individuals) as situated in history is typical of Beauvoir, and informs *The Second Sex* (and her later book, *Old Age*) in ways that are sometimes overlooked, but which must be kept in mind if the full implications of Beauvoir's social philosophy are to be understood.

The genesis of *The Second Sex* has its own deep history. Although the idea of a book on women was one which Beauvoir discussed with her friend and colleague Colette Audry, when they were both young teachers in Rouen in the 1930s, the project interested Audry rather than Beauvoir.[6] For her part, the young Beauvoir still resisted the need to insert herself into the category 'woman' at all. For example, when she suffered a diminution in her sense of purposefulness following the completion of her education and the beginning of her liaison with Sartre, she refused to attribute her distress and remorse to her female position. 'I had refused to be labelled "a child",' she writes, 'so now I did not think of myself as "a woman": I was *me*.' It is the older Beauvoir, writing her memoirs, who recognizes the particularly female aspect of her own youthful dilemma – that is, that women are not supposed to have individual lives, but, preferably, should accept a state of pure alterity which excludes positive experience. At the time, Beauvoir can only report that such an idea was alien to her, and that, therefore, the notion of feminism did not seem to apply to her circumstances, or to offer any means of understanding them. This is entirely in keeping with Beauvoir's view of the importance to her of her youthful sense of her own exceptionalism, which she, at times, stresses with respect to class and age as well as gender, and which she sees both as self-delusion and as a necessary fiction which made her violation of predetermined norms possible. Another example of this, pertinent to the origin of *The Second Sex*, occurs in Beauvoir's account of the enlargement of her circle of friends in the wake of existentialism's first post-Liberation success. She notes how she always regarded her and her women friends' problems as pertaining solely to individuals. The war made an immense impact on her ethical orientation. It taught her that cultural objectifications and definitions – she cites the overwhelming example of Jews and Aryans – are not incidental. The new women she meets, all over 40, have all lived as 'dependent persons'. She listens to their stories with interest while still feeling that their common position has nothing to do with hers.[7]

Beauvoir portrays her realization of the significance of her female status as a moment of awakening. Casting about for a project after the completion of *The Ethics of Ambiguity*, Beauvoir says that she wanted to write about herself. She realized that the first question she needed to address was the meaning of her position as a woman: at first she thought the question negligible. However, encouraged by Sartre to consider it further, the impact of her sex struck her as 'a revelation'. The astonishingly brief two years it took her to write her book about the female condition re-emphasized the centrality of her philosophy of intersubjectivity, and, she says, she considered *The Other, the Second* and *The Other Sex* as titles for the book, until Jacques Bost, Beauvoir's friend and lover, suggested the final title, *Le Deuxième Sexe.*[8]

As Beauvoir extended her analysis of the question of intersubjectivity with regard to sex and gender, various circumstances surrounding the composition of the book also need to be kept in mind. In 1946, when she started her research, she had, as has been noted, just completed *The Ethics of Ambiguity*, her most extended conventional treatment of ethics. The Second World War was only just over when the book was begun, and the war's impact in terms of Beauvoir's intellectual recognition of the force of history on the individual had been absorbed. In many ways, *The Second Sex* can be read as a product of the great euphoria which came with the Liberation of France, in which the imagined political and social possibilities for a new future were very much under discussion, not only among Beauvoir's close associates, but in Europe in general. The questions of religion and race were also very much on Beauvoir's mind: Paris had been shocked when the survivors of the Nazi death camps returned to haunt it; the first detailed knowledge of the Holocaust gave an urgency to finding new ways to address the question of the Other. Further, during the period of the composition of the book, Beauvoir was deeply immersed in an important love affair with the American author Nelson Algren, whose ideas about women were conventional. Beauvoir met Algren when she visited the United States for the first time in 1947, and she registers her disappointment with the lack of freedom shown by American women in the volume she wrote about her lecture tour of the United States, *America Day by Day*, which she produced simultaneously with *The Second Sex*. As we have noted, this book also contains long sections about the condition of black Americans, a topic much on her mind at the time and related to her contemporaneous friendship with the great black novelist, Richard Wright, which opened out Beauvoir's thought regarding intersubjectivity from that of individuals to that of social groups. It must be mentioned, too, that Beauvoir's relationship with Sartre was seriously under threat during the composition of her study of women because of his strong attachment to another woman: there was a real danger that the association between the two philosophers might end. All these factors feed into Beauvoir's analysis of women, which is also an analysis of herself. Finally, and in anticipation of her later, cognate work on the old, it is important to note that Beauvoir was increasingly aware of her own aging as she wrote the book.

The Second Sex, then, was written against a background composed of this concatenation of personal and historical exhaustion, shock, exhilaration and uncertainty. When viewed in this light its sharpness of focus and authority of argument are all the more impressive. The treatise shares a structure with *Old Age*, with each book moving through vast amounts of data on its topic. In both studies, Beauvoir begins with biology, moves through ethology and history, and takes in myth, legend and strategies of representation. Psychological formation and cultural practice are treated at great length in both volumes, while each ends with concluding sections which point the way out of the oppressive cultural formations that the books describe. In each case the purpose of the work is intellectually activist as well as historical and descriptive. The politics of each work, however, are of a particular order. It is not unfair to label these the politics of a philosopher who never separates experience from intellection, and whose investment in whatever matter is at hand is at once personal and impartial. What is definitely the case is that each volume is governed by a philosophical framework into which all aspects of the discussion fit. And while the detail in each volume has attracted sometimes hostile debate, it is the nature of the philosophical argument supporting the edifice of these texts which are most important for this study.[9]

Beauvoir first lays out this argument clearly and precisely in the introduction to *The Second Sex*. All her points contribute to defending the text's overarching principle, stated economically at the beginning of Book Two, that 'One is not born, but rather becomes a woman.'[10] She begins by asking the most fundamental of questions, 'what is a woman', after noting the continuing babel of questioning, exhortation and exasperation which surrounds the still extensive public discussion of the topic (a circumstance which has not altered in the nearly 60 years since *The Second Sex* was published). She cites a range of common definitions, each of which is rejected and each of which will receive extended treatment in the course of the book. The biological definition ('woman is a womb') is the first mentioned and found wanting. If biology was the sole or even main determinant of womanliness, there would be no need for further discussion: it would be redundant to persuade biological females to be women, and there would certainly be no justification for the common discussions of whether certain possessors of uteruses are women or not. Beauvoir then considers the notion of femininity as an essence, whether biological or Platonic. She cites the prevalence of this definition in the time of Aquinas and notes the semi-mystical penumbra which surrounds its invocation. In a comparative point, she argues that the biological and social sciences reject the notion of fixed essences, and uses the linked examples of Jews, black people and women as categories which must not be treated as consisting of fixed entities with unchanging characteristics. However, she also characteristically rejects the claims of those who hold positions which she characterizes as that 'of the enlightenment, of rationalism, of nominalism' who declare that 'woman' has nothing but the arbitrary meaning assigned to it, and that all human beings are the same.[11] This position, Beauvoir argues, is too abstract: it ignores individuals' concrete experiences and neglects to take into account the situation of specific women, unlike science, which is always alert to the impact of environment on the shaping of individuals' characteristics.

Before moving on to Beauvoir's own definition of woman, the implications of her opening statements need further comment. Firstly, by rejecting equally functionalist biological arguments focused on reproductive capacity as well as arguments based on vague and mysterious notions of 'the eternal feminine' as starting points, she clears the ground for her own definition, which is based on cultural practice. Secondly, her early citation of other groups who have suffered gravely from idealist definitions of fixed essences marks the potential of her method for use in other areas, such as the discussions of colonialism, race and age to which Beauvoir herself contributed. Finally, Beauvoir's last point must be noted closely, as her arguments in *The Second Sex* are sometimes dismissed for failing to recognize the difference between men and women, and for arguing for the collapse of the feminine into the more general category of the human, which, almost always, denotes only the masculine. This is, patently, not Beauvoir's argument, and the fact that it is not needs reiteration.

The next part of her argument indicates Beauvoir's awareness that her position might be misread in this way. After insisting that, if she wishes to define herself, she must begin by declaring she is a woman, she underlines the asymmetry of women's need to mark their gender position with men's lack of any need to do so. Men, she says, do not feel the need to declare their sex: the masculine is assumed to be so utterly primary that it is equated with the human, in an absolute sense. The feminine, in turn, is treated as deviant from the absolute human type, which is, by implication, always masculine. Beauvoir argues, anticipating points made by Hélène Cixous, that the terms in the binary oppositions which follow from this sexual polarity between male and female are not of equal value. They are 'without reciprocity', with the female 'representing only the negative', and, therefore, the not-quite-human, given the unspoken elision of the male and the human categories. Under this regime, women are associated with the emotive and the blindly biological, while men theorize and imagine their bodies as vehicles of direct, purposive connection to the world. Calling up the ghosts of Aristotle and Aquinas, and citing the Old Testament, Beauvoir glances at the history of the definition of women as 'lack', as 'defectiveness', as imperfection, as 'an "incidental" being'.[12] Beauvoir encapsulates her discussion in a crucial brief statement by arguing that man is regarded as the Absolute Subject, while woman is imagined as the inessential Other.[13] This is the philosophical formulation which Beauvoir intends to dismantle in the course of her treatise, and she has ready to hand the philosophical tools with which to do this in her concepts of subjection, reciprocity and situation which featured so strongly in *Pyrrhus and Cinéas* and *The Ethics of Ambiguity*.

How she means to proceed is illustrated by her remarks on Lévinas's essay 'Temps et l'Autre'. Beauvoir criticizes Lévinas's comments on the 'full flowing' of 'otherness' in the feminine, by remarking that this position is entirely governed by an unspoken masculine point of view, that woman, too, is possessed of consciousness and ego, and that alterity can only be discussed properly with attention to 'the reciprocity of subject and object'. While noting that the category of the Other is 'primordial' for human consciousness, and citing Hegel's argument that consciousness itself is hostile to all other consciousness (a position to which the Sartre of *Being and Nothingness* holds), Beauvoir goes on to emphasize the means by which the relativity of consciousness is made manifest in ways which counter the idea of the supremacy of the absolute subject. In her view, one aspect of human culture is a series of enactments of the reciprocity of consciousness. Travel, war, festivals, trade, diplomacy and contests among groups all work to strip both individuals and groups of illusions of absoluteness and to school them in the knowledge of the relativity of all human existence.[14]

Beauvoir's account of the interrelationship of consciousnesses as a fundamental part of their nature stresses the ontological position seen in her writing since the composition of *She Came To Stay* in the late 1930s. She now brings her theory of intersubjectivity into play in her analysis of the position of women. In this, her rejection of the idea of the Absolute Subject is of the first importance. Her alternative ontological starting point is, as Sonia Kruks puts it, the 'situated subject: a subject that is intrinsically intersubjective and embodied, thus always "interdependent" and permeable rather than walled'.[15] Further, this intrinsically intersubjective subject is always located in history, and it is to the history of women that Beauvoir now turns to explain why women, unlike possessors of other despised attributes (again she cites people of colour, the colonized and Jews as cognate examples of unjustly dominated groups), have submitted so quietly to their relegation to the category of absolute Other.

The answer to this question lies, argues Beauvoir, in women's history. Unlike the groups noted above, women have never formed a separate collectivity, and therefore possess no cultural memory of a time before domination. No single event can be remembered as the key to their subjugation. This is an interesting point, especially in the light of certain kinds of recent feminist attempts to exhume such a woman's past moment from the tangle of prehistory. Beauvoir, most pointedly, does not pursue this point (though she is highly interested in the representations of women which emerge from prehistory via myth and legend). Instead, she sees women's collective situation as most like that of the proletariat, where the oppressed and oppressor do not live as separate groups, but are intermingled and interdependent. The comparison, which, like Beauvoir's earlier analogies between women and other oppressed groups, is a traditional one for certain kinds of feminists, and it has been used often both before and after *The Second Sex*. It is useful to note that Beauvoir read Engels (whose analysis of women's history in *The Origin of the Family, Private Property, and the State* she criticizes later in the text), among others, in preparation for writing the book, and equally useful to recall that Beauvoir, like many leftist thinkers, believed for decades that improvement of women's position was secondary to, though inextricably linked with, the evolution of socialism. This was, in fact, the chief reason for her refusing the label of 'feminist' until 1971, a decision which followed her revised view that the key issues of socialism and those of feminism were separate.[16] The reasons for this shift, however, which she would not make in her private views for several decades, are already in play in the late 1940s in *The Second Sex*, where she articulates the differences between class and gender clearly.

The proletariat, she notes, is a historical phenomenon. It has not always existed, and, therefore, there is no reason to think it must persist. However, there have always been women: their femaleness is anatomical and physiological. And, as far as the human record knows, their subordination to men is not the result of an event. Instead it is apprehended as a condition, and, as such, is exempt from contingency and from other events which might overturn or modify it. Beauvoir does not let matters rest at this. In a point which is crucial to her argument she argues that 'the nature of things is no more immutably given, once for all, than is historical reality'. What is important, she says, emphasizing a point central both to her ontology and to her ethics since the late 1930s, is assuming the position of subject. Again, she insists that this position is intersubjective. Beauvoir does not say, as might be expected, that women must learn to say 'I': instead, she says, women must learn to say 'we'.[17] The precise kind of recognized historical intersubjectivity she has in mind is illustrated by the examples she gives of the success of groups which have been defined as subservient turning the tables on their oppressors: the proletariat in Russia; black people in Haiti; the Indo-Chinese who were currently fighting against French colonialism. These reversals have only been possible, argues Beauvoir, through each respective groups' members' transformed apprehension of themselves as subjects, of their communal refusal to be relegated to permanent subservience and non-reciprocal Otherness. In agreeing to say 'we', these groups transform their oppressors into 'Others', who can, therefore, be challenged. Action is dependent on this transformation in consciousness taking place.

Beauvoir's illustration of the linkage between consciousness of the self as simultaneously partaking of individual and social elements feeds directly into her analysis of the difficulties faced by women as a caste. And, especially because *The Second Sex* often attracts criticism for its individualist principles, it seems all the more important to note that Beauvoir sees women's lack of belonging to a recognizable social unit, which can define itself against a correlate but opposing social unit as one of women's chief difficulties. Women are not possessed of the kinds of historical experiences which tend to make for group identity: she says, bleakly, that women have 'no past, no history, no religion of their own'. Their various solidarities of class, race and religion align with those of the men to whom they are appended and not to women as a group. Further, argues Beauvoir, borrowing a term from Heidegger, men and women are bound together in 'a primordial *Mitsein*', a biologically fundamental and unbreakable togetherness.[18]

Woman's position as one half of the totality of this fundamental human *Mitsein*, which Beauvoir, giving her own strong emphasis to the commonality involved in such associations, treats as potentially advantageous to women precisely because of the shared nature of the totality formed by the component parts, could have worked to women's benefit. However, it most patently has not. To explain this circumstance, Beauvoir takes Hegel's master-slave dialectic as the starting point for her analysis. Although woman is not precisely in the position of slave to man (and, importantly, unlike Hegel's slave, she does not desire his destruction), she has, however, always been man's dependant. This dependency is ensured by society, which hampers her through legal, economic, educational and customary practice. Further, in such circumstances, to relinquish the one advantage seemingly granted by the culture – that is, men's protection, both economic and moral – is extremely difficult for women, who are left exposed on all sides by refusal of the traditional gendered bargain. The risks run by women who choose the subject position are both 'economic' and 'metaphysical', by which Beauvoir means the assumption of responsibility as both an economic and an ethical agent, each of which carries a high possibility of failure. It is, she says, easier to decline the bargain than to accept it, and, at times, because of the cultural and material constrictions noted above, it is impossible for women to even attempt to choose the status of subject. Beauvoir held to this position fiercely throughout her life, stressing particularly the need for economic independence for women as a condition of their assumption of full status as a subject.[19] Many women, however, cannot or will not avoid this primary kind of concrete dependency. Woman accepts her definition as the Other for three main reasons, thinks Beauvoir: her lack of resources; the *Mitsein* which binds her to man under even disadvantageous terms; and, most disturbingly, because she may actively enjoy and embrace her definition as the Other.[20]

Discouraging, although powerful, as Beauvoir's analysis is, she nevertheless points to the slow change occurring in women's condition. Digging again into the history of the philosophical and political discussion for the origins of woman's relegation to the disempowered position in the duality of the sexes, she argues that men's explanations of women's inferiority must be suspect. She turns here, as she does at many points in the book, to statements by women to support her case. And it must be emphasized that Beauvoir's text is full of the voices of women who are her predecessors and contemporaries, from Mary Wollstonecraft to Susan B. Anthony, from Mme de Sta'l to Virginia Woolf. At this point, she lets the seventeenth-century feminist, Poulain de la Barre, carry the argument about men's lack of disinterestedness in putting women's case.[21] Concurring with de la Barre's point, Beauvoir returns again to the list of culturally significant forces which have been ranged against women. From legend to the law, from religion to science, from philosophy to literature, all have participated enthusiastically in the subordination and objectivization of women.

It was only in the eighteenth and nineteenth centuries, says Beauvoir, that things begin to shift. She links this slow change explicitly to changes in economic conditions attendant on the industrial revolution which brought increasing numbers of women into the labour market. Concurrently, the rise of democratic ideology led a few men to challenge traditional hostile views of women (Beauvoir mentions Diderot and John Stuart Mill as two of these honourable exceptions). As with nineteenth-century racist theorists, the anti-feminists of this period used the most prestigious discourses of the day – in this case the new sciences and social sciences – to promote the notion of separate 'equalities' for male and female. Beauvoir reads the formulation 'equal but separate' as wholly pernicious, and as the basis for justifying extreme discrimination. Again, her cognate cases are those of the Jews and of people of colour. Her antagonism to this position is ontological. By positing separate essences for despised groups, members of those groups appear to be fixed in the historical (and thus alterable) characteristics of inferiority which pertain at the time of definition. The Hegelian sense of the verb 'to be' loses its dynamic properties which denote possibilities of change, and instead takes on an idealist cast. The importance of situation to social conditions is forgotten, and alterity, instead of being understood as a fluctuating reciprocal property of intersubjectivity, is assigned as an essence to the oppressed group.

In all this, Beauvoir deploys her revised Hegelian ideas *contra* Hegel, noting that Hegel, like St Paul, Lenin and Nietzsche, stands with the enemies of women's equality.[22] Further, she outlines precisely what men have to lose in abandoning the conventional illusion of women's essential alterity. If women are no longer automatically defined as the Other, the assumption of the position of subject becomes all the more difficult for men. For men who fear their own powerlessness, the loss of automatic inferiors augments their terror. However, if men have (generally suspect) things to lose by recognizing women as subjects, they also have a good deal to gain. First, and this is very much a philosopher's point, logical consistency will be served. Democratic ideas so infuse modern thought that the very postulation of unequal groups is troubling. Men of the democratic era, argues Beauvoir, no longer postulate women as inferior, and the logical inconsistency in treating women as the Other makes less and less sense within the dominant political and ideological framework. Difficulties here reside in covert male defence of masculine privilege, which is often not even perceived as such. Beauvoir gives the example of women's general difficulty in entering the professions being taken by men as a sign of natural sexual inferiority with no regard to investigating other reasons why this case should pertain. Subordination, she says, takes subtle forms: differences which appear unimportant can have far-reaching effects. Only woman can fully understand her own situation. She must cultivate the ability to disregard male accounts of her position, whether these take the form of violent attack or suspect praise of feminine difference. Equally, she notes, feminist interventions have often proved counterproductive, and allowed men to turn the question of woman's status into useless quarrels. In a move which echoes that of each new wave of feminist thought, Beauvoir declares the language of previous discussions of the issue hopelessly corrupt. She wants to clear the ground, to start afresh.

This is, as she immediately admits, impossible. The best that can be done, she says, is to listen to the accounts given of their situations by women who have transcended some of the limitations imposed on their caste, and who may be in a position to speak with some impartiality. It is difficult to say whether Beauvoir is simply trying to hearten herself and her readers when she announces that as women, 'by and large we have won the game'. Ever historically alert, she points to the importance of the United Nations' positive view of the increase in women's equality, and she points, as well, to the achievement of a group of women, in which she includes herself, who have not had to find their femininity 'an inconvenience or an obstacle'. Following her own argument, she declares herself a member of a female collectivity which possesses an identity, which can say the word 'we', and which has a responsibility to help its 'younger sisters' think with 'clarity and understanding' about the future.[23]

Typically, with her developed theories of ambiguity and uncertainty brought into play once again, Beauvoir immediately critiques her own argument. While noting the emergence of a group of women who can practise impartiality, she then denies the possibility of discussing the position of woman, or any human question, free from bias, and she goes on succinctly to state her own. Any objective discussion, she notes, 'implies an ethical background'. The ethics of *The Second Sex*, she says, implies a society in which the public good is defined in terms of the creation of institutions which promote concrete opportunities for individuals. Her definition is situational and materialist in orientation, and she pointedly discards the romantic notion of 'happiness' from her ethics. Happiness, she says, is a matter for individual consciousness alone, and it has been used too frequently to justify vested interests to serve as a useful principle in ascertaining the public good. The 'existentialist ethics', which she declares the underlying ethical ground of her text, takes liberty as its foundational value. The self-transcending subject, moving from the facticity of immanence to the responsibility of pursuing 'freely chosen projects' provides the model for agency on which Beauvoir's ethics is based. To simply accede to the given, to refuse liberty is to be lost in 'absolute evil'.[24]

With this ethical judgement in mind, Beauvoir turns again to her sensitivity to woman's situation. Beauvoir emphasizes the fact that woman is driven not only by the shared human ontological desire to regard herself as a subject, but also by the elements of ideological and material *compulsion* which equally form part of her situation, and which are designed to force her to accept her definition as the Other. In addition, when Beauvoir's principle of the intersubjective nature of subjectivity is applied to this text, her stated project of analysing women's possibilities in terms of liberty rather than happiness is one which is necessarily undertaken on behalf of and, in some sense, in concert with, the collective 'we' of women who, along with Beauvoir, reject definition as absolute Other.[25] Significantly, Beauvoir completes her map of the territory she is investigating with a philosophically exact gesture of solidarity with her chosen group as she inserts her own 'I' into the collective 'we' and 'they' of women in general as she reaches toward futurity.

The argument which has just been outlined represents the philosophical core of *The Second Sex*, with the detailed material presented at great length in the text serving as an exhaustive fleshing out of these principles. The vastness the text demanded was a surprise to Beauvoir, who did not expect such a massive result from her research on women. That research was, she said, a 'journey into history', from which she returned confirmed in her material principles, convinced that the history of woman was bound up with that of 'inheritance' and was 'a by-product of the economic evolution of the masculine world'.[26] This conclusion made her look at the world afresh, and Beauvoir's own sense of astonished discovery of an unperceived aspect of the familiar world is one reason for the text's energy. *The Second Sex* is one of that handful of books which tends to be a revelation for its readers: it served, first of all, as a revelation for its author, who provides it with a rigorous argument of great force and supports it with a wealth of detail from an encyclopaedic range of sources.

In the third volume of her memoirs, *Force of Circumstance*, Beauvoir provides a narrative account of the reception of the book which itself is designed to underline the contentiousness of her production and to shadow its main arguments. She notes its phenomenal initial success as an economic commodity. This is important in the light of her key argument in the volume (one she reiterated repeatedly in interviews throughout her life) that women can only assume the status of subject from a position of economic independence. Next, she foregrounds comments made to her about her courage in writing the book, an attitude which, she says, did not cross her mind as necessary when writing the book, but one well in keeping with the account she gives of women who challenge their relegation to the position of the Other. And, while she implicitly ranges the men associated with *Les Temps Modernes*, in which lengthy extracts from the book first appeared, along with Diderot and John Stuart Mill as males who were friendly to the emancipation of women, and who therefore welcomed her book, she stresses the outraged attacks her work attracted from others. In a famous sentence she lists the personalized attributes which informed these attacks: 'unsatisfied, frigid, priapic, nymphomaniac, lesbian, a hundred times aborted, I was everything, even an unmarried mother.'[27] Beauvoir's tactics in this narrative continue her drive to refuse a divide between her life and her philosophy, between abstraction and experience. The differences in men's responses to *The Second Sex* points again to the ideological rather than natural status of the ascription of the place of the Other by men to women. The insults she records illustrate the invocation of biologistic factors as the determining ones in the oppressive definition of woman as simply body (in this case, body gone wrong) as opposed to man's intellect. She rehearses the logical inconsistencies in the attacks on her work ('women had always been the equal of men, they were forever doomed to be their inferiors'[28]) in illustration of a main point in *The Second Sex* of the inconsistency of masculine accounts of women, with their sole constant being women's position at the inferior pole of the binary opposition of gender. Noting the hostility of both the Catholic Church (which put the book on its blacklist) and the Communist Party, Beauvoir illustrates the unified endeavour of institutionalized religion and politics, left and right, in insisting on women's subservience. By gracefully citing Colette Audry's published defence of the book, she makes a reciprocal gesture of solidarity to the woman who had first proposed the project and who belongs to that group of privileged women, of which they are both members, who make up the nucleus of the identifiable group to which women can belong. After again insisting on the uselessness of a feminism which does not address the need for a revolution in the position of women in economic production, she records her pleasure in the enormous, if sometimes disturbed response she has received from women readers.

Finally, Beauvoir ends where she began *The Second Sex*, with irritation, but this time an irritation overcome in finding in women her 'most serious public'. In overcoming this highly damaging, but typical part of women's condition which leads even other women to consider members of their own sex as inferior, Beauvoir again uses herself as an illustration of the processes she philosophically analyses in *The Second Sex*. Further, and more generally, her work on women, she says, helped to keep her attuned to the real and saved her from the philosopher's vice of 'drifting in the universal'.[29]

It is, indeed, Beauvoir's short-circuiting of the universalism permeating the Cartesian mind–body split through her insistence that consciousness and material existence are indivisible, and the ways in which she employs her concept of the situatedness of the subject in *The Second Sex* which provide the basis for some of the most vibrant recent work on gender. Two key recent writers provide examples of the continuing impact of Beauvoir's declaration that 'One is not born, but rather becomes a woman'.

In 1981, Monique Wittig's essay, 'One is Not Born A Woman', took Beauvoir's insistence that 'woman' was a cultural rather than a natural category as the starting point for a powerful argument for the privileging of lesbian society which might work to escape the hierarchical master/ slave dichotomy inherent in the persistence of the political categories of 'women' and 'men'. Wittig's influential essay provides one of the landmarks in the current flourishing of Queer Theory and her impassioned call for the dissolution of the myth of universal 'woman' while working against the pernicious hierarchical social relationship which the collective classification as 'women' means. While stressing the effects on consciousness of belonging to the 'class' designated as 'women' for any individual subject who is defined within that class, Wittig argues the case for the exemplary practice of the lesbian as an 'escapee' from binary concepts of gender politics, who are well-placed to work for the destruction of the social system of heterosexuality which has proved so destructive for its female members.[30]

Judith Butler, the most eloquent and influential of the current inheritors of Beauvoir's work in *The Second Sex*, also grounds her writing in Beauvoir's distinction between sex and gender. Like Wittig, she stresses Beauvoir's point that gender is not a natural but a cultural phenomenon. She powerfully reformulated Beauvoir's point in 1986 in 'Sex and Gender in Simone de Beauvoir's *Second Sex*' with her statement that 'all gender is, by definition, unnatural' with its corollary that, if this is the case, the body must be seen as 'a field of cultural possibilities',[31] which is open to any number of interpretations which provide escape from gender polarities. In the intense recent debates on gender identity and embodiment, Butler takes Beauvoir's ideas to their radical consequences by stressing the completely conventional (and therefore transformable) nature of the link between sex and gender. In her major work, *Gender Trouble: Feminism and the Subversion of Identity*, Butler grounds her own view of the contingent and active nature of gender as performance, activity, or becoming in Beauvoir's philosophical principles. (And Butler argues that Wittig has misread Beauvoir in that she has elided distinction between sex and gender, and that, further, unlike Beauvoir, she mistakenly places the lesbian outside gender categories. Most importantly, Butler rejects Wittig's instatement of the lesbian as a discrete category, as this requires equally fixed heterosexual categories to sustain the definition.) Butler's own programme is to promote individuals' possibilities for cultural and social agency by reconceptualizing gender politics in terms that reject notions of static, gendered selves, in favour of understanding the subject as 'a point of agency'.[32] Butler argues that the most effective gender politics support the proliferation of possibilities generated by (rather than identification within) the material structures of signification. Gender does not provide identity, but a repertoire of actions which can be performed subversively. The proliferation of subversive gender acts can, she argues, break down the divide between the self and the Other in precisely the ways suggested by Beauvoir. Butler emphasizes the bodily fissuring of the signs of gender in ways which call attention to its unnatural and therefore political status.

It is important to note that these writers working on the question of women in the tradition initiated by Beauvoir, are not writing solely as academics, or theoreticians, but as intellectuals who have regard for the application of the ethics their thought invokes. Both Butler and Wittig end with philosophically informed calls to political action with regard to gender which can only be of the greatest benefit to women. In this, they are entirely faithful to *The Second Sex* and to Beauvoir's ethical programme on behalf of the half of humankind she refused to define as Other.

Chapter 16
The Second Sex and the Genre Trap

One of the commonplaces of the reception of Simone de Beauvoir's most famous work is to note that, as a text, *The Second Sex* is an anomaly. It does not fit easily into pre-existing bibliographic genres, nor can it be smoothly placed within previously extant classes of intellectual discourse. The many hundreds of essays written about Beauvoir's most influential work themselves illustrate the ways in which her text exceeds, slides around and generally defies boundaries proposed to summarize or describe it. It is, from one point of view, simply an intellectual pleasure to witness the ways in which *The Second Sex* has stimulated discussion in phenomenology, ethics, ontology, sexuality, biology, sociology, politics, history, myth, anthropology, literature and the developments in the second half of the twentieth century both in feminism and in women's studies. The variety and richness of this range of possible ways in which *The Second Sex* can productively be considered, as well as its decided tendency to slip over and around established intellectual categories and genre borders, has led to recent suggestions that it might best be read as a postmodern work. This is an interesting, if anachronistic suggestion, and part of this essay addresses the impetus behind such suggestions. *The Second Sex's* characteristic defiance of category and genre definition is an aspect of the text which intrigues and sometimes perplexes Beauvoir's readers. And, while there is no doubt that *The Second Sex* can be read and is being read in fascinating ways within the confines of a variety of conventional discursive practices, it also seems to us the case that no such reading is completely satisfying as a starting point for understanding the work. What we are interested in examining here are the reasons why Beauvoir did not securely locate *The Second Sex* within the recognized confines of an established field of discourse, and how her refusal to do so is a remarkable part of her compositional and intellectual strategy for the book. Indeed, the power of *The Second Sex* owes much to the fact that it was constructed so that it would have no 'proper' place in the existing scheme of things, thereby allowing it to exist in a space of its own, outside the parameters of masculinist discourse. Beauvoir was so successful at this that, over half a century later, her great work still resists easy categorization.

Precisely why Beauvoir utilized this strategy for *The Second Sex* demands careful attention. For it would have been simple for her to privilege one of the many discourses which already filter through her massive work as the primary governing discourse of the undertaking as a whole. For example, any number of the social sciences could have provided her with a grid for her analysis. Economics, sociology, anthropology or psychology could each have presented recognized categories into which she comfortably could have inserted her study of woman. Equally, the philosophical essay, encompassing epistemology, ethics, political philosophy and her own existentialism, could have provided the determining category for the whole of the work. The arts, too, and some of the varieties of criticism of the arts – especially literary criticism – inform such large portions of the text that these categories of discourse could also have served as the fundamental matrix for the work. Theology offered another route, as did biology, as did study of the law. Finally, the principles of history, or of its rather more literary subgenre, autobiography, could have provided the generic rules to govern Beauvoir's production. From another point of view, Beauvoir could have utilized one variety of ideological commitment, one version of a metadiscourse, to organize her study of women. Marxism was available to her for this purpose, as was psychoanalysis, as was a variety of humanism which has proved particularly influential in the course of French intellectual history. All of these categories, discourses, intellectual orientations and proclivities do feature in *The Second Sex* to a greater or lesser extent. Each has caught the eye of commentators who at times have been frustrated to find that the seam of the particular discourse they trace in the text leads to anomalies, gaps, insufficiencies. There *is* no essential seam of discourse in *The Second Sex*, and the fact that this is the case is crucial for Beauvoir's success.

Equally, there is a range of previous texts which clearly and deeply inform Beauvoir's own undertaking. Gunnar Myrdal's *American Dilemma* suggested profound analogies between the oppression connected with race and that connected with sex. Engels' *The Origin of the Family, Private Property, and the State* provided a base for Beauvoir's analysis of the economic condition of women. Mary Wollstonecraft's *Vindication of the Rights of Woman* and Virginia Woolf's *A Room of One's Own* offered useful templates for the consideration of the general circumstances of women, and patterns for polemic attacks on sexual abuse, as much as the autobiographies of women such as Colette Audry and Marie Bashkirtseff provide instances and ideas which govern various moments in the text. Beauvoir's interest in Hélène Deutsche's work on the psychology of women is evident throughout the production. The work of Hegel and Heidegger, Merleau-Ponty and Sartre, Lévi-Strauss and Lévinas is fed into Beauvoir's mix in a variety of interesting ways. And these examples only constitute a small sample of the categories of discourse and influential individual instances of practice that thread through *The Second Sex* and contribute to its dazzling and kaleidoscopic intellectual effect. Yet despite the omnivorousness of *The Second Sex* in drawing on established perspectives and ideas from extant genres and discourses, and its admirable generosity in naming its sources and pointing out the items Beauvoir considers of value, even in the theories she finds most in need of rejection, the text is delimited by none of its intellectual precursors and partial prototypes. This, in the end, is crucial given the nature of Beauvoir's project which is not to define woman, but to eloquently, even exhaustively, *refuse* to offer such a definition, while demonstrating the inadequacy and misguidedness of earlier attempts to provide such a definition. *The Second Sex*, one of the greatest landmark works of the twentieth century, might best be seen as a considered refusal of definitions, categories, genres. And this refusal moves the text onto very interesting intellectual terrain indeed.

Famously, Beauvoir begins *The Second Sex* by drawing attention to the primacy for her project of the need to address the question 'What is a woman?' What she then does, for two volumes, is to present the case for the inappropriateness, indeed the proven capacity for harm implied in the answers which have been given to this question, a question that it is the primary task of her own work to totally disallow. 'Woman,' she says, radically rejecting, then revising the terms of the question, 'is not a completed reality, but rather a becoming' (Beauvoir 1989, p. 34). Woman, as object, as essence, does not exist. Woman, as much as man, is always situated. Given Beauvoir's location of her own position in the existential lineage, one would scarcely expect her to do anything but repeatedly refuse the legitimacy of such a question as 'What is a woman?' And it is with this refusal in mind that any analysis of *The Second Sex* must rightly begin. However, it also is the case, and this too must be emphasized, that *The Second Sex* identifies as a determining part of the situation of women, the shifting *concept* of woman, which has always been part of the ideological equipment of patriarchy. And it is the history and uses of that *concept* which is Beauvoir's chief concern in *The Second Sex*. Indeed, it is most productive to read *The Second Sex* as a vast tract of conceptual analysis: one addressed not primarily to the history of the *condition* of woman, but to the history of the *concept* of woman, one which explicates the form and use of this concept in a myriad discourses and texts, and describes the application of the concept in a enormous range of lived situations. The text's arguments and case studies provide its own kind of attentive conceptual guide for finding ways through the masculinist minefields littering intellectual and cultural space.

The Second Sex stands as testimony to what a stupendously difficult task this is. Brilliantly and subtly Beauvoir gives example after example of what traps exist for the unwary, of how easy it is to collude, sometimes unsuspectingly, with concepts of woman which fail to register her situatedness and subjectivity. Consider the beginning of *The Second Sex*, where Beauvoir introduces the key idea of the Other as a way of explicating patriarchal concepts of women. This is the first of many ideas and discourses which *The Second Sex* appropriates and brings to bear on constructing its case for refusing the question 'What is a woman?' The way Beauvoir introduces the concept of the Other typifies the method she uses throughout the book for utilizing previous thought and fields of intellectual enquiry. After citing a passage from Lévinas, which ends 'otherness reaches its full flowering in the feminine, a term of the same rank as consciousness but of opposite meaning', Beauvoir says:

> I suppose that Lévinas does not forget that woman, too, is aware of her own consciousness, or ego. But it is striking that he deliberately takes *a man's point of view, disregarding the reciprocity of subject and object*. When he writes that woman is mystery, he implies that she is mystery for man. Thus *his description*, which is intended to be objective, *is in fact an assertion of masculine privilege*. (Beauvoir 1989, p. xxii, emphasis added)

Beauvoir is doing two things here. She is making reciprocity of subject and object part of the concept of the Other, and she also is providing an example of how the *concept of woman* contaminates, like a tasteless, colourless, odourless poison, important intellectual endeavours, thereby forming a strategic part of women's situation. And this is especially so for intellectual women, whose tools must be gathered from the history of ideas, and who therefore must work with traditions which are universally tainted by concepts of woman based on fallacious definitional premises which objectify woman as an essence and which disguise masculinist perspectives as universal.

As Beauvoir moves patiently through the taxonomy of discourses which have addressed the question 'What is a woman?' she puts each selected tradition and genre through a process of decontamination, whereby masculinist points of view are relativized and historicized. The category of 'woman' is treated throughout as a cultural creation, a theoretical entity which despite referring to a nonexistent set, is integral to traditional areas of thought and which has effects which can be historically traced.

This difficult to maintain distinction between 'woman' as disallowed concept and the harmful effects that this fallacious concept has nevertheless had in the world, is the reason why Beauvoir defines her own project in *The Second Sex* without direct reliance on existing discourses. Instead she treats her project as *autonomous*. It is also the reason for her rather weary and exasperated emphasis on the libraries of volumes written on the topic of woman which, she notes, 'have done little to illuminate the problem' (Beauvoir 1989, p. xix). Beauvoir is, indeed, striking out on her own. And while it is the case that she draws upon the ideas of many thinkers from numerous fields, she does so only in so far as they are consistent with her project's autonomy, and she is always ready to give new significance and new interpretations to their facts and conclusions. For example, Beauvoir's opening chapter on biology, justly famous for its convincing conclusion that woman does not have a physiological destiny, should also be prized as an example of Beauvoir's method and audacity. On the face of it, biology, especially for a non-biologist, appears one of the least promising fields for winning a major dispute. But Beauvoir's strategy is already suggested by her chapter's title: 'The Data of Biology' ('Les données de la biologie'), which implicitly distinguishes between biology and the facts which underpin it. Beauvoir clearly distinguishes the difference between the uninterpreted data gathered for use by biologists and the significance which those biologists, and, by extension, society generally, assigns to the biological data. She is also concerned to stress that it is the questions asked by biologists that influence the decisions as to which data to collect as well as the ways in which it will subsequently be explained. Beauvoir's concern is with biological data pertaining to women, and this she sets about disentangling from the significance assigned to it by masculinist science. Once these two realms – the data of biology and its masculinist interpretations – are untangled, new interpretations and significance can be elicited from the facts. Indeed, the gathering of new or other facts might be required under the pressure of different hypotheses. It is not Beauvoir's business in *The Second Sex* to give those alternative interpretations for each of the fields she patiently disentangles from this kind of error (a circumstance which has and continues to annoy some of her most enthusiastic readers but which is altogether in keeping with her project). She shows, over and over again, how the conceptual gives shape to the empirical, how the imaginary and the mythical are predicated upon and formed by prior concepts, how the illusion of objectification produced by the concept of woman (no matter how intellectually bankrupt a concept) not only skews thought but produces real and deleterious effects which can govern and seduce even those who are harmfully subsumed in that definition. As Beauvoir notes, in man's hands 'masculine reasoning becomes an underhand form of force' because 'he has himself chosen the premises on which his rigorous deductions depend'. (Beauvoir 1989, pp. 623–4).

A few more examples will further illustrate this overriding strategy. Notably, the history section of *The Second Sex* offers not the history of women, but rather the history of the idea of 'woman' as conceived and enforced by men through the ages. Beginning with Aristotle, it surveys the various forms which major writers of different periods have given to the notion of 'woman'. But the primary focus of the history section is on how the concept of woman was codified in legal systems from the ancient Egyptians onwards. Beauvoir's brief survey of the history of woman repeatedly identifies the path from concept to law to institutionalized situation as the determining one. Once 'the patriarchate was definitely established,' she writes, 'the males were to write the codes', thereby 'setting up the machinery of woman's oppression' (Beauvoir 1989, p. 79).

The evidence of history is of great interest to Beauvoir in *The Second Sex*, but it is to the part played by the patriarchal notion of woman in myth, including religion and literature, to which the first volume of the text devotes the most attention. '[W]oman sees herself and makes her choices,' writes Beauvoir, 'as man defines her.' It is necessary, therefore, she continues, 'to describe woman such as men have fancied her in their dreams, for what-in-men's-eyes-she-seems-to-be is one of the necessary factors in her real situation.' (Beauvoir 1989, p. 138). Indeed, Beauvoir regards the concept of 'woman' when embodied in myth as perhaps even more determining of women's situation than when encoded in law. As a novelist she appreciates just how insidious, beguiling and invasive of individual and social consciousness ideas can be when veiled in inspiring or entertaining stories. Furthermore, she finds the concept of woman most resistant to critique and change when it appears in the guise of mythical thought. Then the 'contrary facts of experience,' she says, 'are impotent against the myth [of woman]', because it projects the 'contingent, and multiple existences of actual women' 'into the realm of Platonic ideas'. There the patriarchal idea of woman 'is indisputable because it is beyond the given: it is endowed with absolute truth' (Beauvoir 1989, p. 253).

While the first volume of *The Second Sex* magisterially exposes the masculinist concepts governing even the discourses, perspectives and theories which might be considered most congenial to her project (and here one might mention Beauvoir's oppositional treatment of both Marxism and Freudianism), the second and longer volume of the work looks at the ways in which the concept of woman operates as a part of woman's situation. The point that it is again the impact of the *concept* of woman that is the focus of Beauvoir's analysis always needs to be kept in mind as she builds her detailed account of the meanings given at every stage and regarding every aspect of the life course of women. Beauvoir not only continues her work of decontamination by cataloguing the ways in which masculinist descriptions of the details of women's lives are infected by the fundamental conceptual fallacies she pinpoints in volume one of the text, she also shows the ways in which women's own accounts of themselves are deformed by having to work within the cultural and intellectual landscapes skewed by these concepts. Beauvoir can only work toward the demolition of the concept of woman by building great edifices of detailed testimony which stress the variousness of women's accounts of aspects of their experiences even when working with the flawed conceptual tools of cultures which have always defined woman. Beauvoir's accounts underscore the differences women manage to report in their reactions to life events which are conceptually hypothecated as susceptible to universal interpretation. Further, at every point she can, Beauvoir emphasizes *doing* as opposed to *being* as the decisive element in every human life. This is the burden of the most famous sentence in *The Second Sex*, Beauvoir's memorable, and illuminatingly sardonic pronouncement at the opening of the second volume that 'One is not born, but rather becomes a woman'. And, as Beauvoir immediately notes, it takes the entire weight of civilization to crush the human female into the straitjacket of this concept which has so constrained her. Beauvoir's own contribution to civilization is the analysis which clears the ground for women to walk free. In another interesting moment of demystification, which works in a direct but hopeful parallel to her statement on women, Beauvoir notes that 'one is not born a genius: one becomes a genius' (Beauvoir 1989, p. 133). It is the illusion of the fixed category when applied to types of humans which Beauvoir identifies as false in both cases.

This audacious, breathtaking autonomy of *The Second Sex*, and Beauvoir's refusal to allow her text to be captured by previous discourses and genres (while borrowing from them whenever they have something of use to offer to her own project) is the aspect of the text which makes it so central for subsequent feminist writerly practice, and which should make it central to all human writerly practice. Beauvoir was no respecter of previously established genres in any of her work and *The Second Sex* is no exception. For her, intellectual boundaries always existed to be violated in the interest of projects which themselves admitted no such rigid categorization. And by the time that she wrote *The Second Sex* she was practised in the destruction of such boundaries. Beauvoir's literary-philosophical method, devised in the 1930s and used by her throughout her life as a writer, allowed her to disregard the limitation that excluded fiction from philosophy and philosophy from fiction. By the time she wrote *The Second Sex* the violation of traditional intellectual categories was commonplace to Beauvoir, central to her methods and illustrative of her objectives. It is unsurprising that such audacity still intrigues and tantalizes, but sometimes puzzles readers.

Intellectually, then, *The Second Sex* enacts the libertarian tactics which allow it to function as a text dedicated to the demolition of the powerful governing concept of 'woman'. The historical moment of the composition of the text was almost ludicrously appropriate for this task. In 1945 The Second World War ended, and in the same year French women secured the vote. If women had, as Beauvoir stated in the Introduction to *The Second Sex* 'no past, no history, no religion of their own' (Beauvoir 1989, p. xxv), the cataclysms of the first half of the twentieth century had themselves resulted in a brief moment of potentially promising rupture and fracture of which *The Second Sex* itself is a part. Looking back with both admiration and a certain degree of exasperation at the prior history of feminism, Beauvoir noted that previously it 'was never an autonomous movement', but always partly 'an instrument in the hands of politicians, in part an epiphenomenon reflecting a deeper social drama'. Women have always laboured under the sway of, as she put it, 'masculine ideologies', constructed from 'masculine perspectives' (Beauvoir 1989, p. 129). Beauvoir's view was that even her most ambitious female predecessors were always at least partially trapped in a conceptual prison from which there was no known means of escape. If Beauvoir was right in this judgement, then she herself provides the explanation of what made the appearance of *The Second Sex* so historically significant. It cleared the intellectual ground from which women, and men too, could begin to liberate their thought about women and men from masculinist concepts, and masculinist discourses predicated on woman as Other.

Notes and References

Introduction

1. Warnock, Mary, *The Philosophy of Sartre*. London: Hutchinson, 1965, pp. 72–3.
2. *ibid.*, p. 63.
3. Barnes, Hazel., *The Literature of Possibility*. London: Tavistock, 1961, p. 122.
4. See Gerassi, John, *Jean-Paul Sartre: Hated Conscience of His Century*, vol. 1, *Protestantor Protester*, London: University of Chicago Press, 1989, p. 90, and Bair Deirdre, *Simone de Beauvoir: A Biography*. London: Jonathan Cape, 1990, p. 628.

Part I
Chapter 1: Final Exams

1. de Beauvoir, Simone, *Memoirs of a Dutiful Daughter*, trans. James Kirkup. Harmondsworth: Penguin, 1963, p. 104.
2. *ibid.*, pp. 159–60; Bair, *Simone de Beauvoir*, p. 92.
3. *Memoirs*, pp. 160, 158.
4. *ibid.*, pp. 177, 179.
5. Bair, *Simone de Beauvoir*, p. 94.
6. Francis, Claude and Gontier, Fernande, *Simone de Beauvoir*, trans. Lisa Nesselson. London: Mandarin, 1989, p. 51.
7. See Michèle Le Doeuff's perceptive analysis of the importance of the imitation of key teachers in academic growth and the special dangers this holds for women, in her article, 'Women and Philosophy', *Radical Philosophy*, 1977, 17, 2–11.

8. *Memoirs*, pp. 207, 233, 234.
9. *ibid.*, p. 208.
10. *ibid.*, pp. 195, 211.
11. *ibid.*, pp. 284, 278, 284–5, 289.
12. Francis and Gontier, *Simone de Beauvoir*, p. 79.
13. *Memoirs*, pp. 234–5.
14. *ibid.*, p. 239. Beauvoir's later reaction was quite different. In 1983 she was embarrassed by her youthful attitudes: 'Simone Weil was right to dismiss me like that. It took me many years to free myself from what I called in my memoirs "the bonds of my class". I know that even today there are many who accuse me of behaviour instilled by "the bonds of class", especially some feminist women. Perhaps they are right, and one never overcomes the class into which one is born. I don't know.' (Bair, *Simone de Beauvoir*, p. 120).
15. *ibid.*, p. 125.
16. *Memoirs*, pp. 309–10.
17. *ibid.*, pp. 310–14.
18. *ibid.*, pp. 313, 324–5.
19. *ibid.*, p. 323.
20. Francis and Gontier, *Simone de Beauvoir*, p. 82.
21. *Memoirs*, p. 295.
22. See Gerassi, *Jean-Paul Sartre*, p. 90, and Beauvoir, *Memoirs*, pp. 310, 319.
23. *Memoirs*, p. 321. Hayman, Ronald, *Writing Against: A Biography of Sartre*. London: Weidenfeld and Nicolson, 1986, p. 70.
24. *Memoirs*, pp. 331–2.
25. *ibid.*, p. 331.
26. Gerassi, *Jean-Paul Sartre*, p. 91, and Bair, *Simone de Beauvoir*, pp. 144, 142–3.
27. *Memoirs*, pp. 322–4.
28. It must be noted that Sartre's fear of ending his life as a student seems a more likely cause of his examination failure in the previous year than an excess of originality.
29. *Memoirs*, pp. 310, 334.
30. Sartre, *Sartre by Himself*, pp. 21–2.
31. *Memoirs*, pp. 334–5.
32. Sartre, *Sartre by Himself*, p. 23.
33. *Memoirs*, p. 337.
34. The remark is misused in a variety of ways. For example, Michèle Le

Doeuff states that Sartre's remark is 'the conclusion of the first volume of Simone de Beauvoir's autobiography' ('Women and Philosophy', *Radical Philosophy*, p. 8). In fact, the quotation from Sartre appears more than 10,000 words from the end of Beauvoir's book, and Sartre does not figure in either the conclusion or the penultimate section of the volume.

35. *Memoirs*, p. 339.
36. Dayan, Josée and Ribowska Malka, *Simone de Beauvoir*, Paris: Gallimard, 1979, p. 20.
37. Gerassi, *Jean-Paul Sartre*, p. 90, from an interview with John Gerassi, 26 March 1971. Maheu, in another interview with Gerassi, confirmed that he had been Beauvoir's first lover (see Bair, *Simone de Beauvoir*, p. 628).
38. *Le Nouvel Observateur*, 21 March 1976, p. 15, cited in Gerassi, *Jean-Paul Sartre*, p. 91.
39. *Memoirs*, p. 342.
40. *ibid.*, pp. 319, 324–6.
41. *ibid.*, pp. 339–341, 340.
42. *War Diaries*, p. 75. Sartre as a suitor was disinclined to understate his accomplishments, past and future. In 1926 he wrote to Simone Jollivet that he had finished his first novel when he was 8, had created several philosophical systems before he was 17 and had also composed symphonies. See *Lettres au Castor, et à quelques autres*, vol. 1, *1926-1939*, Simone de Beauvoir (ed.). Paris: Gallimard, 1983, p. 9.
43. See Gerassi, *Jean-Paul Sartre*, p. 91; Bair, *Simone de Beauvoir*, pp. 145–6; and Francis and Gontier, *Simone de Beauvoir*, p. 92.

Chapter 2: Courtship and Union

1. Bair, *Simone de Beauvoir*, pp. 155–6.
2. *Memoirs*, p. 345.
3. Francis and Gontier, *Simone de Beauvoir*, p. 92.
4. *Prime of Life*, 13–14.
5. *ibid.*, p. 14, and Bair, *Simone de Beauvoir*, pp. 149–50.
6. Bair, *Simone de Beauvoir*, pp. 150, 155, 156.
7. *War Diaries*, p. 75.
8. *Memoirs*, p. 346, 347, 330, 355, 358.
9. *ibid.*, pp. 358–9, 360.
10. *Prime of Life*, p. 9. The circumstances involved in the hostility to Zaza's

marriage included the uncovering of Merleau-Ponty's illegitimacy, of which he, himself, had hitherto been unaware.

11. *Memoirs*, pp. 326, 314 (emphasis added).
12. *Prime of Life*, p. 12.
13. *Memoirs*, pp. 345, 144, 145.
14. *ibid.*, pp. 340–1.
15. *ibid.*, pp. 342–3.
16. *War Diaries*, p. 282. *Memoirs*, p. 343.
17. *Memoirs*, pp. 343, 344.
18. Evans, Mary, *Simone de Beauvoir: A Feminist Mandarin*. London: Tavistock, 1985, p. 16.
19. *Prime of Life*, p. 24.
20. *ibid.*, p. 22.
21. *ibid.*, p. 23.

Chapter 3: Carousing

1. *Prime of Life*, pp. 23–4.
2. *Letters to Sartre*, trans. Quintin Hoare. London: Radius, 1991, pp. 4–5.
3. *Prime of Life*, p. 56.
4. *ibid.*, p. 8.
5. Sartre, Jean-Paul, *Witness to My Life: The Letters of Jean-Paul Sartre to Simone de Beauvoir, 1926–1939*, Simone de Beauvoir (ed.), trans. Lee Fahnestock and Norman MacAfee. New York: Scribner's, 1992, p. 33.
6. *Being and Nothingness*, trans. Hazel E. Barnes, New York: Philosophical Library, 1956, p. 39.
7. *Prime of Life*, p. 59.
8. *ibid.*, pp. 53–14; Francis and Gontier, *Simone de Beauvoir*, pp. 113–14.
9. *Prime of Life*, p. 54.
10. *ibid.*, pp. 34–8, 55.
11. *ibid.*, pp. 44–6.
12. *ibid.*, pp. 62, 63, 64.
13. *ibid.*, p. 56.
14. *ibid.*, pp. 60, 62, 61.

Chapter 4: Would-be Authors

1. *Witness to My Life*, pp. 35–41.
2. *Memoirs*, p. 329.
3. *Witness to My Life*, p. 41.

4. *Prime of Life*, pp. 88, 89, 90, 92–3.
5. *ibid.*, pp. 93, 100.
6. *ibid.*, p. 103.
7. *ibid.*, p. 106.
8. *ibid.*, pp. 124, 125.
9. *ibid.*, p. 128.
10. Gerassi, *Jean-Paul Sartre*, p. 113.
11. *Prime of Life*, pp. 135–6.
12. *ibid.*, pp. 183–4, 158.
13. *ibid.*, p. 201.
14. Sartre, *Sartre by Himself*, pp. 29–30.
15. *Prime of Life*, pp. 220, 201.
16. Sartre, Jean-Paul, *The Transcendence of the Ego: An Existentialist Theory of Consciousness*, trans. Forrest Williams and Robert Kirkpatrick. New York: Noonday Press, 1957, p. 31.
17. *Prime of Life*, p. 40.
18. *ibid.*, pp. 138, 106.
19. Hemingway Ernest. *A Farewell to Arms*. New York: Scribner's, 1929, p. 185.
20. *ibid.*, p. 227.
21. Sartre, Jean-Paul, *Nausea*, trans. Robert Baldick. Harmondsworth: Penguin, 1965, p. 252.
22. *Prime of Life*, p. 284.
23. *ibid.*, pp. 201, 207.
24. *ibid.*, p. 212.
25. *ibid.*, pp. 209, 210, 210–11, 212.
26. *ibid.*, pp. 217–20.
27. Schwarzer, Alice, *Simone de Beauvoir Today: Conversation 1972–1982*, trans. Marianne Howarth. London: Chatto & Windus, 1984, p. 58.
28. Sartre, *Sartre by Himself*, p. 28.

Chapter 5: More Carousing

1. *Prime of Life*, pp. 246, 245.
2. *ibid.*, pp. 240, 242.
3. *Adieux*, p. 306.
4. See the remarks on the relationship throughout *Letters to Sartre*. See also *Prime of Life*, pp. 257–63.
5. *Prime of Life*, p. 260.

6. *ibid.*, pp. 260, 259–61.
7. *Adieux*, p. 172.
8. *Prime of Life*, pp. 275–85.
9. *Adieux*, p. 159.
10. Bair, *Simone de Beauvoir*, p. 202.
11. *Prime of Life*, p. 293.
12. *Witness to My Life*, pp. 92–5.
13. *Prime of Life*, pp. 293–302.
14. Hayman, Ronald, *Writing Against: A Biography of Sartre*. London: Weidenfeld and Nicolson, 1986 p. 127; and Cohen-Solal, Annie, *Sartre: A Life*. London: Heinemann, 1987, p. 121.
15. *Prime of Life*, 241.
16. Bair, *Simone de Beauvoir*, p. 209.
17. *ibid.*, p. 208.
18. *Prime of Life*, pp. 225, 319, 365.
19. *ibid.*, pp. 327, 336, 346, 337.
20. Bair, *Simone de Beauvoir*, p. 215.
21. See for example, Schwarzer, *Simone de Beauvoir Today*, pp. 112–13.
22. *Letters to Sartre*, p. 260.
23. *Prime of Life*, p. 25.
24. *ibid.*, p. 337.
25. *Lettres au Castor, et à quelques autres*, vol. 1, *1926–1939*, Simone de Beauvoir (ed.). Paris: Gallimard, 1983, vol. 1, p. 274.

Chapter 6: The Family Jewels

1. Simons, Margaret A., 'Beauvoir and Sartre: The Philosophical relationship', *Yale French Studies*, 72, 1986, pp. 165–79.
2. *ibid.*, p. 168.
3. *She Came To Stay*, trans. Yvonne Moyse and Roger Senhouse. London: Flamingo, 1984.
4. *ibid.*, pp. 52, 54.
5. *Being and Nothingness*, p. 304.
6. *Letters to Sartre*, p. 200.
7. *ibid.*, p. 158.
8. Beauvoir, Simone de, *Journal de Guerre: Septembre 1939–Janvier 1941*, Sylvie Le Bon de Beauvoir (ed.). Paris: Gallimard, 1990, pp. 270–3, 280.
9. Hazel Barnes's reading of *She Came To Stay* in 1959 is a partial and interesting exception. As the English translator of *Being*

and Nothingness, Barnes was particularly well placed to identify the philosophical content in Beauvoir's novel and succeeded admirably in delineating its theory of Others. But all the rest – and, as shall be seen, it is a great deal – she missed. Barnes, however, was working with the severe handicap of not knowing the order in which the two books had been written. Although she attributes all the ideas and images common to the two works to Sartre, a striking characteristic of her reading is an acute unease that she may be mistaken on this very point. See Barnes, *The Literature of Possibility: A Study in Humanistic Existentialism*, London: Tavistock, 1959. For other kinds of readings of Beauvoir's fiction see, especially, Fallaize, Elizabeth, *The Novels of Simone de Beauvoir*, London: Routledge, 1988, and Whitmarsh, Anne, *Simone de Beauvoir and the Limits of Commitment*, Cambridge: Cambridge University Press, 1981.

10. *She Came To Stay*, p. 1.
11. *ibid.*, p. 1.
12. *ibid.*, pp. 1–2.
13. *ibid.*, p. 2.
14. *Prime of Life*, p. 13.
15. Russell, Bertrand, *The Problems of Philosophy*. London: Oxford University Press, 1967, p. 6.
16. *She Came To Stay*, pp. 2, 2–3.
17. *Transcendence of the Ego*, p. 103.
18. Sartre, Jean-Paul, *The Emotions: Outline of a Theory*, trans. Bernard Frechtman. New York: Philosophical Library, 1948, pp. 11, 18.
19. *Transcendence of the Ego*, p. 105.
20. *She Came To Stay*, pp. 6–7.

Chapter 7: The 'Lost' Letters

1. Danto, Arthur C, *Sartre*. London: Fontana, 1991, p. 1.
2. *Prime of Life*, p. 328.
3. *Letters to Sartre*, pp. 20–1.
4. *ibid.*, p. 178.
5. *ibid.*, pp. 37, 46.
6. See Sartre's *War Diaries*, pp. 160–2 for a long passage from a letter Sartre received from Bost.
7. *Letters to Sartre*, pp. 54, 86, 92, 120, 149–50.

8. *Witness to My Life*, p. 230.
9. *War Diaries*, pp. 170–1.
10. Hayman, Ronald, *Writing Against: A Biography of Sartre*. London: Weidenfeld and Nicolson, 1986, p. 145.
11. Cohen-Solal, *Sartre*, p. 139.
12. *The Words*, pp. 153, 146, 153.
13. *Witness to My Life*, p. 249.
14. *Lettres au Castor et à quelques autres*, (ed) Simone de Beauvoir, vol. 2, Gallimard, Paris, 1983, p. 27. Translation taken from Cohen-Solal, *Sartre*, p. 142.
15. *Journal de Guerre*, pp. 270, 270–3, 280.
16. *War Diaries*, pp. 197, 208.
17. *Being and Nothingness*, pp. 527–9.
18. *War Diaries*, pp. 208–9.
19. *She Came To Stay*, p. 51.
20. *War Diaries*, pp. 209, 214.
21. *She Came To Stay*, pp. 69, 81.
22. *ibid.*, p. 135.
23. *War Diaries*, pp. 229, 230.
24. *ibid.*, p. 11.
25. *She Came To Stay*, p. 131.
26. *War Diaries*, p. 258.
27. *Letters to Sartre*, pp. 275, 277.
28. *Adieux*, p. 304.
29. *Witness to My Life*, p.198.
30. Hayman, *Writing Against*, p. 128.
31. *Lettres au Castor*, pp. 94, 111.
32. *Prime of Life*, p. 23.
33. Bair, *Simone de Beauvoir*, p. 207.
34. Lawson, Sylvia. 'All in the family', *London Review of Books*, 3 December 1992, p. 16.
35. *She Came To Stay*, pp. 7, 43–4.
36. Gerassi, *Jean-Paul Sartre*, p. 158.
37. *Prime of Life*, pp. 315–18, and Bair, *Simone de Beauvoir*, pp. 228–32.
38. Bair, *Simone de Beauvoir*, p. 228.
39. *ibid.*, pp. 228–9.
40. *ibid.*, pp. 601–2, 678–9, 602.
41. *Letters to Sartre*, p. xi.

Part II
Chapter 8: A 'Preposterous' Thesis

1. Barnes, Hazel E. *The Literature of Possibility: A Study in Humanistic Existentialism*. London: Tavistock, 1961 [1959], p. 15.
2. Heller, Scott, 'Scholars seek to rank Simone de Beauvoir among leading 20th-century philosophers,' *The Chronicle of Higher Education*, 4 September 1998, pp. A22–3.
3. Barnes, *The Literature of Possibility*, p. 113.
4. *ibid.*, p. 121–2.
5. *ibid.*, p. 122.
6. *ibid.*, p. 385.
7. *ibid.*, p. 123.
8. *ibid.*, p. 123.
9. Fallaize, Elizabeth. *The Novels of Simone de Beauvoir*. London: Routledge, 1998, p. 29
10. Barnes, *The Literature of Possibility*, p. 124.
11. *ibid.*, p. 127.
12. *ibid.*, p. 127.
13. *ibid.*, p. 129.
14. *ibid.*, p. 128.
15. *ibid.*, p. 129.
16. *ibid.*, p. 132.
17. de Beauvoir, Simone, *She Came To Stay*, trans. Yvonne Moyse and Roger Senhouse. London: Fontana, 1984, pp. 307–10. Jean-Paul Sartre, *Being and Nothingness: An Essay on Phenomenological Ontology*, trans. Hazel E. Barnes. New York: Philosophical Library, 1956, pp. 259–63.
18. Barnes, *The Literature of Possibility*, p. 134.
19. *ibid.*, p. 135.
20. Merleau-Ponty, Maurice, 'Metaphysics and the Novel', in *Sense and Non-Sense*, trans. Hubert L. Dreyfus and Patricia Allen Dreyfus. Evanston, IL.: Northwestern University Press, 1964, p.39. Originally published as 'Le Roman et la Métaphysique', *Cahiers du Sud*, 270, March 1945.
21. Beauvoir, Simone, *She Came To Stay*, p. 146.
22. Fallaize, *The Novels of Simone de Beauvoir*, pp. 33–4.
23. Merleau-Ponty, p. 33.
24. Beauvoir, *She Came To Stay*, pp. 51–2.
25. *ibid.*, pp. 113–126, 161, 171, 180.

26. *ibid.*, pp. 178–212.
27. Merleau-Ponty, p. 33.
28. Danto, Arthur C., *Sartre*, 2nd edn. London: Fontana, 1991, p. 42.
29. *ibid.*, p. 43.
30. Merleau-Ponty, pp. 28–9.
31. Beauvoir, *She Came To Stay*, p. 3.
32. Merleau-Ponty, p. 30.
33. The first chapter of the Moyse/Senhouse translation of *She Came To Stay* (Beauvoir 1984) has a short series of interconnected errors which do not enhance the intelligibility of Beauvoir's presentation of her theory of appearances. Central to Beauvoirean/Sartrean thought is the distinction between the appearances of non-conscious being and the way those appearances are organized by conscious beings. Beauvoir and Sartre generally refer to an instance of the latter as a 'world'. Thus in her novel's opening chapter, Beauvoir distinguishes repeatedly between *la terre* and *le monde* (Beauvoir 1972 [1943]). But in several places the English translation does not honour this distinction, having translated *terre* as 'world'. It appears that the translators have acted to save Françoise from her bad faith regarding existence of elsewhere. The ellipses in the following passage form part of their translation.

> On the other side of the window-panes, the small, secluded square was asleep under the black sky; and, some way away, a train was moving through an empty landscape ... And I am there, I am there, but for me this square exists and that moving train ... all Paris, and all the world [*terre*] in the rosy shadows of this little office ... and in this very instant all the long years of happiness. I am here [*là*], at the heart of my life ... [pp. 4–5]

Similarly, when Gerbert asks Françoise to identify her regrets, she replies: 'Having to live only in my own skin when the world [*terre*] is so vast.' (Beauvoir 1984, p. 5)
34. Beauvoir, *She Came To Stay*, p. 1.
35. *ibid.*, p. 2.
36. *ibid.*, p. 2.
37. *ibid.*, p. 5.
38. *ibid.*, p. 6.
39. *ibid.*, p. 6.
40. Republished as 1948 'Littérature et métaphysique' in *Existentialisme et la sagesse des nations*. Paris: Nagel, 1948, pp. 103–24.

41. Fallaize, *The Novels of Simone de Beauvoir,* p. 41.

42. Beauvoir, Simone de, 'Mon experience d'écrivain', *Les écrits de Simone de Beauvoir.* Claude Francis and Fernande Gontier (eds). Paris: Gallimard, 1979, pp. 439–57.

43. *ibid.,* pp. 440, 441.

44. *ibid.,* pp. 440–1.

45. Beauvoir, Simone de, *Pyrrhus et Cinéas.* Paris: Gallimard 1944, pp. 34–5, 58.

46. Simons, Margaret A. and Jessica Benjamin, 'Simone de Beauvoir: An interview', *Feminist Studies,* 5, (Summer, part 2), 1979, pp. 330–45.

47. Beauvoir, Simone de, *The Prime of Life,* trans. Peter Green. Harmondsworth: Penguin, 1965 [1960], p. 221.

48. *ibid.,* p. 221; Simons and Benjamin, pp. 337–8.

49. Simons and Benjamin, pp. 338–9.

50. Simons, Margaret A. 'Two Interviews with Simone de Beauvoir', in Nancy Fraser and Sandra Lee Bartky (eds), *Revealing French Feminism: Critical Essays on Difference, Agency, and Culture.* Bloomington: Indiana University Press, 1992 (1989), p. 37.

51. Contat, Michel and Michel Rybalka, *The Writings of Jean-Paul Sartre, Volume 1: A Bibliographical Life,* trans. Richard C. McCleary. Evanston, Illinois: Northwestern University Press, 1974 [1970], p. 82. Thompson, Kenneth A., *Sartre: Life and Works.* New York: Facts On File, 1984, p. 48. Beauvoir, *The Prime of Life,* 501. Gerassi, John, *Jean-Paul Sartre: Hated Conscience of his Century,* vol. 1. Chicago: University of Chicago Press, 1989, p. 168. Hayman, Ronald, *Writing Against: A Biography of Sartre.* London: Weidnefeld and Nicolson, 1986, p. 164.

52. Beauvoir, *The Prime of Life,* pp. 369, 485.

53. Beauvoir, 'Mon experience d'écrivain', p. 45.

54. Beauvoir, *The Prime of Life,* p. 519.

55. Beauvoir, *The Prime of Life,* p. 369.

56. Beauvoir, Simone de, *Journal de Guerre.* Paris: Gallimard, 1990. Sartre, Jean-Paul, *War Diaries: Notebooks from a Phoney War,* trans. Quintin Hoare. London: Verso, 1984.

57. Beauvoir, Simone de, *Letters to Sartre,* trans. Quintin Hoare. London: Radius, 1991.

58. *ibid.,* p. 200.

59. Beauvoir, *Journal de Guerre,* p. 270.

60. *ibid.,* 270–83.

61. Sartre, Jean-Paul, *Quiet Moments in a War: The Letters of Jean-Paul Sartre*

to Simone de Beauvoir 1940–1963, Simone de Beauvoir (ed.), trans. Lee Fahnestock and Norman MacAfee. New York: Scribner's, 1993, p. 61.

62. Sartre, *War Diaries*.

63. Sartre, *War Diaries*, p. x.

64. Hayman, *Writing Against*, p. 149.

65. Thompson, Kenneth A. *Sartre: Life and Works*. New York: Facts on File, 1984, p. 43.

66. Flynn, Thomas R., 'Sartre and the poetics of history', in Christina Howells (ed.), *The Cambridge Companion to Sartre*. Cambridge: Cambridge University Press, 1992, pp. 213–60.

67. McBride, William L., *Sartre's Political Theory*. Bloomington: Indiana University Press, 1991, p. 32.

68. Leak, Andrew, 'Writing and seduction: Sartre's *L'Etre et le néant* I. Actaeon', *Sartre Studies International*, 1, 1995, p. 58.

69. Sartre, *War Diaries* p. 19.

70. Boschetti, Anna, *The Intellectual Enterprise: Sartre and Les Temps Modernes*, trans. Richard C. McCleary. Evanston Il: Northwestern University Press, 1985, p. 55.

71. Fretz, Leo, 'Individuality in Sartre's philosophy' in Christina Howells (ed.), *The Cambridge Companion to Sartre*. Cambridge: Cambridge University Press, 1992 pp. 67–102, pp. 70, 77, 71.

72. Sartre, *War Diaries*, pp. 196–262.

73. *ibid.*, p. 197.

74. Sartre, *Being and Nothingness*, pp. 527–31.

75. *ibid.*, p. 208–9.

76. *ibid.*, pp. 208–10.

77. *ibid.*, pp. 210–15.

78. *ibid.*, pp. 255–61.

79. *ibid.*, p. 258.

80. *ibid.*, pp. 255–6, 261.

81. *ibid.*, pp. 256–7.

82. *ibid.*, p. 258–9.

83. *ibid.*, p. 259–60.

84. Beauvoir, *Letters to Sartre*, p. 356.

85. In her letter of 5 January 1941, Beauvoir, after explaining a broken engagement, writes: 'I telephoned M. Ponty instead, met up with him at the Dôme, and spent the evening with him. He paid me vast compliments on my novel (the 1st part), telling me it was "great": in

spite of everything, that really did encourage me.' (Beauvoir 1991, p. 364).

86. Klaw, Barbara, Sylvie Le Bon de Beauvoir, and Margaret Simons (eds), *Diary of a Philosophy Student, Vol. 1, 1926–1927*. Illinois: University of Illinois Press, 2007.

87. Klaw, Beauvoir, Simons, *Diary*, 1927, 55.

88. Klaw, Beauvoir, Simons, *Diary*, 1927, 54.

89. For further reading about Beauvoir's student diaries and their influence on the careers of Beauvoir and Sartre see Margaret A. Simons, 'Is *The Second Sex* Beauvoir's Application of Sartrean Existentialism?' at www.bu.edu/wcp/Papers/Gend/GendSimo.htm, and Edward Fullbrook and Margaret A. Simons, 'Beauvoir And Sartre: The Problem Of The Other', in Karen J. Warren (ed.), *Gendering Western Philosophy*, New York: Rowman & Littefield, 2008.

Chapter 9: Two Beginnings, One Philosophy

1. Critchley, Simon, *Continental Philosophy: A Very Short Introduction*. Oxford: Oxford University Press, 2001, p. 125.

2. Simons, Margaret A. (forthcoming), 'Bergson's Influence on Beauvoir's Philosophical Methodology'.

3. Warnock, Mary, *Existentialism*. Oxford: Oxford University Press, 1970, p. 133.

4. Warnock, *Existentialism*, p. 136.

5. Sartre, Jean-Paul, *Nausea*. Harmondsworth: Penguin, 1965.

6. Danto, Arthur, *Sartre*. London: Fontana, 1991.

7. 'Two Unpublished Chapters of *She Came To Stay*', p. 2.

8. 'Two Unpublished Chapters', p. 4.

9. *She Came To Stay*, p. 2.

10. 'Two Unpublished Chapters', p. 5.

11. *She Came To Stay*, p. 2.

12. *She Came To Stay*, p. 4.

13. 'Two Unpublished Chapters', p. 5.

14. *She Came To Stay*, p. 1.

15. 'Two Unpublished Chapters', p. 3.

16. *She Came To Stay*, p. 1.

17. 'Two Unpublished Chapters', p. 4.

18. *She Came To Stay*, pp. 1–2.

19. 'Two Unpublished Chapters', p. 5.

20. *She Came To Stay*, p. 6.
21. 'Two Unpublished Chapters', p. 4.
22. *She Came To Stay*, p. 3.
23. 'Two Unpublished Chapters', p. 5.
24. *She Came To Stay*, p. 5.
25. 'Two Unpublished Chapters', p. 4.
26. *She Came To Stay*, p. 2.
27. 'Two Unpublished Chapters', p. 1.
28. *She Came To Stay*, p. 7.

Chapter 10: Whose Ethics?

Notes

1. Anderson 1979, 1993; Bell 1989; Detmer 1988; Dobson 1993; Frondizi 1981; Lee 1985; McBride 1991; Simont 1992.
2. In the penultimate paragraph of *Being and Nothingness*, Sartre, while not yet converted to Beauvoirean ethics, raised in the form of a question the possibility that his partner might be right and he wrong. [p. 627] 'In particular is it possible for freedom to take itself for a value as the source of all value, or must it necessarily be defined in relation to a transcendent value which haunts it?' By omitting both the question mark and the second clause, Sartre's sentence can be used to give a radically false impression. Detmer [1988], for example, writes:
   On this point, the identification of freedom as the good, or at least as the greatest good, Sartre has demonstrated more consistency from his earliest writings to his later ones than he has, perhaps, with respect to any other issue. Thus, in *Being and Nothingness* he urges freedom 'to take itself for a value as the source of all value.' [p. 180]
3. David Pellauer's introduction to Sartre's *Notebooks for an Ethics*, which explains that Sartre wrote these notebooks in 1947 and 1948, offers a recent example of this tendency. He writes:
   'I believe we cannot overlook in attempting to make sense of these notebooks – Simone de Beauvoir's *The Ethics of Ambiguity*. There are so many similarities between the references and examples she uses and those Sartre uses in the notebooks, we must assume *she was well aware of what he was working on*, and vice versa' (p. xii, emphasis added).

The implication that Beauvoir's and Sartre's two works on ethics were written contemporaneously and that the latter influenced the former is given a certain plausibility by a footnote which gives 1947 as the publication date of the 'French original' of *The Ethics of Ambiguity*. But besides not being altogether correct – the first half of Beauvoir's *Ethics* was published in 1946 and the second in January and February 1947 – Pellauer is not comparing like with like. As with Sartre's *Notebooks for an Ethics*, Beauvoir's *The Ethics of Ambiguity* was written *before* it was published. In *Force of Circumstance*, Beauvoir, quoting from her diary, says that, in the office of *Les Temps Modernes*, she turned over all four instalments of *The Ethics of Ambiguity* at 5.30 on 14 May 1946. [p. 92]

4. Her play's opening night, 29 October 1945, was the evening after Sartre's Club Maintenant lecture. [Contat and Rybalka 1974, p. 132; Bair 1990, p. 310]

References

Anderson, Thomas C., *The Foundation and Structure of Sartrean Ethics*. Lawrence, Kansas: University Press of Kansas, 1979.

——*Sartre's Two Ethics: From Authenticity to Integral Humanity*. Chicago: Open Court, 1993.

Bair, Deirdre, *Simone de Beauvoir*. London: Jonathan Cape, 1990.

Beauvoir, Simone de, *The Ethics of Ambiguity*, trans. Bernard Frechtman. New York: Citadel Press, 1948. Originally published as 'Pour une morale de l'ambiguïté', *Les Temps Modernes*, II, 14, 15, 16, 17 (November 1946–February 1947).

——*Pyrrhus et Cinéas*. Paris: Gallimard, 1960 [1944].

——*Force of Circumstance*, trans. Richard Howard. Harmondsworth: Penguin, 1968.

——*The Prime of Life*, trans. Peter Green. Harmondsworth: Penguin, 1969.

——*Who Shall Die?* trans. Claude Francis and Fernande Gontier. Florissant, Missouri: River Press, 1983. Originally published as *Les Bouches inutiles*. Paris: Gallimard, 1945.

——*She Came To Stay*, trans. Yvonne Moyse and Roger Senhouse. London: Flamingo, 1984. Originally published as *L'Invitée*. Paris: Gallimard, 1943.

Bell, Linda, 1989. *Sartre's Ethics of Authenticity*. Tuscaloosa: University of Alabama Press.

Caws, Peter. *Sartre*. London: Routledge, 1984.

Contat, Michel and Michel Rybalka, *The Writings of Jean-Paul Sartre*, vol. 1, trans. Richard C. McCleary. Evanston, Illinois: Northwestern University Press, 1974.

Detmer, David, *Freedom as a Value: A Critique of the Ethical Theory of Jean-Paul Sartre*. La Salle, Illinois: Open Court, 1988.

Dobson, David, *Jean-Paul Sartre and the Politics of Reason: A Theory of History*. Cambridge: Cambridge University Press, 1993.

Frondizi, Risieri, 'Sartre's Early Ethics: A Critique', in P. Schilpp (ed.), *The Philosophy of Jean-Paul Sartre*. La Salle, Illinois: Open Court, 1981.

Jeanson, Francis, *Sartre and the Problem of Morality*, trans. W. Piersol. New York: Newman Press, 1967.

Kruks, Sonia, 'Simone de Beauvoir and the limits to freedom', *Social Text*, Fall, 1987, 111–22.

Lee, Sander, 'The central role of universalization in Sartrean ethics', *Philosophy and Phenomenological Research*, 46 (September), 1985, 59–72.

McBride, William L, *Sartre's Political Theory*. Indianapolis, Indiana: Indiana University Press, 1991.

Manser, Anthony, *Sartre: A Philosophic Study*. New York: Oxford University Press, 1967.

Sartre, Jean-Paul, *Existentialism and Humanism*, trans. Philip Mairet. London: Methuen, 1948. Originally published as *L'Existentialisme est un humanisme*. Paris: Nagel, 1946.

——*What is Literature?* trans. Bernard Frechtman. London: Methuen, 1950. Originally published as 'Qu'est-ce que la littérature?', *Les Temps Modernes*, 17–22 (February–July, 1947).

——*Being and Nothingness: An Essay on Phenomenological Ontology*, trans. Hazel E. Barnes. New York: Philosophical Library, 1956. Originally published as *L'Etre et le Néant: Essai d'ontologie phénoménologique*. Paris: Gallimard, 1943.

——'Materialism and Revolution', *Literary and Philosophical Essays*, trans. Annette Michelson. New York: Collier, 1962, pp. 198–256. Originally published as 'Matérialisme et révolution', *Les Temps Modernes*, 9, 10 (June, July, 1946).

——*Saint Genet: Actor and Martyr*, trans. Bernard Frechtman. New York: New American Library, 1963. Originally published as *Saint Genet: Comédien et Martyr*. Paris: Gallimard, 1952.

——*Anti-Semite and Jew*, trans. George J. Becker. New York: Schocken

Books, 1965. Originally published as *Réflexions sur la question juive*. Paris: Paul Morihien, 1946.

——*War Diaries: Notebooks form a Phoney War, November 1939–March 1940*, trans. Quintin Hoare. London: Verso, 1984.

——*Notebooks for an Ethics*, trans. David Pellauer. Chicago: University of Chicago Press, 1992. Originally published as *Cahiers pour une morale*. Paris: Gallimard, 1983.

Simons, Margaret A., 'Beauvoir and Sartre: The philosophical relationship', *Yale French Studies* 2, 1986, 165–79.

Simont, Juliette, 'Sartrean Ethics', in Christina Howells (ed.), *The Cambridge Companion to Sartre*. Cambridge: Cambridge University Press, 1992, pp. 178–210.

Theunissen, Michael, *The Other: Studies in the Social Ontology of Husserl, Heidegger, Sartre, and Buber*, trans. Christopher Macann. Cambridge, Massachusetts: MIT Press, 1984.

Warnock, Mary, *The Philosophy of Sartre*. London: Hutchinson, 1965.

——*Existentialist Ethics*. London: Macmillan, 1967.

——*Existentialism*. Oxford: Oxford University Press, 1970.

Chapter 11: The *Absence* Of Beauvoir

Notes

1. All translations from this text are our own.
2. All translations from this text are our own.

References

Beauvoir, Simone de, *Pyrrhus et Cinéas*. Paris: Gallimard, 1944.

——'Littérature et métaphysique', in *Existenitalisme et la sagesse des nations*. Paris: Nagel, 1948.

——'Preface', *America Day by Day*, trans. Patrick Dudley. London: Duckworth, 1952.

——*The Prime of Life*, trans. Peter Green. Harmondsworth: Penguin, 1965.

——'Deux chapitres inédits de "L'Invitée"', in *Les Ecrits de Simone de Beauvoir*. Paris: Gallimard, 1979.

——*She Came To Stay*, trans. Yvonne Moyse and Roger Senhouse. London: Flamingo, 1984.

Samuel Guttenplan (ed.), *A Companion to the Philosophy of Mind*.

Blackwell Companions to Philosophy, vol. 5. Oxford: Blackwell Publishers, 1994.

Holveck, Eleanore, 'Can a Woman Be a Philosopher?: Reflections of a Beauvoirean Housemaid', in Margaret A. Simons (ed.), *Feminist Interpretations of Simone de Beauvoir*. University Park, Pennsylvania: Pennsylvania State University Press, 1995.

Howells, Christina (ed.), *The Cambridge Companion to Sartre*. Cambridge: Cambridge University Press, 1992.

Merleau-Ponty, Maurice, 'Metaphysics and the Novel', *Sense and Non-sense*, trans. Hubert L. Dreyfus and Patricia Allen Dreyfus. Evanston, Illinois: Northwestern University Press, 1964.

Sartre, Jean-Paul, *Being and Nothingness: An Essay on Phenomenological Ontology*, trans. Hazel E. Barnes. New York: Philosophical Library, 1956.

——*War Diaries: Notebooks from a Phoney War, November 1939–March 1940*, trans. Quintin Hoare. London: Verso, 1984.

——*Quiet Moments in a War: Letters of Jean-Paul Sartre to Simone de Beauvoir, 1940–1963*, Simone de Beauvoir (ed.), trans. Lee Fahnestock and Norman MacAfee. New York: Charles Scribner's Sons, 1993.

Simons, Margaret A., 'Joining Another's Fight: Beauvoir's Post-Modern Challenge to Racism in *America Day by Day*,' paper delivered to the Midwest Division, Society for Women in Philosophy, October 1994.

Warnock, Mary, *Existentialism*. Oxford: Oxford University Press, 1970.

Chapter 12: Beauvoir in the Intellectual Marketplace

1. Moi, Toril, *Simone de Beauvoir: The Making of an Intellectual Woman*. Oxford: Blackwell, 1994.

2. See Michèle Le Doeuff, *Hipparchia's Choice: An Essay Concerning Women, Philosophy, etc.*, trans. Trista Selous. Oxford: Blackwell, 1991, and Mary G. Dietz, 'Introduction: Debating Simone de Beauvoir', *Signs*, 18, 1 (Autumn 1992), 74–88.

3. Fullbrook, Kate and Edward Fullbrook, *Simone de Beauvoir and Jean-Paul Sartre: The Remaking of a Twentieth-Century Legend*. Hemel Hempstead: Harvester Wheatsheaf, 1993; New York: Basic Books, 1994.

4. See Simone de Beauvoir, 'Pyrrhus and Cyneas', trans. Christopher Freemantle, *Partisan Review*, III, 3 (1946), 330–7.

5. Simons, Margaret A., 'Two Interviews with Simone de Beauvoir', trans. Jane Marie Todd in Nancy Fraser and Sandra Lee Bartky, *Revaluing French Feminism: Critical Essays on Difference, Agency, and Culture*.

Bloomington, Indiana: Indiana University Press, 1992, pp. 27–8. Peter Green translates 'concerted delirium which is a system' as 'conscious venture into lunacy known as a 'philosophical system'. See Simone de Beauvoir, *The Prime of Life*, trans. Peter Green. Harmondsworth: Penguin, 1965, p. 221.

6. Simons, Margaret A., 'Two Interviews with Simone de Beauvoir', p. 34.
7. Simons, Margaret A. and Jessica Benjamin, 'Simone de Beauvoir: An Interview', *Feminist Studies*, 5, 2 (Summer 1979), 338.
8. *Prime of Life*, 225.
9. *ibid.*, 327.
10. *ibid.*, 224, 327–8.
11. Bair, Deirdre, *Simone de Beauvoir: A Biography*. London: Jonathan Cape, 1990, p. 206.
12. *ibid.*, 207–8.
13. *ibid.*, 209.
14. Quotations from the report of Grasset's reader, Henry Müller, which Beauvoir cites in *Prime of Life*, p. 327.
15. Rockmore, Tom. *Heidegger and French Philosophy: Humanism, Antihumanism and Being*. London: Routledge, 1995, p. 14. The following discussion draws, in various ways, on this excellent new study of Heidegger's influence in France.
16. The key texts supporting this view are Victor Far'ias's controversial book, *Heidegger and Nazism*, trans. Paul Burrell and Gabriel R. Ricci, Joseph Margolis and Tom Rockmore (eds). Philadelphia, Temple University Press, 1989, which attracted enormous attention on its first, French publication in 1987 and Richard Wolin (ed.), *The Heidegger Controversy: A Critical Reader*. London, MIT Press, 1993.
17. Rorty, Richard. 'Introduction' to *Essays on Heidegger and Others, Philosophical Papers*, vol. 2. Cambridge: Cambridge University Press, 1991, p. 4.
18. See Rockmore, *Heidegger and French Philosophy*, pp. 94–8.
19. *ibid.*, p. 97.
20. Beauvoir, Simone de. *The Second Sex*, trans. H. M. Parshley. Harmondsworth: Penguin, 1972, p. 66.
21. Simons, 'Two Interviews with Simone de Beauvoir', pp. 33, 34.
22. Rockmore, *Heidegger and French Philosophy*, pp. 72–5.
23. Taylor, Charles. *Sources of the Self: The Making of the Modern Identity*. Cambridge: Cambridge University Press, 1989, p. 503.
24. *ibid.*, pp. 487–8.

Part III
Chapter 13: Gender and Method

1. Merleau-Ponty, Maurice. 'Metaphysics and the Novel' in *Sense and Non-sense*, trans. Hubert L. Dreyfus and Patricia Allen Dreyfus. Evanston, Illinois: Northwestern University Press, 1964), pp. 26–40, originally published as 'Le Roman et la métaphysique' *Cahiers du Sud*, 270, mars 1945. Simone de Beauvoir, 'Littérature et métaphysique', *Existentialisme et la sagesse des nations*. Paris: Nagel, 1948, originally published in *Les Temps Modernes*, 1, 7, avril 1946, pp. 1153–63.

2. 'Littérature et métaphysique', p. 116. All translations from this essay are our own.

3. Holveck, Eleanore. 'Can a Woman be a Philosopher?: Reflections of a Beauvoirean Housemaid' in Simons, Margaret A., *Feminist Interpretations of Simone de Beauvoir*. University Park: Pennsylvania: Pennsylvania State University Press, 1995, p. 70.

4. See *Prime of Life*, p. 221, and 'Littérature et métaphysique', pp. 106–7.

5. *Pyrrhus et Cinéas*. Paris: Gallimard, 1944, pp. 34–5. Unless otherwise indicated, translations from this text are our own.

6. *Pyrrhus et Cinéas*, p. 58.

7. Beauvoir wrote 'Deux chapitres inédits de *L'Invitée*' (*Les écrits de Simone de Beauvoir*), Claude Francis and Fernande Gontier (eds). Paris: Gallimard, 1979, pp. 275–316) in 1937–8. This text treats many of the philosophical issues covered in *L'Invitée*. Its use of the consciousness of the child, Françoise, as the medium through which it raises and explores basic metaphycial questions liberates the inquiry from the pretensions and prejudicial authority of the philosopher. The 'Deux chapitres' are especially strong on the question of point of view, which is woven through large portions of the text. At age 13, Françoise comes to the existentially unremarkable but philosophically noteworthy judgement that *'c'etait impossible d'être partout à la fois'* (p. 283). She then explores what this ontological limitation entails for her grasping of reality. For example, see the passage on p. 286 realating Françoise's experiments with opera glasses.

Beauvoir, 'Preface', *America Day by Day*, trans. Patrick Dudley (London: Duckworth, 1952), n.p.

8. Simons, Margaret A., 'Joining Another's Fight: Beauvoir's Post-Modern Challenge to Racism in *America Day by Day*', paper delivered to the

Midwest Division, Society for Women in Philosophy, October 1994, p. 5.

9. 'Metaphysics and the Novel', p. 27.
10. *ibid.*, p. 27.
11. *ibid.*, p. 27.
12. *ibid.*, pp. 27–8.
13. 'Littérature et métaphysique', p. 114.
14. *ibid.*, p. 119.
15. 'Can a Woman be a Philosopher?', p. 72.
16. 'Littérature et métaphysique', p. 105.
17. *ibid.*, pp. 105–6.
18. *ibid.*, p. 106.
19. *ibid.*, p. 106.
20. *ibid.*, pp. 106–7.
21. *ibid.*, p. 109.
22. 'Littérature et métaphysique', pp. 123–4.

Chapter 14: Gender and Ethics

1. Francis and Gontier, *Simone de Beauvoir*, p. 210.
2. *The Ethics of Ambiguity* was published initially in four instalments in *Les Temps Modernes*, the first two in November and December 1946 and the second two in January and February 1947.
3. Mackie, J. L., *Ethics: Inventing Right and Wrong*. Harmondsworth: Penguin, 1977, p. 15.
4. Wittgenstein, with admirable brevity and characteristic imperiousness, stated his version of the noncognitivist position in 1921 (the first English translation appeared in 1922) as follows: 'The sense of the world must lie outside the world. In the world everything is as it is, and everything happens as it does happen: *in* it no value exists – and if it did exist, it would have no value.' (*Tractatus Logico-Philosophicus*, trans. D. F. Pears and B. F. McGuinness. London: Routledge & Kegan Paul, 1922, Section 6.41, p. 71). Wittgenstein went on to declare that 'ethics cannot be put into words' (Section 6.421, p. 71), that ethics is transcendental, and that ethics and aesthetics are the same.
5. *Pyrrhus et Cinéas*, p. 14.
6. *ibid.*, p. 47. Beauvoir had developed this theory previously in *She Came To Stay*.
7. *ibid.*, p, 16.

8. *ibid.*, pp. 56, 23.
9. *ibid.*, p. 23.
10. *ibid.*, p. 29.
11. *Ethics of Ambiguity*, p. 15.
12. *Pyrrhus et Cinéas*, p. 29.
13. *L'Existentialisme et la Sagesse des Nations*. Paris, Nagel, 1948, pp. 99–100. Our translation.
14. *Ethics of Ambiguity*, pp. 24, 17, 112, 17–18.
15. *The Novels of Simone de Beauvoir*, p. 76.
16. *Ethics of Ambiguity*, p. 29. When doing close comparative analysis of the initial appearance of philosophical theories and ideas in the works of Beauvoir and Sartre, one is often surprised and perplexed by the length of the time lag between their initial appearance in Beauvoir's writing and their subsequent utilization by Sartre. In such cases one cannot help but wonder what were the pedagogical and psychological processes by which the man was eventually brought around. With the theory of situated freedom, however, some of the details of Sartre's tortuous conversion to Beauvoir's position have been made public. In *The Prime of Life*, Beauvoir describes their intellectual conflict in April 1940.

   During the days that followed we discussed certain specific problems, in particular the relationship between 'situation' and freedom. I maintained that from the angle of freedom as Sartre defined it – that is, an active transcendence of some given context rather than mere stoic resignation – not every situation was equally valid: what sort of transcendence could a woman shut up in a harem achieve? Sartre replied that even such a cloistered existence could be lived in several quite different ways. I stuck to my point for a long time, and in the end made only a token submission. Basically I was right. (p. 434).

   A direct result of this disagreement was that Beauvoir began, independently of Sartre, to develop the ethics which is the subject of this chapter and which differs fundamentally from the purely individualist one she had previously held together with Sartre.

   Two years after their initial disagreement, Sartre was still holding out against Beauvoir's theory of situational freedom. To her biographers Francis and Gontier, Beauvoir, explaining how she and Sartre argued about what was to be included in *Being and Nothingness*, spoke as follows:

   In the first version of *Being and Nothingness* he spoke about freedom as though it were equally complete for everybody. Or at least that it was always possible to exercise one's freedom. I, on the other hand, insisted that there exist situations in which freedom cannot be exercised or is nothing more than a hoax. He agreed with that. As a result, he gave a lot of weight to the situation in which the human being finds himself (*Simone de Beauvoir*, p. 210).

But not nearly enough to satisfy Beauvoir. Deirdre Bair says that Beauvoir told her that in September 1942 she 'began her initial version of *Pyrrhus et Cinéas* as an attempt to think through some of her disagreements with what eventually became Sartre's fourth section of *Being and Nothingness*, in particular the chapter dealing with questions of freedom' (*Simone de Beauvoir*, p. 270).

Near the end of their lives Beauvoir recorded a conversation between herself and Sartre on the subject of his conversion to her view of freedom. Having characterized his former position as being that 'freedom and consciousness were the same', Beauvoir asks him how his conversion took place. (*Adieux: A Farewell to Sartre*, p. 352):

SARTRE: I think that's important. I was working on *Being and Nothingness* at that time. It was about 1943. *Being and Nothingness* is a book about freedom. I then, like the old Stoics, believed that one was always free, even in exceedingly disagreeable circumstances that might end in death. On this point I've changed very much. I think that in fact there are situations in which one cannot be free. I explained my thoughts on the subject in *The Devil and the Good Lord* (1951) (p. 358).

The Sartre scholar, Peter Caws, however, notes that 'in 1946 Sartre still believed in radical freedom', whereas by 1952 he found 'the point not quite so obvious. Situations might be more complex, and more confining, than had been allowed for by the heroic version of existentialism' (*Sartre*, pp. 125–6).

17. *Pyrrhus et Cinéas*, pp. 85–6.
18. *Ethics of Ambiguity*, p. 26.
19. *ibid.*, pp. 81, 32.
20. *ibid.*, p. 28.
21. *ibid.*, pp. 28, 30, 32, 81.
22. 'Merleau-Ponty and Pseudo-Sartreanism', trans. Veronique Zaytzeff and Frederick Morrison, *International Studies in Philosophy*, 21 (1989), 10.
23. *ibid.*, pp. 7, 11.

24. *Ethics of Ambiguity*, p. 156.

25. *ibid.*, p. 85.

26. Kruks, 'Gender and Subjectivity', pp. 98, 100, 95.

27. *The Second Sex*, pp. 424–44.

28. Stone, Bob, 'Simone de Beauvoir and the Existential Basis of Socialism', *Social Text* (Fall 1987), 125.

29. Singer, Linda, 'Interpretation and retrieval: Rereading Beauvoir', *Women's Studies International Forum*, 8, 3, 1985, 232.

30. *Ethics of Ambiguity*, p. 72.

31. *Pyrrhus et Cinéas*, pp. 65, 96, 99–101, 116–17.

32. *ibid.*, pp. 114–15.

33. *The Second Sex*, p. 728; *Pyrrhus et Cinéas*, pp. 115, 116; 'Eye for Eye', trans. Mary McCarthy, *Politics* (July–August 1947), 134–40.

34. *Pyrrhus et Cinéas*, pp. 96, 10, 65.

35. *ibid.*, p. 110.

36. See Kruks, 'Gender and Subjectivity', p. 99–101.

37. *Pyrrhus et Cinéas*, pp. 113–14; Kruks's translation in 'Gender and Subjectivity', p. 99.

38. *The Second Sex* as cited by Kruks, 'Gender and Subjectivity', p. 105.

39. *Ethics of Ambiguity*, p. 107.

40. *ibid.*, pp. 12–15.

41. Debra Bergoffen, 'Contesting Intentional Anxieties', Silverman Phenomenology Series. Duquesne University Press, forthcoming.

42. *Ethics of Ambiguity*, pp. 70, 74, 71, 86–7.

43. Mackie, *Ethics*, p. 111 (emphasis added).

44. *Pyrrhus et Cinéas*, p. 112.

45. Singer, 'Interpretation and Retrieval', p. 236.

Chapter 15: *The Second Sex*

1. The book sold over 1 million copies in French and between 2 and 3 million in the more than 20 languages into which it has been translated. It provided Beauvoir with a sufficient income for life. See Bair, *Simone de Beauvoir*, p. 652.

2. *The Second Sex*, p. 13.

3. See Jo-Ann Pilardi, 'The changing critical fortunes of *The Second Sex*', *History and Theory*, 32, 1993, 51–73.

4. *The Second Sex*, p. 15.

5. From an interview in *Ms*, July 1972, republished in Elaine Marks and

Isabelle de Courtivron (eds), *New French Feminisms*, Hemel Hempstead: Harvester Wheatsheaf, 1981, p. 145. For another example of this kind of response see *Prime of Life*, p. 367.

6. See Bair, *Simone de Beauvoir*, pp. 379–80. In an interview Audry told Bair about Beauvoir approaching her at the Café Flore in the summer of 1948, saying 'You know that book you were always talking about when we were in Rouen? The one about women? Well, I'm the one who's going to write it.' Audry remained an associate of Beauvoir throughout her life and was a significant campaigner for women's rights in France. See Francis and Gontier, *Simone de Beauvoir*, pp. 126, 290. Beauvoir quotes Audry extensively in *The Second Sex*.

7. *Prime of Life*, pp. 62, 572.

8. *Force of Circumstance*, trans. Richard Howard. Harmondsworth: Penguin, 1968, pp. 103, 178. In a footnote in *Force of Circumstance* (p. 196) she notes that the book 'was begun in October 1946 and finished in June 1949; but I spent four months of 1947 in America, and *America Day by Day* kept me busy for six months.'

9. With regard to *The Second Sex*, for example, this debate has recently centred on the related questions of Beauvoir's treatment of motherhood, lesbianism, the body and sexual passion, as well as querying the book's historical and class limitations, and its Western and French viewpoint see, for example, Hazel Barnes, 'Simone de Beauvoir and later feminism', *Simone de Beauvoir Studies*, 4, 1987, 5–34; Margaret A. Simons, 'Reclaiming *The Second Sex*', *Women's Studies International Forum*, 8, 3, 1985, 169–71; Moi, *Simone de Beauvoir: The Making of an Intellectual Woman*, pp. 73–92; Le Doeuff, *Hipparchia's Choice*, pp. 55–6.

10. *The Second Sex*, p. 295. This idea has been of immense importance to feminist discussions from the 1960s to the present and stands behind work ranging from Kate Millett's *Sexual Politics* (1970) to Judith Butler's *Gender Trouble* (1990), and, informs, often in submerged ways, much of the current work on the performativity of gender.

11. *The Second Sex*, p. 14.

12. *ibid.*, pp. 15, 16.

13. *ibid.*, p. 16.

14. *ibid.*, pp. 16, 17.

15. Kruks, 'Gender and Subjectivity', p. 98.

16. See Beauvoir's account of her decision to assume the label of feminist in *All Said and Done*, trans. Patrick O'Brian, Harmondsworth: Penguin, 1977, p. 491.

17. *The Second Sex*, p. 19.
18. *The Second Sex*, p. 19. The strength of this point for Beauvoir gives the reason for her interest in Shulamith Firestone's *Dialectic of Sex* (1970), which proposes artificial insemination as a universal substitute for sexual intercourse, thus offering a utopian view of a radical revision of the terms of the biological imperative holding men and women together. On this matter see Beauvoir's interview with Alice Schwarzer in Marks and de Courtivron, *New French Feminisms*, p. 146.
19. See Beauvoir's statement about the importance of her own economic independence in *Prime of Life*, p. 367.
20. See *The Second Sex*, p. 21.
21. Beauvoir's attention to previous women's work is diminished in the English translation of *The Second Sex*, because of editorial decisions about abridging the text. For a history of these decisions and an account of what has been lost see Margaret A. Simons, 'The silencing of Simone de Beauvoir: Guess what's missing from *The Second Sex*', *Women's Studies International Forum*, 6, 5, 1983, 559–564 and Yolanda Astarita Patterson, 'Who was this H. M. Parshley?: The saga of translating Simone de Beauvoir's *The Second Sex*', *Simone de Beauvoir Studies*, 9, 1992, 41–7.
22. *The Second Sex*, p. 25.
23. *ibid.*, pp. 27, 28.
24. *ibid.*, pp. 28, 29.
25. Michèle Le Doeuff, in her superb study of Beauvoir, *Hipparchia's Choice*, is absolutely correct in emphasizing the point that, unlike much recent feminist thought, Beauvoir is not concerned with women's happiness but their subjectivity and their agency, (pp. 115–16).
26. *Force of Circumstance*, p. 195.
27. *ibid.*, p. 197.
28. *ibid.*, p. 198.
29. *ibid.*, p. 203.
30. See Monique Wittig, 'One is not born a woman', *Feminist Issues*, 1, 2, (Winter 1981), 47–54.
31. 'Sex and Gender in Simone de Beauvoir's *Second Sex*' in *Simone de Beauvoir: Witness to a Century*, *Yale French Studies*, 72, 1986, pp. 35, 49.
32. See Judith Butler, *Gender Trouble*. London: Routledge, 1990, pp. 111–28, 143.

Chapter 16: *The Second Sex* And The Genre Trap

Reference

Beauvoir, Simone de, *The Second Sex*, trans. H. M. Parshley. New York: Vintage, 1989.

Books in English by Jean-Paul Sartre

Essays

Anti-Semite and Jew, trans. George J. Becker. New York: Schocken Books, 1965.

Being and Nothingness: An essay on Phenomenological Ontology, trans. Hazel E. Barnes. New York: Philosophical Library, 1956.

Critique of Dialectical Reason, vol. 1, *Theory of Practical Ensembles*, trans. Alan Sheridan-Smith, ed. Jonathan Rée. London: NLB, 1976.

The Emotions: Outline of a Theory, trans. Bernard Frechtman. New York: Philosophical Library, 1948.

Essays in Existentialism, ed. Wade Baskin. New York: Citadel Press, 1990.

Existentialism, trans. Bernard Frechtman. New York: Philosophical Library, 1947.

Existentialism and Humanism, trans. Philip Mairet. London: Methuen, 1948.

Literary and Philosophical Essays, trans. Annette Michelson. New York: Collier, 1962.

Notebooks for an Ethics, trans. David Pellauer. Chicago: University of Chicago Press, 1992.

Politics and Literature, trans. J. A. Underwood and John Calder. London: Calder & Boyars, 1973.

The Psychology of Imagination, trans. Bernard Frechtman. New York: Washington Square Press, 1966.

Life/Situations: Essays written and spoken, trans. Paul Auster and Lydia Davis. New York: Pantheon, 1977.

Sartre on Theater, Michel Contat and Michel Rybalka (eds), trans. Frank Jellinek. London: Quartet, 1976.

Search for a Method, trans. Hazel E. Barnes. New York: Vintage, 1968.

The Writings of Jean-Paul Sartre, vol. 2, *Selected Prose*, eds Michel Contat and Michel Rybalka, trans. Richard McCleary. Evanston, Illinois: Northwestern University Press, 1974.

The Transcendence of the Ego: An Existentialist Theory of Consciousness, trans. Forrest Williams and Robert Kirkpatrick. New York: Noonday Press, 1957.

What is Literature? trans. Bernard Frechtman. London: Methuen, 1950.

Fiction

Nausea, trans. Robert Baldick. Harmondsworth: Penguin, 1965.

Intimacy and Other Stories, trans. Lloyd Alexander. New York: New Directions, 1948.

The Reprieve, trans. Eric Sutton. Harmondsworth: Penguin, 1963.

The Age of Reason, trans. Eric Sutton. New York: Bantam, 1959.

Iron in the Soul, trans. Gerard Hopkins. Harmondsworth: Penguin, 1963.

Drama

Altona, Men Without Shadows, The Flies, trans. Sylvia and George Leeson, Kitty Black, Stuart Gilbert. Harmondsworth: Penguin, 1962.

The Chips Are Down, trans. Louise Verése. London: Rider & Co, 1951.

Crime Passionnel, trans. Kitty Black. London: Methuen, 1961.

Three Plays: Kean, Nekrassov, The Trojan Women, trans. Kitty Black, Sylvia and George Leeson, Ronald Duncan. Harmondsworth: Penguin, 1969.

In Camera and Other Plays, trans. Kitty Black, Stuart Gilbert. Harmondsworth: Penguin, 1982.

Biography

Mallarmé: Or the Poet of Nothingness, trans. Ernest Sturm. London: Pennsylvania State University Press, 1988.

Saint Genet: Actor and Martyr, trans. Bernard Frechtman. New York: New American Library, 1963.

Autobiography, Memoirs and Letters

Baudelaire, trans. Martin Turnell, 1949 rpt. London: Hamish Hamilton, 1964.

Sartre by Himself, trans. Richard Seaver. New York: Urizen, 1978.

War Diaries: Notebooks from a Phoney War, November 1939–March 1940, trans. Quintin Hoare. London: Verso, 1984.

Witness to My Life: The letters of Jean-Paul Sartre to Simone de Beauvoir, 1926–1939, trans. Lee Fahnestock and Norman MacAfee, ed. Simone de Beauvoir. New York: Charles Scribner's Sons, 1992.

The Words, trans. Bernard Frechtman. New York: George Braziller, 1964.

Books in English by Simone de Beauvoir

Essays

The Ethics of Ambiguity, trans. Bernard Frechtman. (1948, rpt.) New York: Citadel Press, 1970.

Simone de Beauvoir: Philosophical Writings, Margaret A. Simons (ed.). Chicago: University of Illinois Press, 2004.

Why Burn Sade? trans. Annette Michelson. London: Peter Nevill, 1953.

Old Age, trans. Patrick O'Brian. Harmondsworth: Penguin, 1977.

The Second Sex, trans. H. M. Parshley. (1953, rpt.) Harmondsworth: Penguin, 1972.

Fiction

All Men are Mortal, trans. Leonard M. Friedman. London: Norton, 1992.

Les Belles Images, trans. Patrick O'Brian. London: Flamingo, 1985.

The Blood of Others, trans. Yvonne Moyse and Roger Senhouse. Harmondsworth: Penguin, 1964.

The Mandarins, trans. Leonard M. Friedman. London: Flamingo, 1984.

She Came To Stay, trans. Yvonne Moyse and Roger Senhouse. London: Flamingo, 1984.

When Things of the Spirit Come First: Five Early Tales. trans. Patrick O'Brian. London: Flamingo, 1983.

The Woman Destroyed, trans. Patrick O'Brian. London: Flamingo, 1984.

Drama

Who Shall Die? trans. Claude Francis and Fernande Gontier. Florissant, Missouri: River Press, 1983.

Biography

Adieux, trans. Patrick O'Brian. Harmondsworth: Penguin, 1985.

Autobiography, Memoirs and Letters

America Day by Day, trans. Patrick Dudley. London: Duckworth, 1952. Also trans. Carol Cosman (London: Gollancz, 1998).

All Said and Done, trans. Patrick O'Brian. Harmondsworth: Penguin, 1977.

Diary of a Philosophy Student: Volume 1, 1926–1927, trans. Barbara Klaw. Chicago: University of Illinois Press, 2006.

Force of Circumstance, trans. Richard Howard. Harmondsworth: 1968.

The Long March, trans. Austryn Wainhouse. London: Andre Deutsch and Weidenfeld and Nicolson, 1958.

Letters to Sartre, trans. and ed. Quintin Hoare. London: Radius, 1991.

Memoirs of a Dutiful Daughter, trans. James Kirkup. Harmondsworth: Penguin, 1963.

The Prime of Life, trans. Peter Green. Harmondsworth: Penguin, 1965.

A Very Easy Death, trans. Patrick O'Brian. Harmondsworth: Penguin, 1969.

Index